WAR ON WOKE

Also by Alan Dershowitz

War Against the Jews

Get Trump

Dershowitz on Killing

The Price of Principle

The Case for Vaccine Mandates

The Case for Color-Blind Equality in an Age of Identity Politics

The Case Against the New Censorship: Protecting Free Speech from Big Tech, Progressives, and
    Universities

Cancel Culture: The Latest Attack on Free Speech and Due Process

The Case for Liberalism in an Age of Extremism: or, Why I Left the Left But Can't Join the Right

Confirming Justice—Or Injustice?: A Guide to Judging RGB's Successor

Defending the Constitution

Guilt by Accusation: The Challenge of Proving Innocence in the Age of #MeToo

Defending Israel: The Story of My Relationship with My Most Challenging Client

The Case Against Impeaching Trump

The Case Against BDS: Why Singling Out Israel for Boycott Is Anti-Semitic and Anti-Peace

Trumped Up: How Criminalization of Political Differences Endangers Democracy

Electile Dysfunction: A Guide for Unaroused Voters

The Case Against the Iran Deal

Terror Tunnels: The Case for Israel's Just War Against Hamas

Abraham: The World's First (But Certainly Not Last) Jewish Lawyer

Taking the Stand: My Life in the Law

The Trials of Zion

The Case for Moral Clarity: Israel, Hamas and Gaza

The Case Against Israel's Enemies: Exposing Jimmy Carter and Others Who Stand in the Way of Peace

Is There a Right to Remain Silent? Coercive Interrogation and the Fifth Amendment After 9/11

Finding Jefferson: A Lost Letter, a Remarkable Discovery, and the First Amendment in the Age of
    Terrorism

Blasphemy: How the Religious Right is Hijacking Our Declaration of Independence

Pre-emption: A Knife That Cuts Both Ways

Rights From Wrongs: A Secular Theory of the Origins of Rights

America on Trial: Inside the Legal Battles That Transformed Our Nation

The Case for Peace: How the Arab-Israeli Conflict Can Be Resolved

The Case for Israel

America Declares Independence

Why Terrorism Works: Understanding the Threat, Responding to the Challenge

Shouting Fire: Civil Liberties in a Turbulent Age

Letters to a Young Lawyer

Supreme Injustice: How the High Court Hijacked Election 2000

Genesis of Justice: Ten Stories of Biblical Injustice that Led to the Ten Commandments and Modern Law

Just Revenge

Sexual McCarthyism: Clinton, Starr, and the Emerging Constitutional Crisis

The Vanishing American Jew: In Search of Jewish Identity for the Next Century

Reasonable Doubts: The Criminal Justice System and the O.J. Simpson Case

The Abuse Excuse: And Other Cop-Outs, Stories and Evasions of Responsibility

The Advocate's Devil

Contrary to Popular Opinion

Chutzpah

Taking Liberties: A Decade of Hard Cases, Bad Laws, and Bum Raps

Reversal of Fortune: Inside the Von Bülow Case

The Best Defense

Fair and Certain Punishment: Report of the 20th Century Fund Task Force on Criminal Sentencing

Courts of Terror: Soviet Criminal Justice and Jewish Emigration (coauthored with Telford Taylor)

Criminal Law: Theory and Process (with Joseph Goldstein and Richard Schwartz)

Psychoanalysis, Psychiatry, and Law (with Joseph Goldstein and Jay Katz)

WAR ON WOKE

WHY THE NEW McCARTHYISM IS
MORE DANGEROUS THAN THE OLD

ALAN DERSHOWITZ

Hot Books

DEDICATION

War on Woke is dedicated to the students who are on the battlefield of the important war against the dangers of woke. These brave young women and men are risking grades, recommendations, popularity, and even occasionally physical safety to stand up for principle, due process, free speech, and democratic values. I hope this book helps them and me stand ready to defend them against unfair retaliation.

ACKNOWLEDGMENTS

My small army of dedicated defenders of liberty include my family, my staff of Maura Kelley and Annie Hoyos, and my friends Alan Rothfeld, Harvey Silverglate, and Aaron Volaj, as well as my supporters who encourage me. My editor Hector Carosso and publisher Tony Lyons are indispensable to my ability to write and publish quickly.

Hot Books may be purchased in bulk at special discounts for sales promotion, corporate gifts, fund-raising, or educational purposes. Special editions can also be created to specifications. For details, contact the Special Sales Department, Skyhorse Publishing, 307 West 36th Street, 11th Floor, New York, NY 10018 or info@skyhorsepublishing.com.

Hot Books® and Skyhorse Publishing® are registered trademarks of Skyhorse Publishing, Inc.®, a Delaware corporation.

Visit our website at www.skyhorsepublishing.com.
Please follow our publisher Tony Lyons on Instagram @tonylyonsisuncertain.

10 9 8 7 6 5 4 3 2 1

Library of Congress Cataloging-in-Publication Data is available on file.

Hardcover ISBN: 978-1-5107-8036-1
eBook ISBN: 978-1-5107-8037-8

Cover design by Brian Peterson

Printed in the United States of America

Contents

Introduction

I came of age when civil libertarians were opposing Senator Joseph McCarthy's targeting of alleged Communists and their enablers, and civil rights activists were battling segregation, Jim Crow, and other bigotry such as anti-Semitism. As a young man I eagerly participated in these righteous causes and fought against hard-right bigots who supported these evils. Now, sixty-five years later, I find myself in a struggle against current hard-left and "woke" versions of McCarthyism, censorship, racial separation, and anti-Semitism.

This book is about these new dangers to civil liberties and racial, religious, ethnic, and gender equality. It does not assert that the past and present evils are identical. They are not. But they have in common certain characteristics associated with closed-minded intolerance.

Although the old McCarthyism may have caused more damage to innocent people in the past, the new woke version is more dangerous to the future of civil liberties and equality in America, because it is espoused and practiced by many young people who will become our leaders in the years to come.

This new McCarthyism challenges the basic tenets of the classic liberal (in the traditional sense) state: Freedom of expression; due process; presumption of innocence; right to counsel; equal application of the law; tolerance and respect for differing viewpoints; an acceptance of the reality that in a democracy, no one always gets their way. And noble ends do not justify ignoble means.

These bedrock principles are rejected by McCarthyite extremists on both the hard left and the hard right. This has been the case, in varying degrees, historically: Communists and fascists alike rejected traditional liberal values and tolerance. Both have espoused anti-Semitic tropes. But these anti-libertarian attitudes have become more mainstream, pervasive, and influential today coming from the woke left in academia, in the media, and increasingly in the business community, especially high tech. They pose a clear and present danger to a way of life that has long served us well, and an even clearer danger to future generations of Americans.

I am writing this book in the recognition that this generation of Americans can change the course of our history—for the better or worse. It is our responsibility to stop the new woke McCarthyism before it becomes the new Americanism that destroys our hard-earned liberties. Inaction is not an option in the face of this growing danger. Hence, this call to immediate action. This is truly a time that tests the souls of all good people who are dedicated to liberty and equality.

Many good people, especially on the left, fought bravely against the evils of the old right-wing McCarthyism, and even some on the right opposed Joseph McCarthy. Now some good people, mainly in the center and on the moderate right, are fighting against the evils of the new left-wing McCarthyism. Too few on the left have joined this opposition. Too few are genuine civil libertarians speaking out today and risking the wrath of partisan advocates who talk the talk of civil liberties, but walk the walk of intolerance. Hardly anyone has fought with equal fervor and nonpartisan political principles against the evils of both. Though I am generally more sympathetic to the political positions of the left than the right (choice, gay marriage, reasonable climate and gun control, separation of church from state, fairness to accused criminal defendants), I have tried to be politically neutral in my condemnation of left- and right-wing McCarthyism. I have condemned both over the past sixty-five years, and I plan to continue to do so as long as my eighty-five-year-old body and mind gives me the necessary strength.

The old McCarthyism targeted Communists, former Communists, "fellow travelers" who were sympathetic to Communism, and civil liberties lawyers who defended accused Communists, even if they themselves were not Communists. Anyone who was associated in any way with the evils of Communism, was lumped together with the actual evildoers, as reflected by this story (perhaps apocryphal) of a pro-Communist rally at City College of New York in the 1930s. The police were beating up protesters, when one shouted, "Stop beating me. I'm an anti-Communist here to protest the Communists." The policeman responded, "I don't care what kind of Communist you are," and continued beating him.

International Communism was an actual threat during the Cold War, when the Soviet Union and its allies took control of Eastern Europe, much of Central Europe, and parts of Asia and Central America. The leader of international Communism threatened to "bury" us, as their nuclear arsenal grew and spread. As elementary and high school students, we were required to practice "duck and tuck"—crouching under our desks to protect us from a Soviet atomic bomb. But the fear of Communist "infiltration" into the highest levels of our government was greatly exaggerated. The major targets of the old McCarthyism were former Communists, who had joined the Communist Party during the 1930s when it was seen by many as a bulwark against Nazism. Many such anti-fascist Communists— especially Jews—left the Party when Stalin made his notorious pact with Hitler, thus becoming an ally of Nazism, at least for a time. Some remained and others rejoined after Germany invaded the Soviet Union, thus ending that alliance of evil. Others supported the ends and sometimes the means of Communism, without actually supporting the Party, as exemplified by Robert Oppenheimer in the recent film by that name.

By the time the old McCarthyism reached its peak of power in the late 1940s to the mid-1950s, the American Communist Party had few members or followers and even fewer in government positions. McCarthyism was about the past, not the present. And certainly not the future. It took an enormous personal toll on former Communists, as brilliantly presented in the film *The Front*. But it had little impact on the future, as demonstrated by the fact that nearly all those responsible for making that great film (with the notable exception of Woody Allen who played a young non-Communist) were old

Communists who had been victimized by McCarthy but had become heroes, or at least were no longer cancelled. The influence of the old McCarthyism began to erode when the Senate censured Joseph McCarthy in 1954—and essentially ended with his death in 1957, though there were residues into the early 1960s. The enduring legacy of the original McCarthyism is its near universal condemnation by the verdict of history.

That is unlikely to be the fate of the new woke McCarthyism that we are currently experiencing. It is likely to increase in influence as the young woke McCarthyites who are now in universities become our future leaders.

In addition to the greater future danger of left-wing McCarthyism, the reason I focus more on it than on its right-wing counterpart is precisely because my political sympathies are closer to the left than to the right. I have always maintained that each of us has greater responsibility to call out the extremists on our side than those on the other side. It's easy to criticize those with whom we fundamentally disagree. It is much harder and more important to criticize the means employed by those with whose ends we generally agree.

Many of the new left-wing McCarthyites—like many of the Communists and fellow travelers who were victimized by the right-wing McCarthyites—seek commendable ends, such as racial and gender equality or "equity," at least as they selectively define it. They want to reduce economic, educational, health, and other significant disparities. They want to protect the environment and reduce gun violence. They oppose undue religious influence in governance. They seek fair elections with equal voting rights. They expect the judiciary to be responsive to the needs of the less powerful. They demand that corporations place the needs of consumers over the profits of executives and shareholders. They advocate a foreign policy that prioritizes international human rights (at least for some) over parochial American interests. They call for goodness of virtue and decency, as they see it, to prevail over the evils of vice and indecency.

Some, but not all, of these desiderata are supported as well by good people on the right, but with less emphasis on equality and more on liberty—as they selectively define it.

I generally support much of the agenda of the left, especially the center-left. But as a civil libertarian, I insist that my goals, even the most commendable ones, must always be achieved within the rule of law, and not by means that endanger the liberty of others. Because of this insistence on proper means, I sometimes fail to achieve my commendable goals, but that is part of the democratic process. Democracy provides no assurance of outcomes. It is a process not a promise. I am prepared therefore to prioritize means over ends.

The democratic process is also based on lack of certainty that the ends one prefers are ultimately the best ones. As the great jurist Learned Hand cautioned (quoting Oliver Cromwell):

> "I beseech ye in the bowels of Christ, think that ye may be mistaken." I should like to have that written over the portals of every church, every school, and every courthouse, and, may I say of every legislative body in the United State. I should like to have every court begin, "I beseech ye in the bowels of Christ, I think that we may be mistaken."

He went on to define the spirit of liberty:

> The spirit of liberty is the spirit which is not too sure that it is right; the spirit of liberty is the spirit which seeks to understand the mind of other men and women; the spirit of liberty is the spirit which weighs their interests alongside its own without bias.

Former Supreme Court justice Robert Jackson echoed these views in the context of Supreme Court justices:

> We are not final because we are infallible, but we are infallible only because we are final.

The hard left and the hard right share in common a certainty that their views, and only their views, are the infallible ones. This certainty engenders intolerance not only for other views, but also for processes that encourage the challenging of accepted truths. Freedom of speech and due process are deemed unnecessary for those who are certain of THE TRUTH, whether it be political truth, racial truth, gender truth, economic truth, or religious truth. For them, the Truth needs no dissent, nor does it need due process. It is simply there to be discovered by authorized truth seekers. A recent example of this ideological certainty was the claim by Professor Lawrence Tribe that the Fourteenth Amendment automatically disqualifies Donald Trump from running for president even though it provides no process or procedure for determining if he, in fact, engaged in "insurrection or rebellion." Tribe asserted that this alleged disqualification was "self-enforcing," and actually "promotes" democracy by denying voters the right to cast their ballot for a candidate of their choice.

What I call "the truthing process"—the never-ending quest for better verities—is anathema to those who believe that the truth is eternal and fixed. I speak not of scientific truths, which though subject to amendment, are more fixed than political or ideological truths. Even for scientific truths, there must be a process not a pronouncement, as Galileo painfully learned and taught us. I speak of the kinds of truth that can never be proved with the empirical certainty of science.

As former justice Felix Frankfurter observed: "The history of American freedom is, in large part, a history of procedure." To which may be added, the history of procedure is, in large part, a history of due process. The truthing process relies on fair procedures applicable to all. This includes the "adversarial process" in litigation.

McCarthyism, both new and old, is the opposite of a truthing process. It bears hallmarks of the Inquisition, Stalinism, and fascism, whose "truths" did not endure. They retained their verisimilitude among the people only through compulsion, force, violence, and censorship. They were rejected in the marketplace of ideas when that marketplace was opened to differing truths—when procedures were put in place that assured equal access at the critical marketplace. Again, Justice Jackson, who served as our chief prosecutor at the Nuremberg trials: "Those who begin coercive elimination of dissent soon find themselves eliminating dissenters. Compulsory unification of opinion achieves only the unanimity of the graveyard." As former chief justice William Rehnquist once ruled: "Under the First Amendment, there is no such thing as a false idea. However pernicious an opinion may seem, we depend for its correction not on the conscience of judges and justices, but on the competition of other ideas." In rendering that important ruling, Rehnquist was paraphrasing a letter written by Thomas Jefferson in 1801, the original of which hangs on my wall. This is what Jefferson wrote to Elijah Bordman on the eve of the 25th anniversary of the Declaration of Independence:

> [W]e have nothing to fear from the demoralizing reasoning of some, if others are left free to demonstrate their errors, and especially if the law stands ready to punish the first criminal act produced by false reasoning. These are safer corrections than the conscience of a judge. . . .

Who knows which of today's certain truths will survive the verdict of history? Only time will tell, and it will tell only if competing truths are not repressed by the certainty of the new woke McCarthyism.

This new McCarthyism, like the old McCarthyism, did not suddenly develop. It grew out of the false certainty of the old left that morphed into the new left during the Vietnam War and its protests. The extreme left, like the extreme right, has never brooked dissent, but until recently this sensorial and intolerant attitude of the left was a minority view, even among most left-wing zealots. The two events that transformed this into an apparent majority or at least plurality view on the left and certainly on the hard left, were 1) the emergence of Donald Trump as the champion of the hard right, and the overreaction to it from many on the left; and 2) the killing of George Floyd and the racial reckoning that followed this horrendous police act. These transforming events contributed largely to the emergence of the new woke McCarthyism as a clear and present danger to the rule of law, free speech, due process, and traditional concepts of color-blind equality. The influence of these events has endured well beyond the events themselves and threatens to become a long-term, if not permanent, fixture in our legal and political constellation.

The election of Donald Trump in 2016, and his loss in 2020, followed by his false claim of victory, turned many traditional liberals and civil libertarians into rabid Get Trumpers. His announcement that he would seek reelection in 2024 turned many of these Get Trumpers into anti-civil libertarians who openly admitted that preventing Trump from becoming president again was more important than preserving the Constitution. They were prepared to dispense with freedom of speech for Trump supporters, the right to counsel and due process for Trump and associates, and the rule of law as applied to him. According to them, this was essentially a state of emergency, demanding that rights be suspended in the interest of the greater good, as in wartime and other national security threats. Jefferson placed the survival of our new republic over the demands of the Constitution, as did Lincoln; Woodrow Wilson denied due process to immigrants who he believed threatened the American way of life; Franklin Delano Roosevelt authorized the racist detention of Japanese Americans; George W. Bush authorized the use of unconstitutional measures to combat the threat of terrorism. And now, following these precedents, even some traditional civil libertarians seem to believe that the threat of Trump is even greater than those that justified previous suspension of rights. They assure us that rights once suspended, can quickly be restored when the crisis has passed.

My disagreement with that short-sighted perspective led me to write a book entitled *Get Trump: The Threat to Civil Liberties, Due Process, and Our Constitutional Rule of Law*, in which I criticized both Donald Trump and those who were advocating unconstitutional means to prevent him from regaining the presidency. Following the publication of that book, Trump has been indicted four times, as I predicted. I address the strengths and weaknesses of the evidence, as well as the processes leading to the indictments in this book.

The horrible murder of a Black man named George Floyd at the hands of a policeman and his associates created a collective sense of guilt among many white liberals and centrists. The call for a racial reckoning that followed increased the influence of Black Lives Matter and other groups that demanded what they called racial "equity" over what had traditionally been called color-blind equality. These demands could not easily be resisted by guilt-ridden corporations, media, academies, and individuals, who overreacted and deemed those who sought color-blind equality to be racist.

Never in recent history has there been such a swift turnabout in attitudes and actions. From boardrooms to Broadway, from kindergarten to medical school, academic priorities shifted from the goal of making race irrelevant to making race the most relevant factor. Everything changed. Almost no institution—private or public—was immune from this collective reckoning and guilt-ridden overreaction. The noble end of making up for our sordid history of institutional racism justified the ignoble means of reinstituting a new form of discrimination—this time against the perceived old discriminators, regardless of whether they, as individuals or institutions, played any role in the discriminations. Because all were guilty as a group, none were guilty as individuals. Reckoning used past discrimination to justify current and future discrimination. Martin Luther King's dream—of a time when children will be judged by the content of their character rather than the color of their skin—became the nightmare of a new form of race consciousness. Short-term, but highly visible, acts of reckoning were seen to justify long-term adoption of policies based on racial differences.

A recent *Wall Street Journal* op-ed by Professor David Decosimo described what occurred at his university:

That summer, many BU departments published [. . .] "antiracist" statements limiting academic freedom and subordinating inquiry to [that] ideology. With their dean's oversight and approval, the School of Theatre passed a plan to audit all syllabi, courses, and policies to ensure conformity with "an anti-oppression and anti-racist ideology." The sociology department publicly announced that "white supremacy and racism" were "pervasive and woven into . . . our own . . . department." In the English department's playwriting program, all syllabi would have to "assign 50 percent diverse-identifying and marginalized writers," and any "material or scholarship . . . from a White or Eurocentric lineage" could be taught only "through an actively anti-racist lens." They even published hiring quotas based on race: "We commit to . . . hiring at least

50 percent BIPOC"—an acronym for black, indigenous, or people
of color—"artists by 2020. . . ."

BU President Robert Brown announced several universitywide
institutions including a task force to examine and expunge racism
from BU. A dean claimed the administration would examine not
only policies and practices but even ideas—and not only for racism
but for whatever might "facilitate racism. . . ."

And to this day at universities everywhere, activist faculty and
administrators are still quietly working to institutionalize [this]
vision. They have made embracing "diversity, equity, and inclusion"
a criterion for hiring and tenure, have rewritten disciplinary standards to privilege antiracist ideology, and are discerning ways to circumvent the Supreme Court's affirmative action ruling.[1]

The means used to create racial reckoning morphed into means that
spread to gender reckoning, where the goal of eliminating discrimination against gay and transgender people was employed in the service of
creating new privilege to make up for past lack of privilege.

"Privilege" became the new racism of the day. All white males were
privileged, regardless of their individual circumstances. All people of
color, gays, transgenders, and even women were unprivileged, regardless of their individual circumstances. The group, as defined by identity
politics, became the unit, rather than the individual. Jews, for example,
were all privileged, despite a long and painful history of discrimination
and genocide, and despite the reality that approximately half of the
world's Jewish and Israeli population are dark-skinned Sephardim and
people of color, or that many Jews live in poverty. The nation-state of
the Jewish people, Israel, was privileged, despite it being surrounded
by enemies sworn to its destruction and being victimized by terrorism
and rocket attacks. Privilege justified discrimination, hatred, silencing,
denial of due process and the other characteristics of McCarthyism.
The bogeyman[2] of the old McCarthyism was Communism. The

---

1   David Decosimo, "How Ibram X. Kendi Broke Boston University," *Wall Street Journal*, September 28, 2023, https://www.wsj.com/articles/how-ibram-x-kendi-broke-boston-university-academic-freedom-progressive-fb92d525.

2   "Bogeyman" is a mythical creature designed to frighten kids into behaving.

bogeyman of the new McCarthyism is privilege. Both were misused to justify repression and denial of fundamental rights to the targets of the McCarthyites, old and new.

The new McCarthyism that has been induced by the candidacy, election, defeat, and new candidacy of Donald Trump is different in kind and degree from its variation that was induced by the George Floyd killing. Both are the product of well-intentioned goals but as the late justice Louis Brandeis once warned: "Experience should teach us to be most on our guard to protect liberty when the government's purposes are beneficent. Men born to freedom are naturally alert to repel invasion of their liberty by evil-minded rulers. The greatest dangers to liberty lurk in insidious encroachment by men of zeal, well-meaning but without understanding." That observation is applicable to a considerable degree in the new woke McCarthyism.

A. The Donald Trump-Induced McCarthyism

The Trump-induced McCarthyism is the product of genuine fear that the reelection of Donald Trump to the presidency will harm America greatly, if not destroy it. When Larry David screamed at me on the porch of the Chilmark store in the summer of 2021, his hatred of Trump—and derivatively of those who he believed enabled him—was genuine. His face turned red, his veins literally bulged, and I thought he was in danger of having a stroke. When he saw me, an old friend who had helped him and his family in numerous ways over the years, he believed he was looking at Joseph Goebbels and other Nazis who had facilitated the rise of Adolf Hitler. His emotions were uncontrollable. He is not a stupid man. At a rational level, he understands the honorable role of a lawyer in defending the Constitution, even on behalf of someone he regards as evil. He has never condemned me for defending O. J. Simpson, Senator Ted Kennedy, Mike Tyson, Bill Clinton, or even Jeffrey Epstein. But Donald Trump was different. He stood for everything people like David opposed to the core of their beings. His rational faculties simply ceased to operate.

Although condemned by many, the concept of a "Trump derangement syndrome" is accurate. I had seen it previously with regard to Israel.

There are certain people with whom I could discuss anything rationally and constructively, but when it came to discussing Israel, an "Israel derangement syndrome" replaced rationality. These people were simply incapable of having a rational discussion about the pros and cons of Israeli policy, or even Israel's existence as the nation-state of the Jewish people. Their brains seem to become scrambled by uncontrollable emotional hatred. I used the term "Israel Derangement Syndrome" back then, and it was accurate, if metaphorical. It is still accurate today, as demonstrated by the immediate reaction by many on the woke left to the Hamas attacks of October 7: blaming Israel and justifying Hamas.

A similar syndrome exists when it comes to discussions of Donald Trump. One cannot talk about any of Trump's positive accomplishments, without a comparison being made to Mussolini who made the trains run on time and Hitler who created full employment for German workers.

In some respects, this was not the fault of those afflicted with the syndrome. It literally took over their minds and bodies and made rational discussion impossible.

Trump was not, of course, the first person to cause this kind of irrational reaction.

Communists in the 1940s and '50s caused it among conservatives. Japanese Americans caused it following the attack on Pearl Harbor. Civil rights workers caused it among Jim Crow Southerners in the 1960s. Jim Crow Southerners caused it among liberals during the same period. And Muslim terrorists caused it following 9/11. In each of these instances, and more, the passions were so high and the hatreds so deep that otherwise rational people were willing to subordinate constitutional rights to what they perceived was the admirable goal of destroying America's enemies. In some respects, they succeeded. The Constitution was ignored when President Roosevelt ordered the confinement of more than a hundred thousand Japanese Americans. It was largely ignored during McCarthyism. It was ignored by Southern judges during the Jim Crow period. It was largely ignored in the aftermath of 9/11. And it is being ignored today by anti-Trump zealots who believe that the noble end of defeating Trump and preventing him from becoming president again is worth any cost, including denying constitutional rights to those who disagree.

B. The George Floyd-Induced McCarthyism

The reckoning understandably caused by the unjustified killing of George Floyd resulted in a different kind of McCarthyism. As with the old McCarthyism, the issue became literally black and white: either you were fully in favor of the racial reckoning; or you were a racist. There was no in-between. For example, those who agreed with the statement made by Justice Sandra Day O'Connor in 2003, that race-based affirmative action might be constitutionally permissible, only as a temporary ameliorative of racial disparity, which had a cut-off date of approximately twenty-five years, were deemed to be racist. Quoting Martin Luther King's dream of a color-blind future became an indicia of racism. Agreeing that black lives matter, but adding that all lives matter became a ground for terminations and cancellation. Rational discussion of differing approaches to achieving racial equality were forbidden in the marketplace of ideas. The core issue became the privileged versus the unprivileged, which meant white versus black.

The Supreme Court decision in June 2023 that held race-based affirmative action unconstitutional, while encouraging non-race-based alternatives in pursuit of equality, was wildly condemned as racist, despite the reality that the same decision would have been rendered by the liberal Warren Court back in the 1960s (see pages 142–145).

C. McCarthyism: The Death of Nuance

The new woke McCarthyism, like the old, eschews nuance, calibration, compromise, and the Learned Hand desiderata of "doubt" as a hallmark of liberty. The essence of McCarthyism is "we versus they": Patriotism and Communism, Black and white, zero-sum division between good and evil. The old McCarthyism divided America into Communists versus patriots, "real Americans" versus "globalists" and "leftists." The new woke McCarthyism divides us into privileged versus unprivileged, and racists versus woke progressives, oppressors versus oppressed. (Both demonized Jews: the old as "Communists and fellow travelers"; the new as "privileged" and Zionists.) The great middle—the vast majority of citizens who think for themselves rather than uncritically accepting any party line or politically correct dogma—are marginalized or ignored. We must all pick sides and be "good Scotsmen" on every issue.

With certainty comes intolerance—for marketplace testing and possible rejection of ideas that we are sure must be true; for procedural barriers to accusations which should not be doubted; for academic freedom to challenge politically correct verities; for political candidates who do not share our Truth; and for blasphemous books that shake our faith in the dogma of the day.

We have not yet begun to burn books but both the right and left are effectively banning some by forbidding them in our schools, libraries, and bookstores. We are cancelling speakers, preventing them from speaking in our libraries and classrooms, as I have been. If not cancelled, they are shouted down. To paraphrase Heinrich Heine: those who begin by shouting down speakers will end by physically attacking them, just as those who begin by burning books, will end by burning people. Or to quote George Bernard Shaw, assassination is the ultimate form of censorship.

Some academic extremists have not shied away from taking censorship to its extreme Shavian conclusion, advocating violence and even murder to stop the spread of ideas they regard as dangerous. An English professor at Wayne State University wrote a post on social media following the shouting down of a federal judge by Stanford law students whose acts of censorship were organized by the local chapter of the National Lawyers Guild. The post read, "I think it is more admirable to kill a racist, homophobic or Islamophobic speaker than to shout them down." He was suspended despite his disclaimer that he does "not advocate violating federal and state criminal codes."

Two New York lawyers were disbarred and sentenced to several months in prison for throwing a homemade bomb into an unoccupied police car during a post–George Floyd protest. The hard-left organization Antifa threatens and practices violence to stop "fascist" speakers from being given a platform. Their definition of fascism includes liberals like me and others who do not follow their Stalinist definition of "political correctness."

The violence from individuals on the hard right has been more lethal, especially against Jews and Blacks attending religious services, but it has been less organized and justified on a larger scale. Both are indefensible. But almost no leaders of even the hard right advocate synagogue and church shootings. These lone gunmen murders are matters for law enforcement, not debate. The bigot who shot and killed Jewish worshippers in Pittsburgh was convicted of murder, with little or no support from the right. On the other hand, some extremists on the hard left do support the violent destruction of property, and some even justify violence directed at police, judges, and other government officials. Violence by left-wing radicals against the establishment is regarded as proper subject for debate among some academics. Since the two events that were central to the legitimization of the new McCarthyism, there has been far more, if less lethal, violence, from the hard left than from the hard right—and much less condemnation from mainstream media, academics, and politicians. Following the Hamas massacres of October 7 and the Israeli military response, there has been violence and harassment directed against pro-Israel students, demonstrators, and speakers. Bridges and terminals have been blocked. Events have been disrupted. Structures have been damaged.

Neither the new nor old McCarthyism require violence to succeed. They require intolerance, the weaponization of law, and a willingness to ignore constitutional rights and liberties for one's opponents. They may both contribute to atmospheres in which violence thrives, because it is central to all forms of McCarthyism that noble ends justify at least some ignoble means. Which ones is often a matter of degree and personal choice, but once the means are subordinated to the ends, principles become subordinated to pragmatism, as defined by zealots.

Since the occurrence of the two central events that facilitated the mainstreaming of the new left-wing McCarthyism, I have written dozens of op-eds and several books arguing against this dangerous development. I have delivered lectures and podcasts about it. In writing about these issues, I have offered prognostication about the directions in which we are heading. Most of my predictions about efforts to prevent Trump from regaining the presidency, about how the courts will deal with affirmative action, and other divisive issues, have turned out to be correct. (TV commentator Mark Levin has called me "the Nostradamus of the legal profession.")

In this short book, I organize and present my advocacy in roughly chronological order, with updates and reorganizations that clarify my thinking. My opposition to the new woke McCarthyism is necessarily a work in progress, since the phenomenon itself is ever-changing with the shifting winds of politics, protests, court decisions, legislative and executive actions, and other unanticipated developments. My writing is necessarily reactive, though I try to anticipate problems before they occur. Because I try to think anew and independently about every issue, my views are not formulaic or partisan. Nor are they always predictable, as some critics who accuse me of inconsistency argue. They are wrong. My views are consistent with my principles that have remained essentially the same since the old McCarthyism. Unlike Groucho Marx, I do not say: "these are my principles. If you don't like them I have others." My principles—my commitment to free speech, due process, equal protection, zealous representation, and fundamental fairness—have stood me well over the last nearly three-quarters of a century. More importantly, they have served our nation well. They "ain't broken" and we should not break them by applying them only selectively to "me but not to thee."

No principle is sacrosanct—certainly not to anyone, like me, who accepts Learned Hand's mantra of constant self-doubt and uncertainty. But principles are always being tested by history and persistent challenges. Some have survived and endured. Others have ended up in the waste bin of history. McCarthyism is among the latter. Let us not repeat the tragic lessons of the past. Rather, let us learn from them and reject McCarthyism, whether old or new, right or left, well or ill-intentioned. We are better than that and we control our destiny for better or worse.

So am I optimistic or pessimistic? In Israel, a pessimist moans, "things are so bad, they can't get any worse." The optimist joyfully responds, "yes they can." I am both. If the young people who are leading the new McCarthyism become our future leaders without changing their current intolerance, certainty, and impatience with due process, we are in for a rough future in which the new woke McCarthyism threatens to become the new Americanism. But I would not have written this book and devoted so much of my time and energy to resisting this new McCarthyism if I thought its ultimate success was inevitable. I believe that the marketplace of ideas can change attitudes and actions. Experience is the best teacher, and bad experience is the best teacher of all—if people are willing to learn from it.

A decade ago, I wrote a book entitled *Rights from Wrongs*, in which I argued that most of our rights derive from experience—from a recognition of wrongs such as slavery, genocide, sexism, homophobia, racism, anti-Semitism, and others evils accepted by past generations that are now widely, if not universally, recognized as wrongs that require the acceptance of rights to prevent their recurrence. I believe that experience will prove that McCarthyism—old and new—is among these wrongs.

Among the wrongs of McCarthyism is that it leaves little room for nuanced debate. As I wrote in an earlier essay:

> We are experiencing the death of nuanced discourse in many parts of the world today. Instead, we see black or white debate between two sides, each insisting that they are right and the other wrong in every respect. Neither side is willing to give intellectual quarter to the other or even to listen to their counterarguments. Unconditional surrender is demanded. Compromise is unthinkable in this war of ideologies.
>
> Gone are days when friends could disagree and yet respect each other's views. Today, long-term friendships end over an unwillingness to acknowledge that there may be two sides to a divisive issue. Counterarguments are not answered by facts or logic but by ad hominem insults.

In that essay, I provided two contemporary examples—one domestic, the other foreign—of this "degrading of discourse." The first was the lack of nuance in the claims and counterclaims regarding Donald

Trump: a large proportion of Americans believe that Trump is the most dangerous public figure in our history, and that the danger he poses justifies any means necessary to prevent his reelection; another large group believes that only he and his reelection can save America from those who seek to destroy it, including the Democrats and President Joseph Biden. There is little tolerance for the views of those of us who believe that Trump's reelection would be bad for America, but that compromising fundamental rights in order to prevent his reelection, would be far more dangerous and enduring. Instead of reasoned debate about this nuanced issue, there is shouting, canceling, and weaponization of our legal system.

A similar, though not identical, phenomenon is currently at play in Israel. As I wrote in that essay:

> The second example of lack of nuance involves the debates here and in Israel about the role and influence of the Supreme Court. Here, the hard left wants to weaken the current Supreme Court by packing it with enough new justices to move it leftward. In Israel, the right wants to weaken its high court by allowing the legislature to override its liberal decisions and by giving the conservative legislature more of a role in selecting the justices.

Left-wing Israelis are taking to the street in mass protests of these judicial "reforms," claiming they will bring an end to Israel as a democracy. Supporters claim they will enhance democracy by transferring power from an unelected elitist court to a Knesset elected by the majority.

Each side has a point. Courts are supposed to be checks on democracy and protectors of minorities and often unpopular civil liberties. In that respect, they are unelected elitists. When the courts rule in favor of minorities over majorities, pure democracy is compromised, but it is compromised in the interest of fundamental civil liberties and human rights for all. The goal is to strike the appropriate balance between majority and minority rights. This requires nuance, calibration, and a willingness to compromise—precisely the elements that are quickly disappearing from political, media, and academic dialogue, both here and in other parts of the world, including Israel.

Throughout the world, opponents of the only "correct" approach—and according to them there is only one correct approach—are subjected to ad hominem attacks, called fascist, and canceled. Demonization has replaced dialogue. The world is the poorer for it.

In several essays in this book, I try to bring nuance and calibration to the Israeli controversy—a controversy about subtle issues that are more suited to academic debate in law schools then to raucous demonstrations and counterdemonstrations on the streets of Tel Aviv and in front of the United Nations. But even these angry protests have been largely peaceful and lawful, especially as contrasted with some in parts of the United States, France, and other democracies. They serve as a model—at least so far—for the right of the people to assemble and petition for a redress of grievances.

Since I wrote those words, priorities have changed dramatically in Israel, with the attack of October 7 and Israel's military response. Israelis are more united around the military challenges they are facing. The McCarthyite, woke, hard left has also become more united, and more deranged about Israel. Even before Israel responded militarily to the Hamas barbarism, the hard left blamed Israel rather Hamas and called for the destruction of the nation-state of the Jewish people.

Nuances and compromise, both essential to democracies governed by the rule of law, are often the first casualties of right- and left-wing, no-nothing McCarthyism. In this short book I fight back against the mindset that is so sure that it is the only right one. I do so in the spirit of the Great American jurist Learned Hand, who, as I've said, defined the spirit of liberty as "the spirit which is not too sure that it is right." I urge my readers to agree or disagree with me in that spirit.

CHAPTER 1

Getting Trump by McCarthyite Tactics

Donald Trump has now been indicted four times by Special Counsel Jack Smith in Florida and the District of Columbia: by Manhattan district attorney Alvin Bragg, and by Fulton County DA Fani Willis. In the op-eds contained in this chapter, in roughly chronological order, I analyze these indictments and their implications, especially in light of the new McCarthyism and weaponization of the justice system.

A. Pre-Manhattan Indictment

Indicting Trump in Manhattan Would Be Targeted Injustice

Does anyone actually believe that if someone else were accused of paying hush money to avoid a sex scandal in the manner that Mr. Trump is suspected of doing, he would be prosecuted?

When I was coming of age in the 1950s, Southern prosecutors would target civil rights workers and search for any possible violation of the law, no matter how technical. If they discovered or invented a violation, they would indict, prosecute, convict, and sentence the target.

Often the violation would be of an obscure statute that had never before been deployed. To paraphrase the late justice Robert Jackson, these anachronistic statutes and precedents lie around "like loaded weapons" ready to be selectively enforced against political enemies.

That, precisely, is what we are now seeing with the Manhattan district attorney, Alvin Bragg, targeting the former president and current candidate, Donald Trump. Does anyone actually believe that if someone else were accused of paying hush money to avoid a sex scandal in the manner that Mr. Trump is suspected of doing, he would be prosecuted?

After spending months searching the criminal code for a law that Mr. Trump might be accused of violating, Mr. Bragg has apparently landed on a highly questionable campaign contribution provision that has never before been used in a comparable situation.

As Jackson also presciently observed: "With the law books filled with a great assortment of crimes, a prosecutor stands a fair chance of finding at least a technical violation of some act on the part of almost anyone."

He added: "In such a case, it is not a question of discovering the commission of a crime and then looking for the man who has committed it, it is a question of picking the man and then searching the law books, or putting investigators to work, to pin some offense on him."

Not to compare Mr. Bragg's NYC to Stalin's Soviet Union, a sordid episode from the past does come to mind: the notorious head of the KGB, Lavrenty Beria, once said to Stalin: "show me the man, and I will find you the crime." Closer to home, J. Edgar Hoover would often target his political enemies for investigation. Or as a South American dictator once threatened: "for my friends everything; for my enemies the law."

All decent people, whether politically opposed to Mr. Trump (as I am) or supportive of his candidacy, should be concerned about this weaponizing of the prosecutor's office for the political purpose of preventing a potential candidate from running for office.

Today this insidious tactic is being used by a Democratic prosecutor against a Republican candidate. In 2016, efforts were made to use it against the Democratic candidate. No one knows who tomorrow's target will be, since the precedent will "lie around like a loaded weapon," to be misused by any ambitious prosecutor in a partisan manner.

It is no answer to say, as supporters of this "get Trump" tactic are arguing, that Mr. Bragg is doing nothing more than fully enforcing

the law on the ground that no one is "above" it. If Mr. Trump or anyone else did the crime, they should do the time. But others have done
things similarly to what Mr. Trump is suspected of doing, and no one
else is being threatened with prosecution.

It is in the nature of partisan selective prosecution that a target
may well be technically guilty of some violation. The question is would
he have been prosecuted for that violation if he were not the political
target.

The Bible sets out two prohibitions for judges. The most obvious
one is "do not take bribes." Interestingly, that comes second in the list
of prohibitions. The first is "do not recognize faces," which means that
justice should never be done based on who the defendant is. Mr. Bragg
has not only recognized the face of Mr. Trump, he has targeted him
specifically for selective investigation and prosecution.

The law does not generally recognize selective prosecution as a
defense to a charged crime. It should. But even if it doesn't, prosecutorial ethics should deter honest prosecutors from recognizing faces. Mr.
Trump should not be indicted for novel and unprecedented technical
crimes for which no one else would be prosecuted.

Equal protection of the law requires equal application and non-
application of criminal statutes. Mr. Bragg would be violating that
important principle if he seeks a grand jury indictment based on what
now appears to be the slim evidence and even slimmer legal basis.

As Bragg Eyes Possible Indictment of Trump, How Will He Surmount the Statute of Limitations

Under New York law, the statute for misdemeanor is two years and for
felony five years.

Statutes of limitations are intended to protect defendants against
stale prosecutions. They reflect the Sixth Amendment to the United
States Constitution that guarantees a speedy trial, as does the due process provisions of New York law. Justice delayed is justice denied to
defendants, because memories fade, witnesses become unavailable, and
exculpatory evidence becomes more difficult to obtain.

There are, of course, exceptions to most statutes of limitations.
Any period of time during which the potential defendant is hiding

or is otherwise unavailable, doesn't generally count in calculating the limitations. Accordingly, the New York State statute expressly exempts "any period [when] the defendant was continuously outside the state" or when "the whereabouts of the defendant were continuously unknown and continuously unascertainable in the exercise of reasonable diligence."

Obviously, President Trump's whereabouts were always known. After all, he was in the White House for most of the time. Moreover, he was never continuously out of New York, having repeatedly returned to the state where he maintained a residence until after he left the presidency.

So what will the district attorney of New York county argue? He will probably try to prove that Trump was not continuously in New York, because he was continuously in Washington and Florida. That argument should fail both as a matter of fact and as a matter of policy. As a matter of fact, Trump will be able to demonstrate visits to New York.

As a matter of policy, an indictment can be filed against the defendant even if he is not physically present in New York. In fact, it is likely that the current indictment against Trump may well be filed while he is in Florida. He will then come to New York where he can be formally arrested, arraigned, and processed.

Why then did the Manhattan district attorney not file misdemeanor charges within two years and felony charges within five years of the alleged offenses? For a very good reason: Alvin Bragg's predecessors did not believe they had a strong enough case to indict and convict.

They could easily have indicted, because, the former chief judge of the New York Court of Appeals quipped, "a prosecutor can get a grand jury to indict a ham sandwich." Yet they obviously felt they did not have a case sufficient to result in conviction and affirmance. So they did not indict.

Indeed, Mr. Bragg himself didn't even indict during the early part of his administration. If he indicts now, it will not be because this case is any stronger than it was within the period of limitations. He will indict now because of increasing political pressures from constituents, donors, and staff lawyers.

None of this is sufficient to evade the policies behind the applicable statutes of limitations. Accordingly, if and when Mr. Trump is indicted, his lawyers will immediately move to dismiss on the basis of the statute of limitations. This will probably require an evidentiary hearing at which prosecutors will be required to demonstrate that Trump was not continuously in New York for sufficient periods of time.

In the unlikely event they were able to do so, a reasonable judge might well conclude the policies behind statutes of limitations and speedy trial guarantees require a dismissal of the indictment, because there was no legitimate excuse for not indicting earlier.

In the usual case, a prosecutor would be hesitant to bring a stale case like this one, knowing that there is a good chance that it will be dismissed, but this is anything but a usual case. This is part of the "get Trump" syndrome, about which I have written in my book of that title. It is not surprising that a prosecutor who would stretch the substantive criminal laws in an effort to "get Trump" would also stretch the statute of limitations.

It seems as if Mr. Bragg doesn't much care if a trial or appellate judge throws out the case on statute of limitations grounds. He will be perceived as having done his job, and the blame will be placed on the judges. But some judges will not want to take the blame for so unpopular an action, because they too face reelection.

In states with elected prosecutors and elected judges, the primary check on abuse lies in the hands of prosecutors themselves. This worked when distinguished lawyers such as Robert Morgenthau and Frank Hogan occupied Mr. Bragg's office. It works less well when an opportunistic politician succumbs to partisan pressures.

Trump's Looming Indictment Is Ridiculously Weak. Bragg Has Disgraced His Office.

In all my sixty years of criminal defense litigating and teaching, I have never heard of a case based on such a ridiculous stretching of the law than the potential indictment of Donald Trump.

New York City district attorney Alvin Bragg is reportedly attempting to charge Trump for conduct related to his alleged $130,000 payment to porn star Stormy Daniels in exchange for her promise not to disclose a consensual, adulterous affair during his 2016 presidential campaign.

As of Friday morning, Bragg has told the grand jury considering these charges to go home until Monday. It's a clear sign of trouble.

In fact, the case may fall apart, and it should. Bragg has disgraced a once proud office.

To state the obvious, while immoral, it is not illegal to pay hush money. So, to turn this relatively benign payment into a state felony, the district attorney must perform a series of legal contortions.

First, he must prove that the payments were fraudulently described in business records.

Generally, one wouldn't be expected to dutifully document "hush money paid to a porn star to remain silent about an adulterous affair," as the whole point of the payoff is to keep it hush-hush. But Bragg wants to make it criminal.

In any event, even if the DA convinces a jury that Trump falsified business records, the worst-case scenario is that this crime is a minor misdemeanor.

That's hardly the scalp that Bragg desires. And so, he must perform another magic trick.

The DA would have to prove that the records were falsified for the purpose of covering up an unreported campaign contribution.

If Trump secretly paid Daniels to keep quiet for the sole benefit of his presidential campaign, then that may well be a federal crime.

And presto! According to Bragg's novel legal theory, that concocts a state felony for which he can prosecute Trump.

Don't try to make sense of it—it's nonsensical.

As it's been said—a prosecutor can indict a ham sandwich. But Bragg may fall laughingly short of even that low bar.

His whole argument hinges on a psychoanalyst's Freudian diagnosis of Trump's motivations. Why did he do what he allegedly did?

At trial, if the defense raises a reasonable doubt that Trump inaccurately recorded the alleged hush payment to prevent damaging embarrassment to his wife, his family, his business ventures, or for any reason other than his campaign, then the charges will not stick.

This case rises and falls on credibility. Unfortunately for Bragg, his key witness, former Trump lawyer and so-called fixer, Michael Cohen, doesn't have much.

If anyone has firsthand knowledge to back up Bragg's theory that Trump paid off Daniels to protect his political aspirations, it would be Cohen, who has already testified before the grand jury. He was the apparent conduit through which Trump paid Daniels. And he existed inside Trump's inner circle for years as a trusted—if not derided—employee.

If the Manhattan DA had any brains, he would have told Cohen to stay home. After all, he's a convicted liar.

In December of 2018, Cohen pled guilty in Manhattan federal court to campaign finance violations for coordinating a payment to Daniels and another woman with whom Trump was alleged to have had an affair.

Now a new letter, obtained by DailyMail.com, shows Cohen's lawyer informing the Federal Election Commission in 2018 that Trump wasn't involved in the hush money scheme.

The letter reads: "Neither the Trump Organization nor the Trump campaign was a party to the transaction with Ms. Clifford, and neither reimbursed Mr. Cohen for the payment directly or indirectly."

The obvious question for Cohen is: Were you lying then, or are you lying now?

On Monday, Cohen's former legal adviser, Robert Costello, testified before the grand jury. After he left the court, he told the media that he informed the jurors that Cohen, "couldn't tell the truth if you put a gun to his head."

Cohen also pled guilty to concealing more than $4 million in personal income from the IRS and lying to a bank to secure a home loan.

He was sentenced to three years in federal prison and ordered to pay a $50,000 fine.

No wonder Bragg sent jurors home for the weekend.

To suggest that Cohen has an axe to grind against Trump would be an understatement—in fact, he wrote two books about it.

In the aptly named *Disloyal* and *Revenge*, Cohen describes Trump as a power mad, wannabe dictator. No matter how inclined a jury is to punish Trump, they can't be completely blind to Cohen's bias.

Even if they are sympathetic to Cohen's antipathy—they can't ignore that he did help Trump when it was convenient.

Cohen plead guilty to lying to Congress about an abandoned project to build a Trump Tower in Russia. In his plea, he said he misled the US Senate Select Committee on Intelligence to protect Trump's campaign messaging.

Finally, Cohen is on tape threatening a journalist investigating the claims of Trump's first wife, the late Ivana Trump, who once accused Trump of spousal rape. She later retracted the claim.

"I will take you for every penny you still don't have," Cohen is heard telling then-*Daily Beast* reporter Tim Mak. "And, of course, understand that by the very definition, you can't rape your spouse," Cohen concluded.

Of course, that's not true. And it won't look good in front of a jury either.

It is still unknown whether there are other, more credible witnesses, who can incriminate Trump.

The publisher of the *National Enquirer*, David Pecker, may testify at a potential trial. He was also caught up in the alleged payments.

Pecker was fined $187,500 by the Federal Election Commission for "knowing and willfully" violating campaign finance law by paying a Playboy model for her story about an alleged affair with Trump for the purpose of never publishing it.

Daniels may also be called to the stand although her testimony would not be directly relevant to how Trump recorded the payments.

I would also advise the defense not to deny in court—if they ever get there—what Trump's lawyer has already denied to the media: that Trump had an affair with Daniels.

The jury will not believe that claim, and it would affect the credibility of the entire defense.

Nor should Trump take the stand in his defense, because to do so would open him up to embarrassing questions which he might be tempted to answer falsely.

If this type of prosecution, with the same facts and law, were directed against an ordinary citizen it would have virtually no chance of succeeding. But because the target is Trump and the location is the very blue city of New York, the likelihood of an indictment and conviction is better than even.

Even so, it would likely be reversed on appeal. In fact, Americans may be voting for president in 2024 as a court considers overturning.

Ironically, Bragg probably didn't care what an appellate court would do in two years. He was looking for his fifteen minutes of fame and for the political benefits that would result from a politically popular "get Trump" prosecution in heavily Democratic NYC.

Now he may be reconsidering. Bragg may be worried that his license to practice law may be on the line if he continues pushing this abject travesty of justice and puts a lying witness on the stand.

Even a political opportunist has limits.

The only real harm that will come from this case is the damage it will do to the country, as our society spirals deeper and deeper into division and distrust.

No matter the outcome of Bragg's case—we all lose.

As Effort to "Get Trump" Ramps Up, Are Leaks from Bragg's Grand Jury a Crime?

The protection of secrecy is as applicable to President Trump as it is to anyone else.

It is likely that a serious felony has been committed right under District Attorney Alvin Bragg's nose and he is not investigating it. Under New York law, it is a felony to leak confidential grand jury information, such as whether the jurors voted to indict. The protection of secrecy is as applicable to President Trump as it is to anyone else.

We know that the information was disclosed while the indictment itself remains sealed and before any official announcement was made or charges brought. It is unlikely that the leak came from the Trump team, which seemed genuinely surprised.

The most likely, though uncertain, scenario is that a person in Mr. Bragg's office or a grand juror unlawfully leaked the sealed information. That would be a class E felony, subject to imprisonment.

It is possible of course that an investigation is underway, but it seems more likely that Mr. Bragg is too busy making up a crime against the man he promised in his campaign to get than investigating a real crime that took place on his watch.

In my new book, *Get Trump*, I predicted that partisan prosecutors would try to get Trump regardless of the lack of evidence or law. That prediction has come true. Since the indictment itself has not been leaked—at least not yet—we don't know its specifics. We do know, based on leaks, that it involves multiple counts, almost certainly involving the payment of hush money to a porn actress.

Under Mr. Bragg's likely theory, Mr. Trump should have disclosed in his public corporate records that he paid the hush money to keep his adulterous affair from becoming public. But no one in history has ever publicly disclosed the reason he paid money for a non-disclosure agreement.

Why would Mr. Trump pay the money in the first place if he had to publicly disclose the embarrassing reason? Furthermore, no one in history has ever been indicted for listing "legal expenses" for sending a potentially embarrassing payment of hush money.

Thus, even the misdemeanor allegation involving false entries is unprecedented and represents selective prosecution. It is also almost certainly barred by the two-year statute of limitations. In order to elevate this bookkeeping case into a felony, Mr. Bragg must also prove beyond a reasonable doubt that the reason Trump made the false entry—if he himself did it—was solely as a campaign contribution to help him win his election.

Mr. Trump was motivated in part by his desire to protect his wife, children, and business interests from harmful disclosures, which would not constitute the crime of making an undisclosed campaign contribution. So this too is a stretch.

It is a fundamental tenet of American law that criminal law should not be stretched to fit targeted defendants. Criminal statutes must be clear and unambiguous. If there is any doubt, the age-old concept of "lenity" requires that these doubts be resolved in favor of the defendant.

Thomas Jefferson once quipped that for a criminal statute to be valid, it must be so clear that a reasonable person could understand it if he read it "while running." A nice image!

I intend to read the text of the indictment, while sitting, with sixty years of experience behind me. I doubt I will find that it meets the constitutional criteria for "fair warning," although I maintain an open mind until I have studied it carefully.

The important point is that when a district attorney runs for office as a Democrat pledging to get Mr. Trump, who is a candidate for president against the incumbent Democrat, that district attorney must have an airtight case.

A weak, questionable, unprecedented, and novel stitching together of two inapplicable statutes will not, and should not, satisfy the American public that this is not a partisan targeting of a political opponent.

Trump Indictment Case Looks Like a Weak Exercise in Creative Prosecution

When a district attorney who ran as a Democrat and promised to "get" Donald Trump indicts the candidate running for president against the incumbent head of his party, he had better have a slam dunk case. Although we don't know exactly what the Manhattan grand jury indicted Trump for, it seems likely, based on what we know, that this is a very weak case which would never have been brought against anyone else.

If this indictment is based on the hush money paid to a former porn star and the manner by which it was recorded in corporate records, this may be one of the weakest cases in my experience. It is a stale case that appears to be beyond the statute of limitations. The DA may argue that Trump was out of the state continuously during the period of limitations, thus tolling—that is, pausing—the statute of limitations, because the former president couldn't be indicted while out of state. But Trump was indicted while he was in Florida, so he could have been indicted any time over the past seven years. Why wasn't he?

Because previous prosecutors decided not to indict Trump based on the facts and law available to them. Has new evidence been discovered? We will see, but it seems unlikely.

This is a case of targeting an individual and then rummaging through the statute books in search of a crime. Prosecutors seem to have come up with nothing under established law, then made up a misdemeanor and then piggybacked it on another alleged crime to create a felony. But one plus one does not equal eleven, and zero plus zero equals zero. That is what we seem to have here.

And even this weak exercise in creative prosecution seems to rely on the testimony of Michael Cohen, who has a long history of lying to federal authorities. No ethical prosecutor can present Cohen to a jury as a credible witness. The DA can try to make the case without Cohen, though he apparently relied on Cohen's testimony to secure the indictment.

Because the case is to be presented to a Manhattan petit jury and judge—unless there is a change of venue—it is certainly possible that Trump could be convicted, against the weight of the evidence and the law. It is also possible that a conviction could be affirmed on appeal by New York courts. It would likely not survive Supreme Court review, but that will not occur for years, if at all.

In the meantime, Trump will continue to run for president. An indictment cannot constitutionally stop him. Neither could a conviction or even a prison sentence. This ill-advised indictment is likely to help his campaign to secure the Republican nomination. If he is photographed, his mug shot may become his campaign poster and the most popular mug shot T-shirt since Frank Sinatra's. I have already received messages from voters who said they had been planning to vote for Ron DeSantis in the 2024 GOP primary but will now vote for Trump as a protest against this indictment.

No one, of course, knows the impact this will have on the election. And that shouldn't matter. What matters greatly is that DA Alvin Bragg has weaponized the justice system to target a political opponent based on a nonexistent or, at best, an extremely weak crime.

When the indictment is unsealed, probably early next week, we will know the extent of the damage to the rule of law. It is not impossible that the evidence and law will surprise us all and present a slam dunk case. But based on everything we know about the long history of this investigation, don't count on it.

B. Post-Manhattan Indictment

No One but Donald Trump Would Be Charged with These Fake "Crimes"

On Tuesday, a historic event took place: For the first time in history, a sitting US president was indicted and charged. In a Manhattan courtroom, former president Donald Trump became the first president and the first presidential candidate ever to be indicted, arrested, and charged.

Since the indictment was announced last week, the nation has waited with bated breath for the indictment to be unsealed in the hopes that there would be something inside that justified such a momentous move on the part of New York's district attorney, Alvin Bragg.

There was not. Bragg's indictment and accompanying statement of facts produced thirty-four absolutely ridiculous charges based on book-keeping and record entries that don't even amount to a prosecutable misdemeanor—certainly not the felony with which former president Trump was charged.

The thirty-four charges hinge on hush money payments the former president allegedly paid to porn actress Stormy Daniels. Yet paying hush money to prevent publication of an adulterous sexual encounter is not a crime. Alexander Hamilton did it. So did thousands of other high-profile Americans. None of them ever disclosed such payments on public corporate records. After all, why pay the hush money if you have to publicly report the reasons it was paid?

Yet DA Bragg assured the American people that prosecuting such false record cases are the "bread and butter" of his office. I challenge Bragg to show us those cases. He won't be able to, because no one who pays hush money to conceal sex, then discloses that fact in public filings.

Yet that is the essence of Bragg's weak case.

There is a bit more to the indictment and the accompanying statement of facts than the sordid Stormy Daniels matter. District Attorney Bragg has sliced the salami very thin and turned this and related episodes into thirty-four separate charges. But at the bottom this is a records case.

In order to turn a questionable misdemeanor into an even more questionable felony, Bragg has had to allege that the reason Trump made false entries was to cover up other crimes. Here is where the indictment is at its weakest. Although the indictment itself does not specify which crimes were allegedly in Trump's mind, the statement of facts indicates that they generally related to election issues. The theory is that Trump hid the real reason for the hush money payments for the purpose of helping his campaign, rather than to hide the adulterous affair from his wife, children, and business associates.

It's weak at best, and nearly impossible to prove at worst.

There are other, more specific allegations in the indictment and statement of facts, and they will be presented to a jury in order to determine whether the specified felonies have been committed. But the jury it will be presented to will consist of Manhattan voters, if Bragg gets his way. Recall that Bragg campaigned on the promise to get Trump, and so the jury pool will undoubtedly include Manhattanites who voted for him to fulfill that pledge. By voting to convict Trump, they can help Bragg fulfill the pledge he made to voters and presumably jury members.

This does not seem to assure a fair trial, and that is why Trump's lawyers will undoubtedly move for a change of venue—something Bragg will no doubt strenuously oppose, because the last thing he seems to be aiming for is a fair trial.

Despite the thirty-four charges and the lengthy documents, it remains clear that no reasonable district attorney would have devoted this much time and this many resources to ferreting out records-keeping violations if there had not been a political motive behind it. Bragg's predecessor had the same evidence and declined to prosecute. So did Bragg at the beginning of his term—a decision which created a backlash and pressure on Bragg to change his mind. Bragg did so, and the result was Trump's appearance in a Manhattan courtroom on Tuesday.

His appearance marked a sad departure from past precedent and a high likelihood that this deeply flawed indictment will create a new precedent under which elected prosecutors of one party will search for possible crimes against their political opponents.

One remarkable aspect of this indictment is that none of the thirty-four charges cites any alleged victim of Trump's crimes. They are the personification of victimless crimes. But there are real victims: the American system of justice and the rule of law.

Manhattan Jury with Trump Derangement Syndrome May Unfairly Convict Donald

The most anticipated indictment in modern history has been released. And, believe it or not, Manhattan DA Alvin Bragg found an alleged crime.

Only it's not the supposed offense that he's prosecuting.

The only potential criminal wrongdoing identified after months of investigation by experienced professional prosecutors appears to be extortion.

But I'm talking about extortion of Trump, not by Trump. That's what it's called when an individual threatens to release damaging information about someone else unless they're paid to keep quiet.

Now, of course, I'm not calling for Stormy Daniels to be prosecuted. I wish her only the best. But this indictment speaks to how laughable and blatantly political this prosecution really is. It's a tragedy.

Bragg labored—mightily—ultimately, he produced a mouse.

Read the indictment documents for yourself. At first glance, the layman may assume that it holds some evidence of wrongdoing. Thirty-four counts laid out over thirteen-pages of an accompanying statement and couched in intimidating legalese.

As expected, the central narrative focuses on the payment of hush money to a former porn star in exchange for a non-disclosure agreement. But the document also broadens out the alleged Trump scheme to include payments to suppress the story of a former Trump Tower doorman, who was peddling an unconfirmed and likely false story of a child that Trump fathered out-of-wedlock, and another payment to former Playboy model Karen McDougal to hide the tale of her alleged extramarital affair with Trump.

Now look closer. All thirty-four counts are relatively similar. Bragg has sliced the salami very thin. In essence, this is a case about bookkeeping.

Stormy Daniels is not a victim. She willingly accepted Trump's money.

The American people are not victims. They elected Trump regardless of his behavior.

Ironically, Bragg—who has failed to go after criminal predators in the streets—has devoted time and resources, which could have been spent going after real killers and rapists and Ponzi schemers to instead go after a man for a victimless, alleged crime.

Clearly, none of the matters to Bragg. He finally has the case that he told the voters of Manhattan he would deliver to them.

During the 2021 race to elect the next Manhattan district attorney, a *New York Times* headline blared, "Two Leading Manhattan D.A. Candidates Face the Trump Question." As the article noted, Bragg wore his animosity towards Trump on his sleeve.

"I have investigated Trump and his children and held them accountable for their misconduct with the Trump Foundation," Mr. Bragg told a December 2020 candidate forum. "I know how to follow the facts and hold people in power accountable."

In November 2021, Bragg was elected.

Now, those same voters will make up the pool from which Trump's jury will be selected.

And by voting to convict Trump, these future jurors would help Bragg to fulfill the pledge he made to them.

This does not seem to assure a fair trial.

The anti-Trump passions in New York City are incredible. I've experienced them myself.

My acquaintance of many years, Caroline Kennedy, told me at a dinner party: "Alan, if I had known you, who have defended Trump on the floor of the Senate, were going to be at this dinner party, I would not have come. But I am too polite to get up and leave now."

A friend, comedian Larry David, confronted me outside a store shouting, "Alan, you're disgusting," over my defense of Trump.

Despite our friendship, they were furious with me, because I simply disagreed with them. You cannot reason with people who have Trump Derangement Syndrome.

That is why Trump's lawyers will undoubtedly appeal to the judge for a change of venue, which Bragg will strenuously oppose. The last thing he wants is a fair trial. He wants a trial that will allow him to realize his campaign promise.

This case should be moved to one of the New York City boroughs, such as Staten Island, or to another part of New York state. But the judge, also an elected Democrat, is unlikely to grant that request.

The American legal system took a body blow yesterday.

Trump's appearance in a courtroom to become the first former president and the first current presidential candidate ever to be indicted, arrested, and charged marked a sad departure from precedent. And this deeply flawed indictment will now create a new precedent under which elected prosecutors of both parties will search for possible crimes against their political opponents.

Whatever the outcome of this Bragg prosecution, Trump should eventually prevail. An appeals court should never uphold such an obvious misapplication of the law.

But I don't know if the American legal system can come back from this as easily. This is a perversion of justice. And if Trump is convicted, it will be a travesty of justice.

Americans everywhere now have cause for concern, because today it is Trump—but tomorrow it could be you.

The Trump-Carroll Verdict Is a Rorschach Test

The mixed verdict delivered by the jury in the Donald Trump civil rape case will be interpreted differently by those who support and oppose the former president.

On the main count that Trump raped E. Jean Carroll, the nine-person jury unanimously found that he did not. The plaintiff could not even satisfy its low burden of proof, namely proof beyond a preponderance of the evidence. In so finding, the jury apparently disbelieved at least part of the plaintiff's testimony. She was very specific about being raped, not merely sexually abused or molested, as the jury did find.

It's a strange verdict. The jury seems to have believed some of her testimony; namely that she had an encounter with Trump at Bergdorf Goodman in the mid-1990s, which Trump has adamantly denied, both in depositions and in public statements. He did not appear at trial either to testify or to sit in the courtroom, but his lawyer presented his denials to the jury.

It is also hard to reconcile the jury's finding that he did not rape her with its finding that he maliciously defamed her by essentially saying that he did not rape her.

Accordingly, the United States Court of Appeals for the Second Circuit to which this case will be appealed, will have its work cut out for it. There will be other substantial issues as well on appeal. They include the extension of the statute of limitations, after it had already expired, which allowed the plaintiff to bring a quarter-century-old case. This may well constitute denial of due process as guaranteed by the Fifth Amendment. Other appellate issues will include the judge's strange ruling that the names of the jurors will remain anonymous even to the lawyers, thus denying them the ability to research them and determine whether any hidden biases may have existed. This may violate the defendant's constitutional right to trial by jury guaranteed by the Seventh Amendment.

Additional appellate issues will include the judge's decision to admit some evidence presented by the plaintiff, such as the infamous *Access Hollywood* tape, in which Trump says that women permit celebrities to touch their private parts, as well as the testimony of other women who were deemed to corroborate the plaintiff's testimony. The judge also excluded some evidence that the defendant sought to admit.

All in all, if the appellant in this case had a name other than Donald Trump, there is a good likelihood that the entire verdict might be reversed. But almost nobody, whether they be a judge or a juror, doesn't have strong views about the former president. Whether these views impact judicial decisions is a question about which reasonable people might disagree.

The impact of this decision on Trump's political aspirations is also uncertain. The mixed verdict is something of a Rorschach test. Supporters of Trump will point to the jury's verdict that he did not commit rape. Opponents of Trump will point to the verdicts against him on the other charges as well as the $5 million that Trump will be obliged to pay her unless he wins the appeal.

The verdict is unlikely to hurt Trump's chances of securing the Republican nomination, since his base is unlikely to be influenced negatively—and that base is probably large enough to secure the nomination. But it may well impact independent voters in the general election. President Biden's sinking polls suggest that if the candidates in November 2024 are Trump and Biden, this will be an election of negatives: Who do you dislike least?

It's a long time until November 2024. During the 2016 campaign, many people thought that the disclosure of the *Access Hollywood* tape shortly before the election would sink Trump's chances, especially among women. That obviously proved untrue: many Trump supporters did not seem to care about accusations regarding his private life. But it remains to be seen whether enough voters care overall—and may be influenced by the unanimous verdict of nine jurors that he abused the plaintiff in this case.

The timing of the appeal may also play a role in voter perception. Under normal scheduling, the appellate verdict in this case could come down either shortly before or shortly after the election. That coming decision is completely in the hands of the judges of the Court of Appeals. They may well postpone the verdict until after the election so as not to influence its outcome.

This verdict is only the tip of a much larger iceberg of charges against Donald Trump. It is the first verdict directly involving his conduct. It is unlikely to be the last. Stay tuned. . . .

The Durham Report: Good People Doing Bad Things

The basic conclusions reached by the Durham report mirror the thesis of my book *Get Trump*: namely that good people have been willing to do bad things in order to prevent Donald Trump from being elected (or reelected) as president. These good people honestly believe that the noble (at least in their view) end in "getting" Trump and preventing him from being president justifies ignoble means, including mendacity and violation of long-established principles.

There can be no doubt that the Durham report is correct in having concluded that government officials—from the top down—viewed the evidence (or lack thereof) through the prism of resolving all doubts against Trump and in favor of his opponents. This was not so much a partisan bias, favoring Democrats over Republicans, because some of the worst offenders are Republicans who honestly believe that the Trump presidency endangered the national security of the United States.

They have the right to hold such a belief, whether correct or incorrect, but as the Durham report made clear, they had no right to distort the facts, the law, and the principles in an effort to prevent the perceived danger from materializing. It was Justice Louis Brandeis who understood the dangers of this approach a century ago, when he warned "The greatest dangers to liberty lurk in insidious encroachment by men of zeal, well-meaning but without understanding." Many of the people involved in the wrongdoing documented by the Durham report were well-intentioned. But they had little understanding of the consequences of their actions.

These consequences include applying a double standard based on who the individual is, rather than what he has done. The biblical command to judges not to "recognize faces" is equally applicable to prosecutors. This is the origin of the blindfold over the eyes of the statute of justice. But the Durham report establishes that many of those charged with doing justice peeked under their blindfolds and saw that the person involved was Donald Trump. They recognized his face, and they applied the double standard of justice or injustice to him.

Reasonable people can and do continue to believe that Trump poses dangers to democracy. I'm not here to argue that they are wrong. Indeed, I plan to vote against him for the third time, because I share some of their concerns. But what these well-intentioned people did poses a far greater danger to the rule of law and our constitutional system than anything Trump has done or is likely to do. Their benighted, even if well-intentioned, actions threatened to establish dangerous precedents that lie around like loaded guns, ready for the hand of any tyrant who is ill-intentioned.

It is important, therefore, that the Durham commission exposed the wrongdoing of these well-intentioned government operatives. The real question is whether the agencies involved will take steps to prevent the recurrence of the wrongs documented in the Durham report. These wrongs will not be easy to fix, because they are subtle and often not visible. They inhere in the minds and souls of those who committed them, even if some of their actions are not subject to external checks.

Another challenge that will be faced by those who want to see change is that critics of the report—even those who have not read it—will point out that it was written by a prosecutor appointed by the Trump administration. Already the media is seeking to discredit its conclusions in that way. The headline in the *New York Times*—"In final report, Trump era special counsel denounces Russia investigation"—highlights Durham's appointment by the Trump administration, as if to suggest partisan bias by the author of the report who has had long experience as a nonpartisan prosecutor.

Many Americans, particularly those who are part of the get Trump at any cost movement, will not see the need for change based on the conclusions of the Durham report. They will continue to believe that the Obama administration and the various governmental agencies taken to task by their report did the right thing. The report itself is written largely in dry technical language and will not well serve the need to educate the American public about the dangers inherent in doing what these wrongdoers did. It is unclear whether John Durham will speak further about this four-year investigation and conclusions. I hope he does. The broad lessons that should be drawn from this report are too important to downplay.

The Durham Report Exonerates Trump, Implicates the Anti-Trump Double Standard

The Durham report documents the double standard employed by the Obama administration in favor of Hillary Clinton. No surprise there. But it also documents a special double standard employed by Democrats and some Republicans specifically against former president Donald Trump.

On the Clinton double standard, Durham points to "highly significant intelligence" received "from a trusted foreign source pointing to a Clinton campaign plan to vilify Trump by tying him to Vladimir Putin so as to divert attention from her own concerns relating to her use of a private email server." He then concludes that "unlike the FBI's opening of a full investigation of unknown members of the Trump campaign based on raw, uncorroborated information, in this separate matter involving a purported Clinton campaign plan, the FBI never opened any type of inquiry, issued any taskings, employed any analytical personnel, or produced any analytical products in connection with the information."

The FBI applied a completely different standard to the Trump campaign, opening a full-scale criminal investigation, despite the absence of "any actual evidence of collusion" between that campaign and Russia. "Indeed, based on the evidence gathered in the multiple exhaustive and costly federal investigations of these matters, including the instant investigation, neither US law enforcement nor the Intelligence Community appears to have possessed any actual evidence of collusion in their holdings at the commencement of the Crossfire Hurricane investigation."

Durham criticized the FBI for failing to take the usual precautionary steps before opening the investigation. They failed to employ "any of the standard analytical tools typically employed by the FBI in evaluating raw intelligence," including "interviews of witnesses" or "significant review of its own intelligence databases" and other routine measures.

The report also documents the special animus toward Trump "at least on the part of certain persons intimately involved in the matter." There was what Durham calls "a predisposition to open an investigation into Trump."

This animus was not limited to partisan Democrats. Many Republicans and independents shared the view that Trump was uniquely dangerous to national security and that anything that could be done to prevent his presidency should be done, regardless of the evidence and lack thereof.

This view continues today among many Trump haters. They don't need evidence of what he has done or not done. They know who he is! And that's enough to justify any means to "get" him.

In my book *Get Trump*, I reach many of the same conclusions reached by Durham, and I extend them to the current investigations designed to prevent or weaken his candidacy. Both in 2016 and now, law enforcement officials who believe that Trump poses a unique danger to American democracy have themselves been willing to endanger our rule of law, by distorting the facts, stretching the law, and ignoring the Constitution—as long as it applies to Trump.

But such compromises of important principles never apply only to one person. They establish precedents that can then be applied to others. As H. L. Mencken cautioned, "The trouble about fighting for human freedom is that you have to spend much of your life defending sons of bitches: for oppressive laws are always aimed at them originally, and oppression must be stopped in the beginning if it is to be stopped at all."

The report provides no road map to avoid repetition of the mendacious, and sometimes illegal, vendetta of documents. Reform will not be easy, because the bias that created the Russia investigation was often subtle, if not invisible. The obvious bias expressed by one particular agent—Peter Strzok—was unusual in its visibility, because he reduced it to writing.

It will also be difficult to reform the FBI because many law enforcement officials think that what they did—and are continuing to do—is the right thing: stretching the law to fit the weak facts. Just look at what the New York district attorney Alvin Bragg is doing to Trump now: making up crimes in order to keep his campaign promise to get Trump.

The Durham report should be required reading for Bragg and all other law enforcement officials who believe it is their job to get Trump, by hook or by crook.

Already some Get Trumpers are criticizing the report, often without even reading it, because its author was appointed by the Trump administration. Of course, they would be praising it and its author's many years of experience as a nonpartisan prosecutor if the Report had favored the Democratic narrative. Most of its conclusions are based on hard evidence that is hard to discredit.

Its findings should be studied by all Americans who care about applying a single standard of justice, regardless of party or personality. It has never been more important, in our deeply divided nation, to guarantee that the law will be applied equally to all.

The Durham Report is a small but essential step in the right direction.

C. Florida Classified Document Indictment: A Smoking Cigarette Butt!

Did Trump Declassify Documents? Criminal Indictment of Former President Has No Legitimate Basis

It seems likely that former president Donald Trump will allege that he declassified the documents that he took to Mar-a-Lago before he left office.

If that claim is presented to the courts, either by legal pleadings or testimony, it will raise several related issues. The first is a question of law, the second is an issue of evidence, and the third is one of procedure.

Let's begin with the law.

There could be little dispute that a president, while in office, has the power to declassify any previously classified documents or material. As the head of the executive branch, he has the last word on what remains classified or declassified. It is possible, though not beyond dispute, that Congress could constrain that power if it enacted clear legislation.

Some would argue that the Constitution precludes the legislative branch from limiting the power of the executive, but that is moot at the moment because Congress has not enacted statutes that specifically prevent the president from declassifying material.

Some think they should, as a matter of policy, formalize the declassification process so as to make it transparent. But absent such legislation, it seems clear that the authority to classify and declassify is an executive function, and the president is the executive. So, if Mr. Trump did declassify documents that were then moved to Mar-a-Lago, mere possession of such documents would not be a crime.

The next question is, did Mr. Trump in fact declassify these documents? If he claims he did, it will be up to the government to challenge that assertion. It could do so in several ways. It could offer evidence designed to disprove Mr. Trump's claim. But proving a negative—in this case, that he did not declassify the documents—is always difficult.

Theoretically, there could be evidence that Mr. Trump told an associate that he was taking classified material with him, knowing it was still classified. It is extremely unlikely, however, that any such evidence exists.

The government could also claim that absent any evidence either way, it must be presumed that a document once classified remains classified. But that ignores the fact that a statement by Mr. Trump to the contrary, if given under oath, would be evidence. And if Mr. Trump decides not to testify, there may be no admissible evidence either way.

In addition, the government could argue that the circumstantial evidence, especially the failure to announce any declassification until the criminal investigation began, can be weighed against his allegation. This is a weak argument, especially if there is no requirement in the law that declassification be announced or recorded.

These factual disputes would have to be resolved by twelve jurors if the government were to present sufficient evidence to warrant its submission to a jury.

The third basic issue, and the one that could determine the outcome of any criminal case, is closely related to the second: Who has the burden of proof on the claim of declassification? That is an issue of legal procedure.

In the usual criminal prosecution, the government has the heavy burden of proving every element of the crime beyond a reasonable doubt. The status of the documents as classified is an element of crimes that prohibit the unauthorized possession of classified material. The government may claim that the question of whether documents once classified have been declassified is a matter of law to be decided by the judge. That is a weak argument under the Fifth and Sixth amendments and their history.

The bottom line is that if Mr. Trump or his lawyers allege— even without his testifying—that he declassified the documents, a criminal charge of unauthorized possession of classified documents would be difficult to prove. That doesn't mean that a prosecutor could not get a grand jury to indict this particular ham sandwich. It does mean that it's unlikely that a conviction against Mr. Trump would be sustainable.

The government is certainly aware of these difficulties, so it may be seeking to indict Mr. Trump on some process crime, such as obstruction of justice. But it will be difficult to establish that Mr. Trump crossed the line from vigorously and lawfully defending his conduct to engaging in criminal obstruction.

No citizen is required to cooperate in a Department of Justice criminal investigation, as President Biden and others have commendably done. Nor can he actively obstruct such an investigation by unlawful means. The government will have a hard time proving beyond a reasonable doubt that Mr. Trump willfully crossed this line.

Based on what we know, we believe that there is no legitimate basis for a criminal indictment of Mr. Trump based on the material that was found at Mar-a-Lago.

Indictment of Trump—the Leading Candidate to Unseat the Administration—Is a Moment to Keep an Open Mind and Wait for the Facts

The burden is on this administration to demonstrate that the case is so strong that failing to bring it would be a great injustice.

The indictment of President Trump better be the strongest case of obstruction of justice since Richard Nixon. Anything short of that will smack of a partisan double standard. For never before in American history has the leading candidate to unseat the incumbent President been indicted by the incumbent President's administration.

The burden is on this administration to demonstrate that the case is so strong that failing to bring it would be a great injustice. It must be far stronger than the cases that were not brought against Hillary Clinton, Joseph Biden, Sandy Berger, and Mike Pence. Perhaps it passes that test, and if it does there will be no basis for any complaint.

If it does not, the indictment of Donald Trump will seriously damage the neutrality of America's rule of law. So let's see what the indictment says, what the facts are, and what the law is. Let's not rush to judgment on either side. Let's be certain that this passes a rigorous test that must be applied when a candidate for president is indicted.

Elections should be decided by the voters, not by prosecutors, judges, or jurors. If there is any doubt about whether a serious crime has been committed by a presidential candidate, that doubt should be resolved by the voters, not by prosecutors who come from an administration that the indicted candidate is trying to unseat.

The Biden administration has a heavy burden to demonstrate that they had no alternative but to prosecute. Maybe this case can meet that high standard, but citizens have a right to be skeptical. Recall that President Nixon was forced to resign not because Democrats demanded that he leave office, but because his fellow Republicans did so.

The indictment against Mr. Trump must be strong enough to generate the kind of bipartisan support that led Richard Nixon to leave office. To be sure, times have changed since the Nixon resignation. We are a more partisan and more divided nation, but there are reasonable Republicans and Democrats who are not necessarily part of the extreme partisanship that afflicts today's Republicans and Democrats.

Let us see whether moderate Republicans support this indictment. I predicted in my book "Get Trump" that he would not be indicted merely for unauthorized possession of classified material, because so many Democrats have been guilty of the same crime. I predicted that if he were indicted it would be for process crimes such as obstruction of justice.

It must be understood that obstruction of justice requires more than refusing to cooperate with prosecutors. To their credit, President Biden and the former vice president, Mike Pence, did cooperate when it was discovered that they had unauthorized possession of classified material. Mr. Trump's failure to do so, though, is not a crime.

The Constitution empowers people being investigated for criminal conduct to refuse to cooperate with prosecutors and indeed to obstruct their efforts by constitutionally authorized means, such as invoking the Fourth, Fifth, and Sixth Amendments. Whether Mr. Trump went beyond that and crossed the line into unlawfully obstructive behavior is a matter of evidence, to which we are not privy.

So let us all keep an open mind until we know all of the facts, but let's remain skeptical about an incumbent administration prosecuting the leading candidate to unseat that administration in the forthcoming election.

A Most Dangerous Indictment

For the first time in American history, the leading candidate to defeat the incumbent president has been indicted by the incumbent's Justice Department. Former president Donald Trump has been indicted by a federal grand jury for illegally retaining classified government documents and obstructing justice.

This is a momentous occasion, and not only for President Trump. This moment portends a massive change in the norms of this nation that all Americans who care about the neutral rule of law should pay close attention to, for it raises the specter of the partisan weaponization of the criminal justice system—not just by the Democrats targeting Trump but by Republicans who will certainly retaliate when they regain control of the criminal charging process.

How do we know this is about political retribution, not the rule of law? Look at the case. One would expect that such an unprecedented criminal prosecution would be the strongest one in political history. And yet, what information we do have suggests a weak case that would never have been brought if it wasn't being brought against Donald Trump.

Indeed, in my book *Get Trump*, I predicted that Trump would be indicted. But even writing a book about the massive attacks President

Trump sustained from his political adversaries, I could not have imagined that the Department of Justice would suffice with a charge as meager as the mere possession of classified documents. I thought they would go after Trump over some process crime growing out of the investigation. I assumed that before proceeding, they would develop a far stronger case—certainly stronger than the extraordinarily weak case put forward by District Attorney Alvin Bragg in Manhattan.

It appears that I was wrong. I gave them too much credit.

The indictment has yet to be unsealed, and there is still a slim possibility that there is a smoking gun, as there was in the obstruction cases against Richard Nixon that led his Republican colleagues to demand his resignation. We will know better when the seven-count indictment is made public, presumably on Tuesday. But based on what we know now, this does not seem like a strong case, especially if it is based on the Espionage Act of 1917, as a charge of illegally retaining documents is.

Ironically, the Espionage Act has been condemned by liberals, progressives, and Democrats since it became the open-ended weapon of choice aimed at political dissidents such as *Eugene v. Debbs* and other anti-war icons. It is vague and capable of being stretched to cover political enemies. So are the other two charges that have been referenced: conspiracy to obstruct justice and lying to law enforcement officials.

Contrast these flimsy accusations with those made against Richard Nixon, which included bribing witnesses, destroying evidence, and other concrete crimes.

At the moment, there is no suggestion of such open and shut accusations. Instead, they seem closer to the accusations made against presidential candidate Hillary Clinton, which never resulted in an indictment.

In order for the public to believe that the soon to be disclosed indictment is not politically motivated, it must be far stronger than the cases that were not brought against other political figures and at least as strong as that against Nixon. That is a high bar, but it must be reached if our Justice Department is to maintain any semblance of impartiality.

It will not be enough to show technical violations that are sometimes prosecuted but often not. It is unlikely that the recording of

Trump showing classified material to a writer will suffice, unless prosecutors can establish the contents of these documents and that they were actually read by an unauthorized person. There must be evidence of willful conduct that violates clear and unambiguous laws and that gives honest prosecutors no choice but to indict.

I doubt that these rigorous but necessary criteria have been met in the current indictment against Trump, but I have an open, if skeptical, mind. As matters stand now, this "momentous" political case threatens to be a momentous challenge to our system of impartial justice.

A Strong Trump Indictment—but Is It Strong Enough?

The evidence against the former president is powerful, but the jurors aren't the only ones who will need convincing.

Special counsel Jack Smith is both confident in his case against Donald Trump and sensitive to political considerations—though those considerations are subtler than the kind of partisan advantage that Manhattan district attorney Alvin Bragg is after.

That's why Mr. Smith brought the charges in Florida. He thinks the case is strong enough that a jury will convict Mr. Trump even in a jurisdiction of diverse party affiliations. His confidence may also explain why he alleged that Mr. Trump willfully rather than negligently mishandled classified material. He might also have wanted to distinguish Mr. Trump's case from those of Hillary Clinton, Joe Biden, and Mike Pence, none of which allegedly involved willfulness.

What should have begun as a routine civil investigation under the Presidential Records Act has ended up with a multi-count criminal indictment, the first federal prosecution ever of a former president or a leading candidate for the presidency. This is partially because prosecutors targeted Mr. Trump and partially because of the unwise way he responded.

Mr. Bragg campaigned for his office on a promise to hold Mr. Trump accountable and delivered when he persuaded a grand jury to hand up a weak indictment. Mr. Smith was appointed specifically to investigate Mr. Trump, and he did his job well. The problem inheres in the office of special counsel, which by its nature selects its target and looks for evidence against him.

Mr. Smith had a lot of help from Mr. Trump. Had the former president cooperated with investigators and immediately returned all the classified material in his possession, as Messrs. Biden and Pence did, charges would have been unlikely. But Mr. Trump did what he always does. He attacked Mr. Smith and resisted his efforts. That provoked investigators to double down, which in turn led Mr. Trump to engage in the allegedly obstructive conduct that forms the basis for several counts in the indictment.

Mr. Smith subpoenaed Mr. Trump's lawyers and persuaded a judge that Mr. Trump had violated the attorney-client privilege by instructing them that it would be "better if there are no documents." The defense team will claim that Mr. Trump was entitled to maintain possession of classified material under the Presidential Records Act of 1978, which establishes detailed procedures for handling the records of former presidents and a civil process for resolving disputes about them. It doesn't carry criminal penalties for noncompliance. Remarkably, the indictment never mentions the Presidential Records Act, despite its apparent relevance to any possible prosecution under the Espionage Act of 1917.

The indictment quotes tape-recorded conversations that form the basis for several charges under the Espionage Act. The critical recording is of a conversation between Mr. Trump, a writer, a publisher, and two Trump staffers, who were discussing a claim that a senior military official had persuaded Mr. Trump not to order an attack on "country A," which in context is surely Iran. Mr. Trump points to some papers he found and tells his guests they prove that military officials supported an attack. "This totally wins my case," he says. "This is secret information. Look, look at this." Mr. Trump then says: "See, as president I could have declassified it. Now I can't, you know, but this is still a secret."

It is possible that Mr. Trump merely waved the papers in front of his guests and never gave them an opportunity to read them, which is apparently not in evidence because the prosecutors don't have the document. But even those hypothetical facts would be enough to support the charge of willfully possessing classified material in an unauthorized manner.

The reason this recording is so powerful is that it is self-proving. It doesn't rely on testimony by flipped witnesses or antagonists of

Mr. Trump. It is the kind of evidence every defense lawyer dreads and every prosecutor dreams about. This is particularly important because an appellate court could find legal error in the ruling that Mr. Trump had violated attorney-client confidentiality and reverse convictions based on his lawyers' compelled testimony. A conviction that rests on a consensually recorded conversation would be harder to challenge.

Mr. Smith has made a stronger case against Mr. Trump than many observers, including me, expected. The question remains: Is it strong enough to justify an indictment of the leading candidate to challenge the president in next year's election? Even with the recorded statements, this case isn't nearly as strong as the one that led to President Richard Nixon's resignation in 1974. Nixon was almost certainly guilty of destroying evidence, bribing witnesses, and other acts of obstruction. Many of the charges in this case are matters of degree. Nor have prosecutors any evidence that Mr. Trump's actions damaged national security more than those of Mr. Biden, Mr. Pence, and Mrs. Clinton did.

When an incumbent administration prosecutes the leading candidate against the president, it should have a case that is so compelling that it attracts the kind of bipartisan support that forced Nixon to resign. No such support is currently apparent, since many Republicans continue to be troubled by the targeting of Mr. Trump. Mr. Smith will have to convince not only a Miami jury but the American public, on both sides of the partisan divide.

Trump and the Case of the Audio Evidence

The playing of the most recent Trump audio recording on CNN raises several important questions. First, how did CNN acquire the recording, which is part of an ongoing criminal investigation and prosecution? The only people who should have had access to it were prosecutors, the Trump aides who made the recording, and perhaps the Trump legal defense.

If prosecutors leaked it, that would almost certainly constitute a crime or at the very least a violation of Justice Department rules. If the Trump defense leaked it without Mr. Trump's permission, that too would raise serious legal and ethical questions. CNN will almost certainly not disclose the source but others in the press should be asking these questions.

The second issue is whether there is any possible defense that the Trump legal team can offer to what the prosecution regards as a smoking gun with fingerprints. Mr. Trump has claimed in an interview that what he showed the writer and publisher were not classified documents but rather newspaper and magazine reports on the issue.

Listening to the recording, however, suggests that Mr. Trump showed them a document that he said was secret and that he could have declassified, but did not, while he was president. It is likely, therefore, that the prosecution will be able to prove at trial that Mr. Trump showed the writer and publisher material that he believed was still classified.

It is possible, however, that although Mr. Trump believed the material to be classified, its contents had already been made public, and it had thereby lost its status as top secret and classified. Mr. Trump may not have known this, but some previously classified material may automatically lose that status when the contents are made public. If this is the case, then Trump could not be charged with unlawfully possessing and showing classified secrets.

Now here's an interesting twist that grows out of my fifty years of teaching criminal law: What if Mr. Trump mistakenly believed that he was showing material that was still classified and secret? He said he believed it on the recording, but his belief may have been incorrect. Could he be charged with attempting a crime if he erroneously believed that material that had become declassified were still classified?

That question has been a staple of criminal law classes for centuries. Indeed, I won such a case nearly fifty years ago, when I successfully defended a man who shot his acquaintance believing he was alive when in fact he was already dead. This defense is denominated as "impossibility." There are two kinds of impossibility under the law: legal and factual.

It is a matter of dispute and degree whether these defenses are valid, and it is unclear whether they would be successful in a case like this one. But before we even get to that perplexing issue it would have to be established that the documents had not been declassified by prior publication.

The next question is who would have the burden of proof on that issue. Would the government have to prove beyond a reasonable doubt that the contents of the documents had not been publicly disclosed and thus effectively declassified? Or would the defense have to offer proof of prior publication? This, too, is a complex and difficult question.

Beyond the fascinating issues posed by CNN's release of the audio tape, the burden of proof has now been shifted in the court of public opinion. In the court of law, the burden always remains on the prosecution. Yet the public is entitled to draw its own conclusions from the available evidence.

Listening to the recording with one's own ears, rather than reading it through the filter of an indictment or press bias, places the burden on the Trump team to explain what everybody can now hear from Mr. Trump's own mouth. So far the explanations have been less than satisfactory, but this is just the beginning of what promises to be a long process, both in and out of the courtroom.

Normally defendants are instructed by their lawyers to remain silent before a trial, but here the defendant is running for president and complete silence is not really a political option. So let's see how the Trump teams—both legal and political—handle the most recent disclosure, namely the recording of what appears to be incriminating statements.

Mr. Trump has already stated that the recording is exculpatory. Perhaps that is wishful thinking, or perhaps the former president knows something that he is not yet sharing.

What If Both Trump and His Prosecutors Are Guilty?

The most intriguing question—legal, political, and moral—about the Trump indictment can best be understood through the vehicle of several hypotheticals: What if a white Southern prosecutor announced that he would only investigate crimes committed by blacks; he then devoted all of his resources to looking for black crimes and none to white crimes; as a result he uncovered evidence of a crime committed by a black citizen.

Would the selective prosecution of the black person be legally valid under the equal-protection clause of the Constitution? Would it be morally acceptable? Would it depend on the nature and seriousness of the crime? Would it depend on whether similar crimes had been committed by whites and not prosecuted?

Now change the hypothetical slightly. It is a prosecutor elected on the Democratic ticket or appointed by a Democrat; he announces that he will investigate only crimes committed by Republicans; and his selective investigation turns up a crime committed by a Republican.

Finally, a third and most relevant, "hypothetical": a prosecutor elected or appointed by Democrats announces that he is focusing his investigation on the leader of the Republican Party, who is running against the incumbent Democratic president; and his selective investigation uncovers an actual crime by that Republican.

It's the third hypothetical that troubles many objective observers, including moderate Democrats as well as Republicans, because it seems clear that Donald Trump has been and is being targeted. Justice Robert Jackson's warning against selective targeting—picking the man and then searching the law books, or putting investigators to work, to pin some offense on him—must be heeded.

Some will argue that regardless of the means used, special counsel John Smith did uncover evidence—some out of Trump's own mouth and the mouths and pens of his lawyers—that proves his guilt. Would they make the same argument about strong evidence uncovered by the racist prosecutor who only investigated black (or Jewish, or gay, or Catholic, or Muslim) crime? If not, how would they distinguish the cases?

Would they deny that Trump was targeted? Both Manhattan district attorney Alvin Bragg and New York attorney general Letitia James campaigned on "get Trump" platforms, and special counsel Smith was assigned a specific target: namely, Donald Trump. Would they argue that racial targeting is worse than partisan political targeting? Would they assert that Trump deserved to be targeted?

Would they condemn the targeting and perhaps punish the targeters, but at the same time prosecute the guilty targeted person?

These are issues worthy of serious debate in a society committed to equal justice. As Smith said in his post-indictment news conference: "We have one set of laws in this country, and they apply to everyone."

But Smith's job isn't to apply the law equally to all. It is to investigate only one person and to indict and prosecute him if the selectively obtained evidence warrants it—regardless of whether others may have committed comparable crimes.

I have long opposed the appointment of special counsel to investigate and prosecute targeted individuals. Just as to a hammer, everything looks like a nail, so to a special prosecutor, evidence points to his target. Investigating events—such as Iran-Contra—is different. Had Smith been appointed to probe the mishandling of classified material by all former high-ranking officials—not just Trump, but also President Biden, former vice president Mike Pence, and former secretary of state Hillary Clinton, among others—and had found that only Trump violated the law, then he could credibly say that the law applies equally to everyone. But by investigating only one such official and prosecuting him without any comparison to others, his claim of equal justice rings hollow.

Moreover, Smith went further than other prosecutors in seeking to violate the lawyer-client privilege. The judges have supported him—mistakenly in my view—and much of his case rests on disclosures made by Trump's lawyers. Other subjects of investigations haven't had their confidential communications challenged under comparable circumstances. This too raises questions about the equal application of the law.

So the questions raised by the indictment of Trump go beyond whether the evidence gathered against him rises to the level of prosecutable crimes; they raise issues of process and equal justice. Some of these issues may be tried in a court of law. But even those that don't raise justiciable claims may raise moral and political concerns that should be subject to debate in the court of public opinion.

Trump's Trials Should Be Televised

The American public has the right to view legal proceedings regarding former president Donald Trump, including pretrial, trial, and post-trial courtroom appearances. At the moment, federal trials are not televised, although many state trials are. The two impeachment trials of President Trump were televised. Transparency and accountability require that both of the Trump trials now pending—the one in Manhattan and the one in Miami—should be televised. Both sides should agree and should petition the judge. If the judge refuses, Congress should enact immediate legislation opening this federal trial to television cameras.

I don't know whether either side favors or opposes televising the trial, but I am certain the public supports maximum transparency.

I have long believed that all trials, except perhaps those involving minors and other select exceptions, should be televised. Citizens have a right to see all three branches of their government in action. Today Congress is on television. So is the president's State of the Union and other important addresses and events. There is no good reason for making an exception for the judiciary. This is especially true now when there is so much public distrust of the courts.

If the Trump trial is not televised, the public will learn about the events through the extremely biased reporting of today's media. It will be as if there were two trials: one observed by reporters for MSNBC, CNN, the *New York Times*, and other liberal media, the other through the prism of reporters for Fox, Newsmax, and other conservative outlets. There will be nowhere to go to learn the objective reality of what occurred at trial.

There are of course some small risks associated with televising a highly publicized trial, such as Trump's in Florida. Participants may play to the camera, but that is already true of members of Congress and other officials whose hearings are currently televised. The public can generally distinguish pomposity from authenticity. But whatever small risks that there are, they are more than outweighed by the benefits of transparency.

As with state trials that are now televised, jurors' faces would not be revealed, and information sealed by the judge should be kept from viewers. But the testimony, the cross-examination, the physical evidence, and other important elements of the trial should be made available for all to see and judge. There can be a brief delay in transmission to protect against any glitches.

I have argued several cases that were televised. The participants quickly forget the cameras and focus on the judge and jurors. There are some distractions, but they don't have a major impact on the case.

In the O. J. Simpson case, the judge and some of the lawyers played to the cameras, but their presence had no discernible effect on the trial or verdict. Those who watched it learned a lot about the legal system. The same is likely to be true in a trial involving Trump. Today, people have chosen sides. They are rooting for an outcome consistent with their side and they are likely to read newspapers and view media that support their perspective. These biases may not be completely eliminated by observing the trial in its entirety, but they will be moderated by seeing the evidence and testimony for themselves.

Most important, the American legal system is under attack from both the right and the left. Although it is far from perfect, our legal system is, in general, better than how it is perceived by partisans. Most of the participants—judges, jurors, lawyers, and even litigants—try to do their jobs honestly. Some do better than others, and we the public are entitled to see the good, the bad, and the ugly.

There will be resistance from some, especially judges, who would rather operate behind the cloak of relative secrecy, but the Constitution forbids that. It requires public trials. At the time of the Constitution's framing, there was of course no TV or radio. A public trial consisted of townsfolk and newspaper reporters being present. Today, "public" has an entirely different meaning. I believe that the framers would have required the trial to be as open as technology permits, consistent with other important considerations. A public trial today is a trial that every American can see and evaluate. TV should become a part of our legal system. This is true of every trial, federal and state, civil and criminal.

It should be especially true of the first trial in American history in which the leading candidate to unseat the incumbent president is the defendant. Justice must not only be done, it must be seen to be done. And the more people see it, the more justice there will be. So let's do whatever it takes, whether through judicial opinions or legislation, to open our courthouses—especially the one in the Southern District of Florida, which will become the focus of the world when Trump goes on trial.

Why Donald Trump Is Having Trouble Getting a Top-Tier Lawyer

Former president Donald Trump has now been arraigned and pleaded not guilty. He was represented by two lawyers, neither of whom he apparently wants to lead his defense at trial. He has been interviewing

Florida lawyers, and several top ones have declined. I know because I have spoken to them. There are disturbing suggestions that among the reasons lawyers are declining the case is because they fear legal and career reprisals.

There is a nefarious group that calls itself The 65 Project that has as its goal to intimidate lawyers into not representing Trump or anyone associated with him. They have threatened to file bar charges against any such lawyers. When these threats first emerged, I wrote an op-ed offering to defend pro bono any lawyers that The 65 Project goes after. So The 65 Project immediately went after me, and contrived a charge based on a case in which I was a constitutional consultant, but designed to send a message to potential Trump lawyers: If you defend Trump or anyone associated with him, we will target you and find something to charge you with. The lawyers to whom I spoke are fully aware of this threat—and they are taking it seriously.

There may be other reasons as well for why lawyers are reluctant to defend Trump. He is not the easiest client, and he has turned against some of his previous lawyers, as some of his previous lawyers have turned against him. This will be a difficult case to defend and an unpopular one with many in the legal profession and in the general population.

Good lawyers, however, generally welcome challenges, especially in high-profile cases.

This case is different. The threats to the lawyers are greater than at any time since McCarthyism. Nor is the comparison to McCarthyism a stretch. I recall during the 1950s how civil liberties lawyers, many of whom despised Communism, were cancelled and attacked if they dared to represent people accused of being Communists. Even civil liberties organizations stayed away from such cases, for fear that it would affect their fundraising and general standing in the community. It may even be worse today, as I can attest from my own personal experiences, having defended Trump against an unconstitutional impeachment in 2020. I was cancelled by my local library, community center, and synagogue. Old friends refused to speak to me and threatened others who did. My wife, who disagreed with my decision to defend Trump, was also ostracized. There were physical threats to my safety.

Our system of justice is based on the John Adams standard: he too was attacked for defending the British soldiers accused of the Boston Massacre, but his representation of these accused killers now serves as a symbol of the Sixth Amendment right to counsel. That symbol has now been endangered by The 65 Project and others who are participating in its McCarthyite chilling of lawyers who have been asked to represent Trump and those associated with him.

Trump's lawyers have now alleged that one of the prosecutors has suggested to Stanley Woodard, the lawyer for Walt Nauta, Trump's co-defendant, that his application for judgeship may be negatively affected if he persists in defending Nauta vigorously rather than encouraging him to cooperate against Trump. If that is true—I have not seen the evidence to support it—then it represents a direct attack on the Sixth Amendment.

Whatever one may think of Trump or the charges against him, all Americans must stand united against efforts to intimidate lawyers and chill them from defending unpopular clients pursuant to the Sixth Amendment. Bar associations must look into the threats and actions of The 65 Project and of prosecutors who try, by subtle or other means, to influence the representation of clients by threats to their careers or other means.

Hard cases may make bad law, but partisan cases endanger constitutional rights. We must do everything to assure that all defendants, including Donald Trump, get the zealous representation to which the Constitution entitled all Americans.

Trump's Prosecutors Shouldn't Get to Use the Word "Espionage"

Former president Donald Trump has been charged with a variety of crimes, including violation of the misnamed Espionage Act.

That 1917 statute is misnamed because it covers a great many offenses that don't involve spying or giving secrets to the enemy.

In fact, over the years it has been used extensively against patriotic Americans who have opposed wars and dissented from other government actions.

In Trump's case, he is being accused primarily of unlawful possession of allegedly classified material.

But because he has been charged under the Espionage Act, many people have been misled into believing the accusations against him have something to do with espionage, spying, or even treason.

The use of the term espionage is extremely prejudicial to Trump in the court of public opinion. It would be even more prejudicial in a court of law if the jury were to hear that word in connection with his case.

Accordingly, Trump's lawyers should immediately move for what's called a motion in limine prohibiting the use of the word espionage by prosecutors, either inside the courtroom or outside it, but especially in front of the jury.

"Espionage" has no relevance to the upcoming trial. It associates Trump with some of the worst offenses imaginable.

Julius and Ethel Rosenberg were executed for espionage. Several former government officials have served long terms for espionage.

Those defendants actually provided classified and other secret information to our enemies.

Trump should not be painted with that invidious brush, based on the evidence in his case.

It's common for judges to prohibit prosecutors from using prejudicial terms in front of the jury.

The judge generally weighs the probative versus the prejudicial impact. In criminal cases, judges should always err on the side of protecting the rights of defendants.

This is not a hard case for barring the use of the term espionage since it has little or no probative effect and a vast potential for prejudice.

That the name of the statute uses the word is no excuse to let the prosecution use it. Often statutes have broad names that have little or nothing to do with the charges in a particular case.

Imagine this hypothetical: Congress passes a statute and entitles it "The Protection Against Child Molestation and Insider Trading Act."

Should prosecutors be allowed to mention the first part of that statute in a case that does not involve child molestation? Of course not.

Nor should the prosecution in this case be allowed to mention the word espionage, even though Congress misnamed the statute with that loaded term.

For this case, the law should be referred to only by mentioning the allegedly unlawful possession of classified material.

That is the essence of this prosecution, and the defendant should not be prejudiced by reference to other aspects of the statute that have no direct bearing on this case.

It's not too early for the defense to file this motion or for the court to grant it. Already, Trump has been prejudiced by media references to the law's "espionage" title.

The court can't stop the media from using that word, but by explicitly ruling it out of the trial, it can have an impact on public opinion and thus on the potential jury pool.

Espionage is a word that denotes some of the most evil intentions on the part of those accused of it. The impact could be subtle, even unconscious, but it is real.

The government would suffer no prejudice from a ban on the term in court. It can still argue Trump's actions may have endangered our national security, but it won't have the help of a misnamed statute.

True, any improper possession of highly classified material may pose some danger to national security if it gets into the wrong hands.

But that would be true as well of the improper possession and use of classified material by others who have not been charged, such as President Joe Biden, former vice president Mike Pence, and former presidential candidate Hillary Clinton.

The American public has the right to judge how serious these dangers were in each case, but its judgment shouldn't be influenced by prosecutors throwing around the word espionage just because it's in the statute.

Indeed, the media themselves should be more responsible and explain that the charges are under provisions of the statute that have nothing to do with spying.

In any trial of Donald Trump, there will be prejudice on both sides. He is hated and loved by people who have already chosen sides.

It'll be hard enough to select jurors who are able to consider the evidence without predisposition and prejudices.

The court should go out of its way to reduce those risks to a fair trial.

Among the ways to do that is to eliminate all reference to the word espionage in the courtroom.

Trump Indictment: Rule of Law or Politics?

Is the recent indictment of Donald Trump in Florida a victory for the rule of law, or a defeat for the concept of equal justice? The answer is: a little bit of both.

There is evidence that Donald Trump was aware that he possessed material that was still classified. That evidence comes from his own mouth and was recorded by his own staff. If valid, it demonstrates that Trump waved a piece of paper in front of a writer and a publisher and said that he could have declassified it while he was president but didn't do so. Prosecutors don't have the piece of paper and so it would be difficult for them to prove its content, but from the context of the conversation it may be the outlines of a possible battle plan against Iran. We don't know whether the people he showed this document to were actually given the chance to read it, or whether they were just told about it as it passed under their eyes. But this tape recording alone may be enough to get the case before a Florida federal jury.

At the same time, we know that government officials—both state and federal—have been out to "get Trump." Indeed, I wrote a book by that title based on the campaign pledges of a Democrat who ran for New York attorney general and another who ran for Manhattan district attorney. The Manhattan district attorney also indicted Trump, but on the flimsiest of charges. In my sixty years of practicing law, I have never seen a weaker or more politically motivated indictment.

So the question is whether or not the Florida federal indictment is part of this "get Trump" process, or whether it is simply an independent and fair application of the law?

One problem with the Florida federal indictment is that it resulted from the appointment of a special prosecutor whose sole target was Donald Trump. The prosecutor was not asked to investigate all former officials who may have taken classified material after they left office. As noted earlier, these include President Joseph Biden, former vice president Mike Pence, former secretary of state Hillary Clinton, and former national security advisor Sandy Berger. They probably also include other former officials who have not yet been caught. It is common for former officials to take material with them when they leave, and inevitably some of the material may well include classified papers.

The special prosecutor held a press conference following the indictment in which he proclaimed that there is only one set of laws, and everyone is equally bound by them. But he was not in a position to say that, because he was not asked to investigate whether others violated the law as well and were not prosecuted.

America is a deeply divided country in which people quickly pick sides and view the evidence through the prism of partisanship. The enemy of partisanship is nuance, calibration, and the equal protection of the law. It is possible therefore that there is fault on both sides: that an improper process of targeting Trump produced proper evidence of a crime.

If that turns out to be the case, there may be different outcomes in the court of law and in the court of public opinion.

In the court of law, it is difficult to prevail on the claim of selective prosecution or unequal justice, except when race, religion or ethnicity are involved. When the claim of differential treatment is based on political or partisan differences, the courts are unlikely to throw out a selectively prosecuted case.

But in the court of public opinion, it matters greatly whether the public perceives the process as fair and equal. The phony indictment in New York lends weight to the "get Trump" claims, while the somewhat stronger indictment in Florida lends weight to the claim that the rule of law has been satisfied.

Both trials will proceed, probably with the New York one coming first. It is likely that the first case will taint the second one in the minds of objective observers. They will be understandably suspicious of the Florida case, even in the face of the somewhat more compelling evidence. This suspicion will only be exacerbated if the Florida case is not televised for all Americans to see. They will understandably ask why they are being denied the ability to judge for themselves, rather than to read and hear about the case through the prism of often biased media. It would be far better if both trials were televised so that people could see their legal systems in action. But at the moment, federal trials are not televised or even broadcast.

There can be exceptions, however, as demonstrated by the fact that the Supreme Court allowed the appeal in the case seeking to overrule *Roe v. Wade* to be broadcast. Many Americans listened to the argument.

In the O. J. Simpson trial a quarter of a century ago, television was allowed, and polls showed that people who watched the trial on television were less surprised at the outcome than people who read or heard about it through the prism of biased media.

Everyone should withhold judgment until all the evidence is in. But in the end, the verdict may be a divided one: they did manage to get Trump on the basis of selective and targeted investigations and prosecutions.

D. Trump's Third Indictment

The DC Election Case

On Tuesday, US special counsel Jack Smith revealed felony charges against the former president for allegedly subverting the will of the American people and attempting to overturn the results of an election.

Yes, Trump's behavior following his 2020 loss was wrong. But was it criminal?

Not on the basis of what I've seen thus far.

Have no doubt, corrupting the US justice system to punish a former president and current candidate nudges the country ever closer to tribalism, chaos, and collapse.

If the attorney general appointed by the incumbent president authorizes the prosecution of the president's chief election rival, the evidence of a serious crime should be overwhelming.

His guilt should be clear beyond doubt, so as to avoid any reasonable suspicion that the prosecution was motivated, even in part, by partisan consideration.

The paradigmatic "gun" must indeed be "smoking."

I call this the "Nixon standard," under which the guilt is so evident that even the defendant's political allies—and certainly less sectarian independents—are satisfied that it is fair.

That admittedly daunting but entirely appropriate standard has not been met by any of the three indictments currently pending against Trump, who stands tied in recent polls against President Joe Biden.

Manhattan district attorney Alvin Bragg's indictment of Trump for falsely reporting the payment of hush money to adult film star Stormy Daniels is scandalously inept. The legal contortions Bragg performed to criminalize a possibly immoral, yet perfectly legal, pay-off are too convoluted to recount here.

Evidence related to Trump's alleged illegal retention of classified materials at Mar-a-Lago are strong, but the supposed crime itself is rather technical and relatively minor. Hillary Clinton, who stored highly sensitive government documents on her "home brew" server, never faced federal charges, nor did President Biden, Vice President Pence, or Bill Clinton's former national security advisor, Sandy Berger.

Why, then, charge the candidate who is in a virtual tie with the incumbent against whom he is running?

The current indictment involves far more serious accusations, but the evidence seems speculative.

In order to establish the underlying charges, the government would have to prove beyond a reasonable doubt that Trump himself actually knew and believed that he had lost the election fair and square.

That he intended to subvert the will of the people.

I doubt they can prove that.

I did not believe that the government would bring this indictment unless it had corroborated evidence that Trump had told people that he knew he had been defeated and was challenging the results for fraudulent and corrupt purposes.

But from what I have read and heard, they don't appear to have any such evidence.

When his son-in-law Jared Kushner was summoned before the grand jury, it was widely expected that he might provide that smoking gun, but he apparently said the opposite: that Trump actually believed he had won.

Others who spoke to Trump during the relevant time period also believe that he was persuaded that the election had been stolen.

I think he is wrong, but it's not what I or the grand jurors think: it's what Trump himself believed.

If the government fails to prove Trump's state of mind beyond a reasonable doubt, the indictment against him may well backfire politically.

He may gain rather than lose support among independents and marginal supporters who oppose the weaponization of our criminal justice system.

But perhaps, most notably, Smith's case against Trump is novel, untested, and unique.

It may collapse under its own weight.

Our Constitution prohibits ex post facto prosecutions—that is, prosecutions that are not based on clear rules easily knowable to defendants at the time of the alleged offenses.

Put simply, the law must be clearly established by firm precedents. There are few in this indictment.

As Thomas Jefferson once put it: the criminal law must be so clear that the average person can understand it if he "reads it while running." The spirit, if not the letter of this prohibition is violated when statutes are stretched, and precedents are ignored.

Smith is charging Trump under a Reconstruction era law, adopted in 1870, that makes it a crime to "conspire to injure, oppress, threaten, or intimidate any person" exercising their Constitutionally protected rights, including the right to vote.

The provision was intended to aid African American citizens emerging from the horrors of slavery. But it has not been used to prosecute someone for contesting the legitimacy of an election.

If it were, it could have been employed against House Democrats, who challenged Trump's 2016 election victory, citing supposed voter suppression and Russian interference.

Of course, it should not have.

But prosecutor Jack Smith has a history of bringing speculative cases.

He won a corruption conviction against former governor of Virginia, Robert McDonnell, in 2014 only for it to be overturned by the U.S. Supreme Court in a unanimous 8-0 decision.

The Court concluded that there was no explicit proof of the charges and warned that "the uncontrolled power of criminal prosecutors is a threat to our separation of powers."

Yes, Smith is known for his creativity, but creativity has no proper role in the criminal justice system, especially when it comes to prosecuting political opponents.

Prosecutor Smith is probably counting on the fact that a District of Columbia jury will be comprised primarily of anti-Trump citizens, because the district is overwhelmingly Democrat and only a tiny percentage of potential jurors voted for him in the last election.

That is why Trump's lawyers will certainly move for a change of venue, perhaps to Virginia, which is far more purple than the neighboring District.

If that motion fails, a conviction is virtually assured, but it is likely that that conviction will be scrutinized carefully on appeal by the Circuit Court and Supreme Court.

No one can ever predict the outcome of an appeal, but affirmance is far from assured.

The bottom line is that the attorney general should not have approved this indictment, based on speculative nature of its legal foundation and the absence of smoking-gun evidence.

No one is above the law and every defendant must be treated equally, but the reality is that when the potential defendant is the candidate running most strongly against the incumbent president, the attorney general should be certain that the case is strong.

This indictment and the evidence on which it is apparently based does not seem to meet that standard.

Long after the champagne buzz wears off, America will only be left with a constitutional hangover.

Being Wrong Doesn't Make Trump a Criminal

The bottom line of the recent Trump indictment alleges that he knew or should have known that he lost the election fair and square, and that his actions in challenging the result were therefore corrupt and unlawful.

The problem with the indictment is that the Supreme Court has repeatedly held under the First Amendment that there's no such thing as a false opinion. Every American, and especially politicians, have the right to be wrong about their opinions. They also have the right to express their false opinions, at least as long as they honestly believe they are true.

Imagine what the world would look like if every politician who told a fib in order to get elected were to be prosecuted and imprisoned. Our legislative sessions would have to be held in the Allenwood prison rather than in the halls of Congress. Lying has long been endemic in politics. That's why we honor George Washington and Abraham Lincoln as truth-tellers among the array of politicians who don't meet that standard.

Indeed, this indictment itself fails to meet the standard of honesty that it requires of Donald Trump. In describing his speech of December 6, this is what it says: "Finally, after exhorting that 'we fight. We fight like hell. And if you don't fight like hell, you're not going to have a country anymore,' the defendant directed the people in front of him to head to the Capitol, suggested he was going with them, and told them to give members of Congress 'the kind of pride and boldness that they need to take back our country.'"

Yet the indictment omits two key words from that speech—"peacefully" and "patriotically"—which suggest that the speech itself was protected advocacy under the First Amendment rather than unlawful incitement. A lie by omission is as serious as a lie by commission, especially in the context of a legal document such as an indictment.

Accordingly, for the US government to win its case, it will have to prove beyond a reasonable doubt that Donald Trump actually believed at and around January 6 that he had lost the election.

The indictment alleges that many of his associates told him he had lost, but I am aware of no smoking gun testimony that Trump actually admitted that he believed them. On the contrary, many people can testify that Trump told them the election had been stolen and that they believe he believed that.

As Thomas Jefferson wrote more than two hundred years ago: "We have nothing to fear from the demoralizing reasoning of some, if others are left free to demonstrate their error..." The constitutionally appropriate response to false political opinions is the open marketplace of ideas, not the closed prison cells of censorship.

If this trial is held in the District of Columbia—one of the most anti-Trump areas of the nation—a skewed jury may well disregard the First Amendment and convict. But the appellate courts, especially the

Supreme Court, could prioritize the First Amendment and reverse any conviction that violates the Constitution.

The indictment endangers not only free speech but also the right to counsel. It describes several people who are believed to be Trump's lawyers as unindicted co-conspirators. This makes it difficult for Trump to claim that he relied on their legal advice in challenging the election. It also sends a dangerous message to creative lawyers whose advice may be second-guessed by a prosecutor after the fact. As one of Trump's lawyers in his first Senate impeachment trial, I am particularly concerned about the impact this indictment could have on the willingness of lawyers to represent him or other controversial politicians.

All in all, this indictment does not seem to serve the interests of non-partisan justice. It appears to be yet another manifestation of the weaponization of the criminal justice system for partisan advantage.

When an attorney general authorizes the prosecution of his president's main political opponent in an upcoming election, the case must be so strong that it leaves no doubt as to its non-partisan credibility. It should meet what I call the "Nixon standard."

The case against Richard Nixon was so strong that members of his own party and independents supported his impeachment and possible prosecution. That standard does not seem to have been met in this case.

Biden, Prosecuting His Rival, Fails to Meet the "Nixon Standard"

More than a year ago press accounts were published of conversations President Biden had with associates. He allegedly complained about the attorney general not being aggressive enough in pursuing President Trump for his role in the January 6 events. This is what the press reported: "Biden had 'said privately that he wanted Mr. Garland to act less like a ponderous judge and more like a prosecutor who was willing to take decisive action over the events of January 6th.'"

I take Mr. Biden at his word when he says that he has never directly interfered with prosecutorial decisions made by the Justice Department, but there can be little doubt that Attorney General Garland, who serves at Mr. Biden's pleasure, was aware of the president's strong feelings when he authorized the prosecution of Mr. Trump for his inexcusable,

but in my view constitutionally protected, role in the terrible events of
January 6.

As I have said for years now, when the leading candidate against
the incumbent president is prosecuted, especially at the urging of the
incumbent president, the case against him must be bulletproof, airtight, and beyond any reasonable doubt. To paraphrase Mr. Biden, the
prosecutor in such a case should act more "like a ponderous judge" and
less like a zealous prosecutor. He should lean over backwards to assure
not only that justice is being done, but also that it is seen to be done by
all reasonable people.

The only alleged crime that meets this high bar is the indictment
in Florida based on the videotape of Mr. Trump waving classified
material in front of journalists and admitting that he had not declassified them and that they are still secret. This piece of evidence is
indeed a smoking gun, but the crime itself is not nearly as serious as
the ones charged in the January 6 indictment. The remaining indictments—the one at New York City and the current one in DC—are
highly questionable and certainly subject to criticism by reasonable
and objective people.

The essence of a Banana Republic—the description applies equally
to some Eastern European and Asian authoritarian regimes, as it does
to South American—is the criminal prosecution of political opponents
by incumbent leaders. We are not a Banana Republic, and we are not
close to becoming one. Yet this most recent indictment, following Mr.
Biden's public demand for the prosecution of his political opponent,
brings us one step closer to banana land.

I have no doubt that if the shoe were on the other foot Mr.
Trump would be demanding prosecution of his political opponents,
but two constitutional wrongs do not make a constitutional right.
It is true that the law must apply equally to all, but it is equally
true—and it has always been the case—that the law should take into
account the realities of our democratic electoral system. Thus, the
standard for an incumbent administration prosecuting its political
enemies, and especially the strongest opposition candidate, must be
considerably higher than in the ordinary case because Democracy
itself is at stake.

In describing the standards that must be employed in such highly political cases, I have articulated two criteria—the first is the "Nixon standard." When President Nixon was threatened with impeachment, prosecution, or both for his obvious crimes, members of his own party joined in the call for his resignation. I am confident that if Mr. Trump had been caught on tape offering or accepting a personal bribe, many Republicans would join the demand for his prosecution. But the current indictments, and especially the most recent one, do not come close to meeting the daunting Nixon standard.

The indictment against Mr. Trump for possession of classified material meets the highest evidentiary standard, but it does not meet the standard for a crime that is sufficiently serious to warrant prosecution in the midst of a presidential campaign. Perhaps the superseding indictment alleging that Mr. Trump ordered the destruction of videotapes may meet that standard, but the evidence cited in the indictment seems questionable and based largely on hearsay statements.

This brings us to the January 6 indictment. Here the crime is very serious, but the evidence seems lacking. I am aware of no direct eye- or ear-witness testimony that would prove beyond the reasonable doubt that Mr. Trump himself knew and believed that the election was fair and that he had lost. Indeed, the evidence of which I am aware strongly suggests that Mr. Trump had convinced himself—quite wrongly in my view—that it had been stolen from him. If this is the case, then any prosecution under this indictment would fail to meet the Nixon standard.

The other standard that must be met is what I have called the "What Aboutism" question. It is entirely fair to ask: "What about Hillary Clinton? What about Joe Biden? What about Mike Pence? They too possessed classified material after they left office." There are, of course, considerable differences among these cases, especially with regard to cooperation. But failure to cooperate is not a crime; it is a right under the Fifth and Sixth Amendments.

No incumbent administration should ever prosecute a leading candidate against its president unless there is a widespread consensus among reasonable Americans of all parties and backgrounds that the prosecution is beyond legitimate controversy. None of the current indictments, in my view, meet that daunting standard.

Can Trump Get an "Impartial Jury" in DC? What the Law Requires

The Sixth Amendment to the United States Constitution guarantees the accused the right to "an impartial jury." But it also states that the trial should take place in "the state and district wherein the crime shall have been committed." What should happen, therefore, when it is virtually impossible for the defendant to get an impartial jury in that state or district?

In federal cases, the law provides for a change of venue under appropriate circumstances. The prosecution of Donald Trump for the events around January 6, 2021, would seem to call for a change of venue. The District of Columbia is the most extreme Democratic district in the country. Approximately 95 percent of the potential jurors register and vote Democrat. Whereas approximately 5 percent voted for Trump. Furthermore, the anger against Trump is understandable in light of the fact that the events of January 6th directly involved many citizens of the district. Moreover, the judge randomly selected to preside over this case has a long history of bias against Trump and his supporters, and her law firm has a long history of conflicts and corruption.

The goal of the Sixth Amendment is to assure not only that the defendant is treated justly, but that the *appearance* of justice is satisfied as well. A jury and judge that are impartial, and seen to be impartial, are essential to achieving this goal. It is imperative, therefore, that in a case where the incumbent president has urged his Attorney General to pursue his political opponent aggressively, that all efforts must be made to ensure fairness. Prosecutors must lean over backwards to persuade the public that partisan considerations played absolutely no role in the decision to indict. Agreeing to a change of venue and judge would go a long way toward seeing that justice is done.

Change of venue motions are only rarely granted, as are motions to recuse a selected judge. But this is a case where justice demands that these motions be granted, both in the interests of the defendants and in the interests of justice. The government should not oppose such motions, though they generally do if it gives them a tactical advantage.

It is likely, therefore, that these defense requests will be denied by the trial judge. Trump's lawyers will try to take an immediate interlocutory appeal before trial.

Though such appeals before trial are generally disfavored, the arguments for allowing it in this case are strong. The trial itself promises to play an important role in the 2024 election, especially since the prosecution wants it to occur in the middle of the campaign season. If an unfair trial results in a conviction, the impact will already be felt, even if it is reversed on appeal after the election, as the prosecution likely anticipates.

So the appellate courts should be able to assure in advance that a fair trial occurs in a fair venue presided over by a fair judge, especially if it takes place before the presidential election.

If the prosecution case is strong, it should have no fear of a jury and judge outside of DC. As the Supreme Court has repeatedly said: the job of a prosecutor is not merely to maximize the chances of winning, but to assure that he wins fairly and justly. In order to achieve that goal, the prosecutors in this case should not oppose defense motions for a change of venue and judge. Nor should it oppose an appeal if the trial judge denies these well-founded defense motions.

In all likelihood, prosecutors will vigorously fight all efforts by the defense to assure an impartial jury and judge, because they want every advantage that will help them secure a victory. They will point to defense efforts to secure advantages for their client and argue that the adversary system of justice requires them to do the same. But that is not the law. The Supreme Court clearly delineated a different role for prosecutors who represent the government:

> The United States Attorney is the representative not of an ordinary party to a controversy, but of a sovereignty whose obligation to govern impartially is as compelling as its obligation to govern at all, and whose interest, therefore, in a criminal prosecution is not that it shall win a case, but that justice shall be done.

The prosecutors in the January 6th case should study this opinion before they deny Trump an impartial jury.

E. Trump's Fourth Indictment: Fulton County, Georgia

Trump's Georgia Prosecutor Is Not Being Truthful

The Georgia prosecutor who indicted Donald Trump and eighteen co-defendants—yes, she indicted them, the grand jury merely rubber-stamped—has said she will try to bring the case to trial within six months. I have been practicing criminal law for sixty years, and I have never seen a trial with nineteen defendants, a ninety-plus page indictment, and this degree of complexity brought to trial in anywhere close to six months. It simply can't happen.

Why then did she begin this case, which is about lying, by misleading the American people? Because to her, this case seems entirely political. Is she using it to run for office, or is she bringing it to garner favor with other Democrats?

This sprawling indictment rests largely on the so-called RICO law—a law that was designed to prosecute and bankrupt members of organized crime. I recall a client of Italian American heritage complaining that the law was targeted at the mafia: "Why else would they call it RICO instead of Morris or John?" He was being perceptive.

Subsequent to its enactment, the RICO law became a favorite of prosecutors, although many RICO convictions were later overturned on appeal. It turned out that RICO prosecutions were more appealing to jurors than they were to judges. That is because jurors want to convict racketeers, while judges need to apply the law fairly.

One serious problem with this indictment is that the nineteen defendants may not all share the same state of mind or intent. Surely some of them, including Donald Trump himself, actually believed and still believe that the election was unfair. Others may have joined in that erroneous belief, while still others may have their doubts.

I am aware of no evidence that Trump himself ever expressed doubts about his certainty that the election was stolen, but it is possible that prosecutors may be able to introduce testimony that other defendants had expressed doubts, or may even have admitted that the election was not stolen. This diversity of viewpoints may pose problems for the prosecution, as well as for the judge who must instruct the jury on the law applicable to each defendant.

Even when RICO and conspiracy are charged, individual guilt must be proved beyond a reasonable doubt. American law does not recognize guilt by association. Every defendant must have the requisite intent, and that intent must be proved in every case beyond a reasonable doubt.

Some courts have been sloppy in applying the intent requirement to RICO and conspiracy prosecutions, but the Supreme Court has never deviated from the requirement that individual guilt must be proved beyond a reasonable doubt.

Because there are nineteen defendants, this trial will take an enormous amount of time to conduct. Some defendants may choose to take the witness stand, others may not. Some may move for separate trials, others may not. Lawyers will argue with each other about certain rulings which may benefit some but not others of the defendants. A trial of nineteen defendants guarantees a logistical mess.

There will be pre-trial efforts to move the case to federal court on behalf of some of the defendants but not others. There may also be efforts to change the venue of the case to a different Georgia county, even if it remains in state court. There will be arguments about the trial dates, because the forty or more lawyers that are likely to be involved in this case will have different trial schedules.

Justice must not only be done, it must be seen to be done. This is especially true when the main defendant is also the main candidate against the incumbent president. Although this is a state, rather than a federal, case, it is being brought by a highly politicized Democrat who is clearly seeking to serve the interests of her party and her preferred candidate. At the moment it appears that Trump will be required to be fingerprinted and to provide a mug shot (the inevitable T-shirt with the mugshot picture will probably be among the best sellers of all time!) The prosecutor appears to be trying to milk this case for every partisan benefit she can secure, both for herself and for her party.

One key issue is going to be whether there are any motions that can be made, which, if they are denied, can be immediately appealed. Such an appeal would probably delay any trial, possibly even beyond election day. The law varies from state to state regarding the immediate appealability of certain motions, but the motion to move the case

to federal court is almost certainly appealable. The current indictment on its face seems strong: it tells a sad tale of claims of corruption, perjury, and malfeasance. But as the prosecutor reminded her
listeners, all of these defendants are presumed innocent. We must
await the presentation of evidence and the cross-examination of witnesses to assess the actual strength of the case. I predict that the case
will be weaker and more subject to challenge as it progresses to trial
and verdict.

Trump Case Could Turn on Which of Three Possible Jury Instructions Is Given by the Judge

The guilt or innocence of President Trump on charges relating to the
2020 elections may well turn on which of three possible jury instructions the judge will give.

The core of the charges against Mr. Trump is that he took actions
and made statements that were corruptly intended to undo President
Biden's legitimate victory. Essential to these charges is the allegation
that Mr. Trump knew and believed that Mr. Biden had won the election fair and square—and that he acted corruptly in falsely claiming
victory for himself.

The prosecution will try to prove that the election was entirely legitimate, that Mr. Trump was told that he had lost—and that he believed
he had lost.

The judge will have to instruct the jurors as to what they have to
find beyond a reasonable doubt before they can vote to convict him.
The defense will seek an instruction that requires all twelve jurors to
find beyond a reasonable doubt that Mr. Trump actually knew and
believed that the election was fair and that he had lost.

It will be difficult for the prosecution to get into Mr. Trump's mind
in order to establish his subjective beliefs. It is likely that at least some
jurors may conclude that the prosecution failed to prove beyond a reasonable doubt that Mr. Trump did not believe he had won.

For that reason, the prosecution will seek an instruction that
would make it much easier to convict. They will ask the judge to
instruct the jury that even if Mr. Trump subjectively believed he had
won, that belief has to be "reasonable." They will present evidence

that many of Mr. Trump's closest advisers told him he had lost, and so any belief he may have held to the contrary would be unreasonable.

If the prosecution presents evidence of what some people told Mr. Trump, the defense will have to be allowed to show that other people supported his view that the election had been stolen.

Mr. Trump would also be allowed to introduce external evidence—such as the Dinesh D'Souza film *2,000 Mules* purporting to depict electoral fraud—that many voters believed that the 45th president had actually won. This would bolster Mr. Trump's claim that his belief, even if wrong, was reasonable.

If a reasonableness instruction is given, and Mr. Trump is denied the right to present evidence of others who believed the election was stolen, it is likely that any conviction would be reversed on appeal.

The third possible instruction would require the jury to find beyond a reasonable doubt that the election was actually stolen. Such an instruction would open the door to Mr. Trump's legal team presenting evidence that the election was actually stolen or unfair.

That would turn the trial into a political debate about the 2020 election, so it is unlikely that such an instruction would be given.

Accordingly, the two most likely instructions would be the one that requires the jury to find that Mr. Trump did not believe Mr. Biden had won legitimately, or an instruction that required the jury to find that even if the former president believed that the election was stolen, his belief was unreasonable.

The centrality of the judge's instruction makes it imperative that the judge presiding over the trial be entirely objective and without biases. Count on the defense to raise questions as to whether Judge Tanya Chutkan, who was selected randomly out of the wheel, satisfies that criteria, especially in a case as controversial as this one is among our deeply divided voters.

The fact that President Obama appointed her is not a disqualification, but Mr. Trump could zero in on the fact that she worked for years in a heavily Democratic law firm—Boies, Schiller & Flexner—in which Hunter Biden was not only employed, but a client.

Considering that Mr. Trump claims that the press and social media repression of the disclosures relating to Hunter Biden's business dealings could have influenced the outcome of the 2020 election, this could well prove to be a question in the case.

When the leading candidate running against the incumbent president is being prosecuted by the attorney general, who serves at the pleasure of the president, the trial must not only be fair beyond any doubt. It must also be seen to be fair by Americans.

No, the Fourteenth Amendment Can't Disqualify Trump

Several academics—including members of the conservative Federalist Society—are now arguing that Section 3 of the Fourteenth Amendment prohibits Donald Trump from becoming president. They focus on the language that prohibits anyone who "shall have engaged in insurrection or rebellion . . . or given aid or comfort to the enemies thereof" from holding "any office." The amendment provides no mechanism for determining whether a candidate falls within this disqualification, though it says that "Congress may by a vote of two-thirds of each house, remove such disability." Significantly, the text does not authorize Congress—or any other body or individual—to impose the disqualification in the first place.

A fair reading of the text and history of the Fourteenth Amendment makes it relatively clear, however, that the disability provision was intended to apply to those who served the Confederacy during the Civil War. It wasn't intended as a general provision empowering one party to disqualify the leading candidate of the other party in any future elections.

First, the text. Section 4 of the Fourteenth Amendment provides the following: "But neither the United States nor any State shall assume or pay any debt or obligation incurred in aid of insurrection or rebellion against the United States, or any claim for the loss or emancipation of any slave." It seems clear that this provision was intended to apply to a particular insurrection and rebellion—namely the Civil War that resulted in the "emancipation" of enslaved people. There were no slaves to be emancipated in the United States after that war.

Moreover, the absence of any mechanism, procedure, or criteria for determining whether a candidate is disqualified demonstrates that the amendment did not lay down a general rule for future elections involving candidates who were not part of the Confederacy. It was fairly evident who participated in the Civil War on the part of the South. No formal mechanism was needed for making that obvious determination. If the disqualification had been intended as a general rule applicable to all future elections, it would have been essential to designate the appropriate decision maker, the procedures, and the criteria for making so important a decision.

In the absence of any such designation, it would be possible for individual states to disqualify a candidate, while others qualify him. It would also be possible for the incumbent president to seek to disqualify his rival, or for a partisan congress to do so. There is no explicit provision for the courts to intervene in what they might regard as a political question. So elections might be conducted with differing interpretations of eligibility and no procedures for resolving disputes about them. It is absolutely certain that if Trump were disqualified by some person or institution dominated by Democrats, and if the controversy were not resolved by the Supreme Court, there would be a constitutional crisis.

Finally, there is the hypocrisy of some who argued in defense of race-specific affirmative action that the equal protection clause of the Fourteenth Amendment should be interpreted in light of its post–Civil War history to protect only previously enslaved people and their descendants, rather than members of the white majority. They would interpret the equal protection clause narrowly and limited by its immediate history, while interpreting the disqualification clause broadly to apply to all candidates in all elections. A fair reading of the amendment leads to the opposite conclusion: the broad language of Section 2 of the equal protection clause ("nor shall any state . . . deny any person within its jurisdiction the equal protection of the laws") strongly suggest general application without being time-bound; whereas the more specific language of Sections 3 and 4 (referring to emancipated slaves and using words that were commonly used to describe the confederate insurrection and rebellion against the Union) suggests a more time-bound application.

"The decision should be made by voters."

Interpreting this post–Civil War amendment as a general provision for disqualifying candidates who some people may believe participated in what they regard as an insurrection or rebellion—as distinguished from a protest or even a riot—would create yet another divisive weapon in our increasingly partisan war. It would be used by Republicans against candidates who may have supported (gave "aid or comfort" to) riots such as those that followed the killing of George Floyd or other violence-provoking events.

The Constitution articulated limited qualifications for presidential eligibility. Beyond those neutral criteria, the decision should be made by voters, who are free to consider the participation of a candidate in activities with which they disagree. Unless an amendment was clearly intended to further limit these qualifications, the voters are the ones to decide who is to be their president. The vague language of the Fourteenth Amendment falls far short of what should be required for so radical a departure from our electoral process.

Donald Trump Is Being Denied His Constitutional Right to Due Process

The four criminal trials currently scheduled for former President Donald Trump are amongst the most significant and controversial trials in American history. It is imperative that they also be among the fairest trials in our history. Regardless of the results—acquittal, conviction, hung jury—the trials must be perceived as having been fair. The defendant must receive the benefit of all of his constitutional and statutory rights. Not only is Donald Trump on trial in these cases, but the American system of justice is on trial, not only in America but around the world.

The defendant is not only a former president; he is also the leading candidate to run against the incumbent president. Never before in our history has a leading presidential candidate been indicted, especially in the run-up to the election. If the trials themselves are unfair or even reasonably perceived to be unfair, our nation will be further divided and our standing in the world of democracies will be further damaged.

There is great desire among those who strongly oppose what Trump did in the past and what they believe he is likely to do in the future to "get" him. Many believe that the noble end of preventing Trump from being our next president justifies ignoble means, including stretching the Constitution and the law so as to assure his conviction. They believe that the reelection of President Trump would be more dangerous than compromising his constitutional rights.

That is a shortsighted view that endangers future generations of Americans.

At the moment, it appears as if Donald Trump will be denied his most fundamental constitutional right—to present his defenses to an unbiased jury. In this respect, there are two major constitutional issues: the timing of the trials and the location of the trials.

When it comes to the timing of Trump's trials, the goal of the "get Trump" posse is to secure convictions and try to influence the November 2024 election. Even if these convictions were subsequently to be reversed on appeal, they will have served their intended purpose in influencing centrist voters, which is why they are prepared to rush to legal injustice—to serve what they view as "political" justice.

As of now, with the exception of the one trial that's scheduled to begin next month, the rest are scheduled right in the middle of the primary season, beginning in March.

As a lawyer with sixty years of experience litigating and teaching about complex criminal cases, I have absolutely no doubt that a fair trial cannot be accomplished within this time frame.

Consider the Fulton County RICO prosecution. There are nineteen defendants, some of whom have demanded a speedy trial as soon as October, while others have insisted on their right to prepare fully for what promises to be a many-months-long trial. The prosecutors insist on trying all the defendants together rather than allowing each of them or at least groups of them to be tried separately.

I am aware of no RICO trial involving multiple defendants, millions of documents, and extremely complex legal and factual issues having ever been fairly tried in such short a period of time.

The same is true of the DC case, where the judge insisted the public has a right to a speedy trial under the Sixth Amendment. "There is a societal interest in providing a speedy trial separate from, and at times in opposition to, the accused," Judge Tanya S. Chutkan said when setting the date.

This is nonsense: only the defendant has the right to demand a speedy trial.

The interest of the government lies solely in providing the defendant a fair trial. If a speedy trial will result in an unfair trial, the Constitution demands a reasonable delay sufficient to assure every defendant the right to present the defense fully and effectively.

Convicting Trump in a speedy but unfair trial absolutely undermines the neutrality of our legal system. In the District of Columbia case, the government has already produced more than 12 million pages of discovery. In this haystack of material, there will be some exculpatory needles, and it will take time to find them and to investigate. It will certainly take many months of work to permit effective assistance of counsel, which is required by the Constitution. At this point, that important right is being denied to Donald Trump.

The second issue is the location of Trump's trials. It is difficult enough to seek twelve objective and neutral jurors anywhere in our divided country, but three of the four trials are now scheduled for areas that are overwhelmingly anti-Trump.

In the District of Columbia, more than 90 percent of the potential jury pool voted against Trump. Many of those potential jurors hate him with a passion that would surely influence their deliberations. In New York, more than 70 percent of potential jurors voted against Trump, and many of them harbor a hatred that would make deliberations impossible. The numbers in Fulton County are somewhat similar to those in New York. Only the Florida federal trial is in a place where neutrality is possible.

Nor is it likely that biased jurors can be weeded out by the imperfect jury selection system. Accordingly, the juries in three of these cases will likely begin with a presumption of guilt rather than the constitutionally required presumption of innocence.

Changes of venue are permitted for good cause, and there is more than good cause here to do so in order to assure the former president a fair jury.

But as of now, Donald Trump is being denied his constitutional right to due process. The world is watching.

Prosecuting Lawyers for Their Legal Representation Is Dangerous to Us All

"How in God's name could so many lawyers get involved in something like this?" That question, asked by John Dean about Watergate half a century ago, is again being asked about the January 6 indictments involving lawyers who were associated with Donald Trump's wrong-headed attempts to challenge the 2020 presidential election. But there are considerable differences among the roles lawyers were alleged to have played in the two situations: the Nixon lawyers were generally accused of conduct outside of their professional roles as advice-givers and litigators. They were charged largely with participating in crimes such as bribery, planning and covering up an illegal break-in, and other acts of obstruction of justice. Some of them just happened to be lawyers, but they could just as easily been laypeople committing criminal acts. They didn't commit their crimes as lawyers.

The lawyers who are currently indicted or were included as unindicted co-conspirators were, at least in part, accused based on their rendering legal services: giving legal advice, filing lawsuits on behalf of clients, and making statements, both oral and written, as part of their legal representation of clients. That is why these charges are much more questionable and controversial than the ones that were brought against former Attorney General John Mitchell, former White House counsel John Ehrlichman, and other Nixon aides who were lawyers.

It is true, and important, that a license to practice law is *not* a license to commit crimes. But it *is* a license to explore and press controversial, even extreme, legal claims and to challenge existing legal precedents in the interests of one's clients. Creative lawyers generally lose their cases because law is a conservative enterprise that relies on past precedents and is resistant to change. But lawyers should be encouraged to push the envelope. That is how progress (and sometimes regress) is achieved in the legal system. The adversary system of justice is based on constant confrontation and challenge.

To be sure, lawyers can sometimes go too far in failing or refusing to accept binding and well-established precedents or existing rules, by bringing lawsuits for improper purposes, such as delay or extortion, or by lying to the court.

But the lines between acceptable and unacceptable legal challenges are generally too uncertain to warrant criminalizing what in retrospect may have been a mistake in judgment or overzealousness.

As mentioned earlier, Thomas Jefferson once quipped that for a criminal law to be fairly applied, it must be so clear that a reasonable person could understand it if he read it "while running." Well, I have read, while comfortably sitting, the criminal charges against attorneys John Eastman, Kenneth Chesebro, Rudolph W. Giuliani, Sidney Powell, and others, and based on sixty years of teaching and practicing criminal law, I do not understand in all cases the line between zealously mistaken advocacy and criminal conspiracy on which these indictments seem to be based. Yes, the courts rejected the legal challenges based on current law but losing a case—even losing badly—should not be a crime. To criminalize advice and advocacy that turns out to be wrong, misguided, or even false will chill lawyers from bringing out-of-the-box lawsuits that might someday prevail and change the law.

Lawyers, like the law itself, tend to be cautious, especially with regard to their own tolerance of risks to their careers. If they have to consider not only their client's best interest, but their own possible exposure to criminal liability, they will refrain from giving risky advice or bringing questionable lawsuits. Judges can quickly reject improper suits—as most did with regard to the Trump suits—so little harm beyond inconvenience is caused by their being brought. But a lawyer failing to bring a questionable suit that might have changed the law could have serious, if largely invisible, consequences for all Americans.

So, the balance of public interest lies with more not fewer challenges to existing law, even if some are unmeritorious. It also lies with not expanding the criminal law to reach questionable conduct that is not clearly illegal under existing precedent. The irony is that the current prosecutions of lawyers for giving advice and commencing litigation that is beyond existing civil law, are themselves based on prosecutors creatively seeking to expand existing criminal law beyond current precedents. And there is more justification for seeking to expand the civil law than for retroactively stretching the criminal law.

The prosecutions against Trump's former lawyers will be vigorously defended against by their lawyers. But bar associations and civil liberties groups should be heard as well, because the unjustified prosecution of lawyers for advising their clients and litigating on their behalf—even if overzealously—endangers the adversary system of justice and thus the rights of all Americans. (I am litigating against a bar complaint brought against me by The 65 Project—an organization that targets lawyers who have defended Trump or anyone associated with him—based on a sanction for challenging the future use of voting machines by a company that refuses to subject them to adversarial testing).

The Shakespearian villain Dick the Butcher advised: "The first thing we do, let's kill all the lawyers." Tyrants such as Hitler, Stalin, Russian President Vladimir Putin, Pol Pot, and Fidel Castro took that advice and targeted lawyers who opposed them. Prosecuting opposition lawyers for challenging the incumbent administration is a dangerous first step away from the rule of law. So, the law and facts should be crystal clear before such prosecutions are authorized. There is real doubt whether this standard has been met in these criminal prosecutions.

Republicans Who Voted against Impeaching Trump Should Not Vote to Impeach Mayorkas

When I represented then President Trump in his first impeachment case, many Republicans praised me for proving that the constitution permits impeachment only for "treason, bribery, and other high crimes or misdemeanors." Trump had not been charged with any of those offenses but rather with vague allegations of abuse of power and obstruction of Congress. The Senate voted to acquit Trump of the unconstitutional charges brought by Democrats. Republicans applauded that result.

Now many of the same Republicans are seeking to impeach Secretary of Homeland Security Alejandro Mayorkas on equally vague and unconstitutional grounds. Whatever else Mayorkas may or may not have done, he has not committed bribery, treason, or high crimes and misdemeanors. Indeed, most Republicans do not even claim that his actions or inactions meet these daunting constitutional standards, but they are prepared to apply a double standard based on partisan considerations.

Double standards are an anathema to justice under our Constitution. There must be one Constitution for all regardless of party affiliation.

If Republications want to amend the Constitution, let them try, but neither the Republicans nor the Democrats have the right to redefine constitutional standards on an ad hoc basis in order to serve their partisan interests.

So, let's hear from some principled Republicans who may dislike what Mayorkas is doing but who understand that they have previously voted for a standard which has not come close to being met.

The philosopher François de La Rochefoucauld said that "Hypocrisy is the compliment that vice pays to virtue." It is also the currency of politics in present day Washington. But it is wrong regardless of which side promotes it.

Congress has the power to issue a statement condemning Mayorkas, just as it had the power to issue a statement condemning Trump. But the extraordinary power of impeachment should be reserved for constitutionally impeachable offences and not invoked simply because one party has the votes to do so.

In the Federalist Papers, Alexander Hamilton warned that the "the greatest danger" regarding the power to impeach would be if it were "regulated more by the comparative strength of parties, than by the real demonstrations of innocence or guilt."

We experienced that danger when Bill Clinton was impeached by Republicans and when Trump was impeached by Democrats. Now we are seeing it play out once again with Republicans in control of the House of Representatives.

Hopefully, there will be enough principled Republications to prevent this abuse of the Constitution. But even if not, our system of checks and balances which requires a two-thirds vote for conviction by the Senate, will prevent Mayorkas's unconstitutional removal. Even if Mayorkas remains in office, a House vote to impeach him would add to the dangerous precedents established by previous partisan abuses of the impeachment provision.

The time has come, indeed it is overdue, for members of Congress who claim to be originalists when it comes to constitutional interpretation to recognize that the Framers explicitly refused to allow impeachment and removal for "maladministration" or other such vague abuses of duty. It is the voters who are allocated the power to vote against those who fail at governance. Congress, like the executive and judiciary, is bound to follow the Constitution.

Just because the Democrats were hypocritical when they impeached Trump on nonconstitutional grounds, does not give Republicans the right to do the same. Two wrongs make a fight, not a right. And the real losers are the American people who count on Congress to uphold the Constitution, especially in areas of impeachment, where the courts have taken a hands-off view.

We live in an age in which partisanship too often trumps principle, and in which noble ends are thought to justify ignoble means. There is a reasonable dispute about how to achieve border security. I may agree with some Republicans who are critical of the current administration's border policies and who place the blame on Mayorkas. But these criticisms—whether one agrees or disagrees with them—do not justify distorting the Constitution.

It is particularly essential in an age of partisan division that the nonpartisan principles of our Constitution be scrupulously obeyed. So, I urge principled Republicans who care about the Constitution to oppose those in their party who are seeking to impeach and remove Mayorkas based on nonconstitutional accusations.

CHAPTER 2

Trying to Get the Bidens by McCarthyite Tactics

Biden Impeachment Articles Are Unconstitutional

When I defended former president Trump against Democrat effort to impeach and remove him on grounds that I believe are unconstitutional, I predicted that when the Republicans gained control of the House, they would use that precedent as a justification for trying to impeach the next Democratic president. Sure enough, Republican representative Lauren Boebert has now introduced articles of impeachment that replicated what the Democrats had done just three and a half years earlier.

In January of 2020, Democrats charged Trump with "abuse of power" and "obstruction of Congress." I argued, successfully, that these articles did not satisfy the constitutional criteria for impeachment: treason, bribery, or other high crimes and misdemeanors. Nearly all the Republicans in both houses agreed with my argument that criminal-type behavior akin to treason or bribery is required, and they voted against the articles of impeachment passed by the Democratic House. Now many of these same Republicans are supporting Biden's impeachment on grounds similar to the ones they rejected when they were directed against the Republican president: "Abuse of power" (Article I), and "dereliction of duty" (Article II).

These alleged grounds do not appear in the Constitution, and the second one was implicitly rejected by the Constitutional Convention when proposals to include "malpractice for neglect of duty," "neglect in the execution of his office," and "maladministration" were withdrawn at the insistence of James Madison, the father of our constitution.

Once again partisanship trumps principle, and consistency is regarded as a weakness in the game of political hardball.

The irony is that there might actually be constitutionally valid grounds for impeaching President Biden under two possible circumstances: 1) if it turns out to be true that Hunter Biden was actually sitting next to his father and was aware that he invoked the former vice president's name when he communicated a threat to a Chinese businessman; and 2) if a high crime committed by a former vice president and future president during his interregnum as a private citizen, can satisfy the criteria for impeachment. The first is a question of fact; the second is a matter of constitutional interpretation.

I personally doubt that Joseph Biden was aware that his son was invoking his name and power when and if he sent that possibly extortionate message. But if that message is real, it certainly requires that Hunter Biden be placed under oath to A) admit or deny he sent the message; B) admit or deny that he was telling the truth when he said his father was sitting next to him; C) admit or deny that his father was aware he was sending the message; D) admit or deny that his father was aware of the content of the message.

The allegation that a former vice president and current president may have been complicit in an arguable extortion plot is a serious one that requires further investigation. In the unlikely event it was to be confirmed, it would raise a profound, difficult, and unresolved question of constitutional interpretations: namely whether a president can be impeached and removed for a high crime committed before he assumed the presidency. Extortion or attempted extortion is a high crime akin to bribery and thus—if proved—would be a constitutional ground for impeachment if it had been committed by a sitting president during his presidency. But what if it had been committed earlier?

Vice President Spiro Agnew was accused of engaging in extortion and bribery. Although the accusation was made during his vice presidency, the alleged crimes were committed while he was still governor of Maryland. He pleaded nolo contendere to a tax felony as part of a plea bargain that included his resigning the vice presidency. Accordingly, we do not know whether he could have or would have been impeached for conviction while vice president of a serious felony he committed before assuming that office.

It is unlikely that this question will be presented in the Biden case, because it is credible that evidence may not exist proving that Joseph Biden committed any impeachable offenses between the time he served as vice president and president—or at any other time. But we won't know that until and unless the current allegation, that include claims of incriminating recordings, are thoroughly investigated. If Republican House members are determined to impeach him, they would be well advised to focus their investigative resources on specific allegations of serious crimes which, if true, may rise to the level of possible impeachable offense, rather than on vague partisan accusations of misconduct which, even if true, they themselves recently argued would not satisfy the criteria for impeaching and removing a duly elected president.

Judge Rightly Rejected Hunter Biden Plea Bargain, Opening Door to Full Investigation

I predicted that the Delaware federal judge would refuse to accept the plea bargain between Hunter Biden and the Justice Department without making further inquiry. Most other commentators believed she would.

The Constitution limits the power of federal judges to deciding actual cases and controversies. They are not given roving commissions to do justice if there is no dispute in front of them. Therefore, judges are reluctant to interfere in agreements that have been arrived at by both parties, since there is no longer a controversy after an agreement has been reached.

The courts have ruled, however, that judges have a responsibility to decide whether a plea bargain is in the interests of justice. This is especially so when the specter of politics hangs over the plea bargain, as it truly does when it involves the son of the sitting president.

Justice must not only be done; it must be seen to be done. In this case it is anything but clear whether justice has been done, and it is crystal clear that it has not been seen to be done by many rightfully skeptical Americans.

Both sides must now go back to the drawing board and see if they can come up with a resolution that satisfies the judge. I predict they will because both sides benefit from resolving this case without a contentious trial.

Yet it will not be easy to resolve at least one important difference: the defense wants this plea bargain to resolve all matters and to allow Hunter Biden to be free of any possibility of future prosecution.

The prosecution would prefer to hedge its bets in the event that further evidence shows that crimes other than the ones already investigated may have been committed. Both sides are worried that if Donald Trump were to reclaim the presidency, he would have his justice department go after what he calls the "Biden crime family" with a vengeance.

A compromise is still possible whereby the prosecution agrees that the matter is closed, subject only to new information of serious crimes—potential crimes that can be identified in the plea bargain itself.

Even if the two sides can agree, the judge should still hold a hearing at which Attorney General Garland and US Attorney to the District of Delaware, David Weiss, are questioned as to whether Mr. Weiss did or did not have the authority to investigate beyond the borders of Delaware.

If he did not have that authority, or if he believed he was limited to his own state, then the judge should refuse to accept the plea bargain, because it would have been based on an incomplete and inadequate investigation. This would be especially true if the plea bargain were to be changed or interpreted to preclude further investigation or prosecution.

In a case such as this one, transparency is essential. The final plea bargain itself should be made public so that Americans can decide whether or not it appears fair.

Tragically, the election of 2024 will likely revolve—at least in part—around the criminal justice system, which both sides have sought to weaponize to their partisan advantage. The judiciary can play an important role in depoliticizing the justice system and reassuring voters that lady justice remains blindfolded.

The Bible commands judges not to recognize faces when they decide cases. They should be blind to political parties, races, genders, or any factors other than the evidence and the law. We are a long way from that paradigm, but Judge Noreika took at least one small step towards approaching it.

Now she should take the next important step of assuring that the investigation that produced the plea bargain was thorough and not artificially constricted by geography. A prosecutor must be free to follow the money trail wherever it may lead.

It is still not clear whether this prosecutor had, and believed he had, that authority. If he did not, he should be told in no uncertain terms that he may continue his investigation until he, and the American public, are satisfied that all potential crimes have been thoroughly pursued.

Garland Illegally Appointed Weiss as Special Counsel

When Attorney General Merrick Garland announced that he was appointing David Weiss as special counsel, he failed to mention § 600.3(c) of the Code of Federal Regulations entitled "Qualifications of the Special Counsel." These qualifications include the following: "The special counsel *shall* be selected from *outside* the United States government." (Emphasis added)

This requirement is the law. The regulations were authorized by Congress under 5 U.S.C. 301, 509, 510, 515-519. The attorney general is the chief law enforcement officer of the United States. It is certainly expected that he would obey the law in its entirety.

If he feels that somehow there is an applicable exception to this requirement, he is obliged to explain why. Particularly when the special counsel is appointed to investigate the son of the incumbent president, who appointed Garland, every T should be crossed and every I should be dotted. Here we have what appears to be a clear rule using the word "shall" rather than a more permissive word such as "may." The regulation on its face seems mandatory, and not advisory. If it is not, why not?

There are good reasons for this requirement. Special counsel is supposed to be independent of the current government, not an employee who serves as US attorney for Delaware and can be fired from that job by the president. He is supposed to look at the evidence through the eyes of an outsider.

Garland may well say that he had little choice but to pick David Weiss, because Weiss has been conducting this investigation for five years. But that sounds like a good reason for *not* appointing the man who already agreed to make what many regard as a sweetheart deal, limited to minor tax and gun violations. Whether consciously or unconsciously, Weiss is likely to want to defend that highly criticized decision—a decision that was (as I predicted) rejected by the judge because of its ambiguity.

As to the five years of investigation, they were conducted not by Weiss himself but by his underlings, who could be kept on if a new special counsel were to be appointed. But even if there were persuasive reasons for naming Weiss as special counsel, Garland had an obligation to explain his apparent violation of a binding regulation. He did not do so at his press briefing. He can still do so now. And he should.

Garland's defenders argue that he may have merely skirted, rather than violated, the law because the appointment was made under his general authority and not expressly under the relevant regulations. This is a stretch especially since he relied on those very regulations to give the special counsel the powers authorized by the regulations. In any event, we rightly expect our attorneys general to comply with both the letter and spirit of the law and not to cut sharp corners.

Democrats frequently say that no one is above the law. Yet they have been silent about Garland apparently placing himself above the law in choosing Weiss in violation of governing legal regulations.

Under our constitutional system of checks and balances, it is within the powers of Congress to summon Garland and ask him to explain why he believes he is justified in ignoring a federal regulation that seems to limit his authority to appoint special counsels. He was surely aware of the regulation and of its apparently binding application. Maybe his explanation will be acceptable. Maybe he will admit he was wrong. Maybe he will decline to respond. The public is entitled to hear him and judge for themselves.

His decision to ignore the regulation was surprising. Many, including this author, have high regard for Garland as a "by the book," politically neutral and fair-minded attorney general. Many of us strongly supported his nomination to the Supreme Court and condemned the refusal of the then-Republican majority of the Senate even to give a hearing based on the lame excuse that it was early in the presidential election year. (The Republicans then rushed Justice Amy Coney Barrett through just weeks before the election). But this decision, along with some others, has been extremely disappointing.

With few exceptions, attorneys general generally become more partisan after they are appointed. This should be expected because they are cabinet members who are supposed to be loyal to the administration they are serving. But they are also supposed to be entirely nonpartisan in conducting criminal investigations and filing charges. It is difficult if not impossible to perform this schizophrenic role.

The ultimate solution is to divide the Justice Department into two separate units: one political, whose incumbent serves at the pleasure of the president; the other a non-partisan prosecutor, who cannot be fired except with consent of Congress. If this were done, perhaps there would be less need for special counsel.

Will the Second Amendment Save Hunter Biden from Prison Time on Gun Charges?

The indictment of Hunter Biden for falsifying a gun application was inevitable once the judge turned down the original plea bargain. This does not mean, though, that there will be a trial, at least not a full-blown trial.

The likely scenario is as follows: Hunter Biden's lawyers will try to negotiate a new deal under which he admits the *factual* allegations in the indictment, but denies that these allegations can be prosecuted as a crime under the Second Amendment.

Mr. Biden's lawyers may also claim that by previously agreeing to diversion for that offense, this incitement constitutes double jeopardy. This is called a stipulated plea, under which the basic facts are stipulated to be true, but the law is challenged.

Such a plea allows the defendant to appeal the inevitable guilty verdict and raise the Second Amendment and double jeopardy issues, eventually perhaps in the Supreme Court. Both the prosecutor and the judge have to agree to such a stipulated plea, and either may refuse to do so.

In that case, Mr. Biden and his lawyers would have to decide whether to plead guilty, perhaps in exchange for a recommendation of probation, or plead not guilty and have a full trial that they would almost certainly lose.

The reality is that few people in Mr. Biden's situation are actually prosecuted for misstatements—even deliberate ones—on their gun applications. If they are prosecuted and plead guilty, they generally get a probationary sentence, especially if there are no prior relevant offenses.

The original plea bargain called for a diversionary judgment, without a plea of guilty or a conviction on Biden's record. This indictment ups the ante, but probably not enough to result in a sentence of imprisonment, especially if there is not a full trial.

Mr. Biden may well also face an additional indictment on his alleged failure to pay several years of taxes in a timely manner. This crime is, too, not often criminally prosecuted for first offenders who eventually paid their taxes.

When it is prosecuted, it usually results in a plea bargain and a probationary sentence. Although the statute of limitations has passed on some other possible crimes, it is likely that investigations are continuing with regard to Mr. Biden's more recent business history.

There is also the possibility, though it seems unlikely, that Attorney General Garland would appoint a special counsel to investigate connections between Hunter Biden and his father, based on allegations made by several Republican politicians and press pundits.

The opening of an impeachment investigation by Speaker McCarthy may produce evidence warranting the appointment of such a lawyer. But in the absence of such developments, the most likely scenario is some kind of a plea to avoid a full-blown trial in the gun application case, as well as a plea bargain to avoid a trial if there were to be an indictment in any tax case.

Were a full-blown trial to occur in the gun permit case, it would likely be scheduled right in the middle of the presidential campaign season, and at about the same time that President Trump would be on trial.

If there is an indictment in the tax case and a plea of not guilty, that trial too might well occur in the run-up of the 2024 election. What is certain is that the 2024 presidential campaign will be influenced by the trials of Mr. Trump.

Whether they will also be influenced by trials involving President Biden's son remains to be seen. It will surely be influenced by the charges against him, and the uncharged allegations regarding his business affairs, which Republicans will try to use to counteract the charges against Trump.

What is also relatively certain is that President Biden will not pardon his son—at least not before the election. That would be a political non-starter. The tragedy is that the coming presidential campaign is likely to be as much about our criminal justice system as about the economy, foreign policy, immigration, and other issues that affect all Americans.

Equal Injustice: Menendez Indictment Does Not Prove Equal Justice

Many Democrats are claiming that the recent indictment of Senator Robert Menendez (D-NJ) proves that the current Justice Department provides equal justice to Democrats and Republicans. Although it is necessary to wait for the evidence to emerge before judgment is passed on this most recent indictment, what appears so far may be closer to equal injustice.

In both the Menendez and Trump cases, prosecutors are engaging in the questionable tactic of seeking to influence the jury before trial. The photographic display of gold bars and cash in the Menendez case is an image that will remain with everyone who saw it. The same is true of the contrived photographic display by the Justice Department of allegedly classified documents spread on the floor. This "show and tell" was produced by the Justice Department and published in virtually every media outlet in the country.

Both show and tells are wrong. Both are intended to prejudice potential jurors and witnesses and to try the case in the court of public opinion before it is subject to the adversarial process to the courts of law. Both come close to ethically impermissible lines. And both should be opposed by all Americans who care about impartial justice for all defendants.

Two wrongs do not make a right—nor do they cancel each other out. They simply compound the injustices and demonstrate that this Justice Department—and several others that came before it—are willing to violate the spirit if not the letter of the law, Justice Department regulations, and legal ethics.

It is unclear whether either of these photographs will be allowed into evidence at the upcoming trials. That would depend on whether it was staged—as the Trump one obviously was—or whether the Menendez display simply recorded what was found and not touched by investigators. If the photographs were to be ruled inadmissible by the trial judge, the prejudice to the defendants would be compounded.

I don't know whether Robert Menendez is guilty, innocent, or somewhere in between. The courts have thrown out several cases in which it was alleged that items of value were given to elected officials in exchange for favors—including a previous one against Menendez. I suspect this will be an easier case to prove in the media than in the courtroom.

Menendez has been a very good Senator, especially with regard to foreign relations regarding the continuing threat to global security from Iran. He is among the more moderate and centrist Democrats in the Senate and is well known for performing constituent services. Whether he stepped over the line here will be determined by a jury after both the government and the defendant present their evidence and each is subjected to the adversarial check of cross-examination and confrontation.

No one should rush to judgment before all the evidence is seen and heard. Nor should Menendez be compelled to resign his seat in the

Senate based on allegations, photographs, and the kind of one-sided testimony that is heard by grand jurors. The presumption of innocence means just that: at this point in time, Menendez should be deemed no more guilty than other officeholders who have been accused of wrongdoing.

Menendez is up for reelection soon, and already a candidate has announced a challenge. It is fair for voters to look at the totality of information before casting their ballots, but the indictment itself should not become the heavy thumb on the electoral scale, since it is only a one-sided accusation.

One irony of the Justice Department's publication of prejudicial photographs clearly intended to influence the jury and potential witnesses is the fact that the same Justice Department is seeking to impose a gag order on Trump, in part because of the claim that he will try to influence jurors and witnesses against the government.

Both Trump and Menendez have the constitutional right—under the First and Sixth Amendments—to defend themselves in the court of public opinion. The government, on the other hand, has no constitutional right to try to influence jurors or witnesses. Its only legitimate role is just to seek objective and fair justice. In that regard, the Justice Department is starting off on the wrong foot in both the Menendez and Trump cases.

So stay tuned. This case may unfold quite differently from the illustrated indictment we have seen thus far.

CHAPTER 3

Media McCarthyism

The "fourth branch" of government—the media—is supposed to be a part of our system of checks and balances. But it has become part of the problem by taking sides and reporting its "truths," rather than objectively, as these essays demonstrate.

If AT&T Can Silence Newsmax, Who Is Next?

AT&T's recent deplatforming of Newsmax, one of America's most influential cable news channels, should alarm everyone, including liberals. We are all at risk when censorship occurs—when one is silenced based on his or her point of view.

The facts strongly suggest that partisan and ideological motives played a sizable role in AT&T and DirecTV's decision to remove Newsmax on January 24, when some 13 million homes were deprived of the channel—including my own. After the recent State of the Union address, I turned to Newsmax for their coverage, but was surprised to find it suddenly missing from my channel guide.

Newsmax has been quite familiar to me: For several years now, I have been a legal analyst for the network. While the channel is center-right in its political orientation, my liberal positions are welcomed without any hesitation.

In my book *The Case Against the New Censorship*, I studied the growing movement to silence dissenting views, of which Newsmax now appears to be a victim.

Publicly, DirecTV and AT&T (DirecTV's 70 percent owner, with financial firm TPG owning the remaining 30 percent) say the move to deplatform Newsmax was about "cutting costs" and saving customers money. But when one notes that Newsmax was the fourth-highest-rated cable news network and that its license fee requests are modest (about $1 per subscriber per year), the DirecTV decision doesn't make much business sense. Indeed, there are dozens of channels that DirecTV carries that cost much more than Newsmax but have much lower ratings.

While DirecTV's decision may have been legally permissible, it was wrong and frankly un-American to deny Newsmax access to its platform, making it impossible for viewers to see the channel and exercise their civic right to take part in the marketplace of ideas.

Over a year ago, DirecTV carried three conservative-leaning channels, including One America News Network (OANN), a hard-right network. Meanwhile, DirecTV has continued to offer a panoply of left-leaning channels. In the past year, then DirecTV and AT&T have deplatformed two of their only three conservative news channels.

As one of America's largest companies, AT&T has a duty to abide by "good corporate citizenship," and thus to provide ideological balance in its choice of platformed TV networks. It clearly has not done so.

While private censorship is often legal, there are potential constitutional concerns if the government encouraged AT&T to shut down Newsmax.

As the case may be, in 2021, Democrats on the House Commerce Committee held hearings to investigate pay-TV systems for carrying conservative channels that were allegedly spreading "misinformation." On February 22, 2021, Reps. Anna Eshoo (D-CA) and Jerry McNerney (D-CA) wrote to AT&T CEO John Stankey demanding to know if he was "planning to continue carrying Fox News, Newsmax, and OANN on U-verse, DirecTV, and ATT TV, both now and beyond any contract renewal date."

A year later, in February 2022, as its contract with OANN neared its end, AT&T announced it was deplatforming the channel. It cited—surprise!—"cost-cutting" as the basis for its decision. OANN never had Newsmax's ratings, but it's not clear why AT&T eliminated it from its lineup while keeping many other low-rated channels.

Newsmax says that when it was up for renewal with AT&T/DirecTV last month, DirecTV's position was, and continues to be, that Newsmax is not eligible for any license fees. Meanwhile, all US cable news channels get fees, and nearly all top cable channels do as well. Newsmax asserts that DirecTV's demand it take zero fees would impact all its other cable broadcaster agreements, essentially demonetizing and censoring the network.

So why doesn't DirecTV cut costs by reducing fees for the many lower-rated networks it carries? Why, again, has DirecTV decided everyone in cable news gets license fees except for Newsmax?

This is not just a "business dispute"; it is a prima facie case of discrimination against Newsmax.

After Elon Musk's release of the "Twitter Files," we know the FBI worked to censor private parties—a serious potential breach of constitutionally protected free speech rights. Did something similar happen when AT&T shut off OANN and Newsmax?

The relatively small amount of money DirecTV saved by removing Newsmax—with the ensuing loss of customers and brand reputation—makes one wonder if a larger hand was at play that forced its deplatforming decision.

House Speaker Kevin McCarthy (R-CA) says Congress will hold hearings on AT&T's targeting of Newsmax and OANN. These hearings must be bipartisan: The rights of all Americans are at stake.

Recently, I signed a letter along with twenty-two major Jewish leaders calling on AT&T and DirecTV to return Newsmax to its platform. (Disclosure: *Newsweek* opinion editor Josh Hammer was another signee of the same letter.)

This letter was remarkable in its support from major Jewish leaders spanning the political spectrum. At a time of rising antisemitism at home and abroad, Newsmax has consistently offered fair and invaluable coverage on issues of concern to American Jews.

As a liberal, I am truly troubled that a major conservative cable news channel—and one that is reliably pro-Israel, like Newsmax—was silenced by AT&T. If AT&T and DirecTV can get away with silencing Newsmax, who will be next?

Lawsuits against Networks for Challenging Elections Endanger Free Speech

Companies that make vote counting machines are suing Fox and others for defaming them. I'm advising clients in several lawsuits involving voting machines, and I'm a frequent contributor to some of these media. So, I am not unbiased. Nor am I unbiased regarding the First Amendment, which I believe is endangered by these lawsuits.

My own personal view is that the 2020 election was generally fair, and President Joe Biden was properly elected. But I am not so sure about the widespread use of machines in counting votes. My general concern about all machines is underlined by the apparent refusal of the voting machine companies to allow experts to examine their inner workings to determine if they are susceptible to hacking in future elections. When the government delegates a governmental function like vote counting to private companies, these companies must be transparent: they should not be permitted to hide behind claims of private business secrets. And the media should be allowed to challenge and criticize them without fear of being subjected to expensive lawsuits by giant corporations.

Moreover, the media should be free to challenge the results of any elections—even if the claims turn out to be false. I am convinced that the 2020 election was fair, but millions of voters believe—or claim to believe—otherwise. The open marketplace of ideas permits the media to give voice to dissenting views, even if they themselves disagree with them.

In the Fox case, discovery has revealed that many at the network, including owners and anchors, had serious doubts about the claims of vote fraud being espoused by some of their guests. Yet they put them on the air, and the network is now being subject to defamation suits because of what the guests falsely claimed, and the anchors didn't dispute. The implications of these suits for the First Amendment rights of the network and its viewers are serious. As a result of these suits, several of the networks stopped showing guests who challenged the elections or who raised questions about the machines. Must all networks present only the majority narrative on controversial issues of national importance? Should they be permitted to present guests who honestly but wrongly believe a counter narrative? Shouldn't the viewers be permitted to choose among competing narratives?

It is interesting to contrast these lawsuits with the lawsuit I'm currently bringing against CNN, which is very different. CNN doctored and edited tapes in which I had argued that a president could be impeached for unlawful, illegal, or corrupt criminal behavior. Their paid commentators and employees then maliciously lied, claiming that I said that a president could not be impeached even if he committed serious crimes such as extortion, bribery, or murder—the exact opposite of what I actually said. The First Amendment does not protect such malicious and deliberate defamation designed to discredit individuals with views different from the networks. It does protect honestly held opinions which turn out to be untrue. As former chief justice William Rehnquist put it: "Under the First Amendment there is no such thing as a false idea." But there are such things as false defamatory facts that are maliciously published in an attempt to destroy the credibility of a person with opposing views, which is what CNN did to me.

The line between the Fox and CNN lawsuits may not always be clear, but it is an important line to preserve. Fox is being sued for allowing opinions and ideas that are essential to an uncensored discussion of controversial and disputed theories regarding a past presidential election, as well as future elections in which votes are to be tabulated by machines. I have accused CNN of maliciously lying about a single recorded statement that I made in the past, concerning which their commentators deliberately and maliciously lied. This is an important distinction to maintain.

We are a deeply divided nation in which passions run high and opinions dramatically differ. As Pat Moynihan used to say: "Everyone is entitled to their own opinions, but not to their own facts." The line between the two is also not always clear: zealots have wrongheaded opinions about facts. Different media "report" facts differently. Distrust in reporting is rampant and often justified. So let the open marketplace be the judge of who is right and wrong. There is no guarantee that the marketplace will always get it right. But to paraphrase Churchill, it may be the worst method, except for all the others that have been tried over time.

Should the Names of Stanford Student Disrupters Be Published?

Once again, a conservative speaker had been shouted down by censorial law students who didn't want him to speak. This time it was Stanford, last time it was Yale. Then it was Georgetown.

If the Stanford Dean of Diversity, Equity, and Inclusion gets her way, this censorship of conservative speakers will spread to other campuses. Among the worst offenders in this all-too-common censorship fest was Dean Tirien Steinbach. In what appears to be a written statement prepared in advance, she effectively silenced the speaker, federal Judge Kyle Duncan, by monopolizing his space. She sought to justify not inviting speakers who might offend the sensibilities of students who she claims to be responsible for "protecting" and providing "safe spaces" against uncomfortable ideas.

After paying lip service to free speech, she suggested reconsidering Stanford's speech policy, repeatedly asked whether "the squeeze is worth the juice." She questioned whether Judge Duncan, whose opinions and views cause "hurt" to students, should have been invited to speak. Her bottom-line message was that offending some students is worse than allowing others to hear from a controversial speaker. This from a high-ranking administrator who was purporting to speak on behalf of the university.

The real victims of this censorship were the students who were denied the opportunity to hear Judge Duncan's full presentation.

An angry Judge Duncan responded, "Don't feel sorry for me. I'm a life-tenured judge. What outrages me is that these kids are being treated like dogshit by fellow students and administrators."

As the late justice Thurgood Marshall once observed, "The freedom to speak and the freedom to hear are inseparable; They are two sides of the same coin."

To her credit, the dean of the law school, Jenny Martinez, condemned the disrupters, writing, "However well-intentioned, attempts at managing the room in this instance went awry. . . . The way this event unfolded was not aligned with our institutional commitment to freedom of speech." She gave no indication of whether anyone would be disciplined.

To be sure, protesting, picketing, and even brief heckling of speakers is also protected free speech, but shouting speakers down with the intent to silence them is not. It is explicitly prohibited by Stanford's rules. Yet that's exactly what occurred without apparent consequences to the disrupters.

The disrupters also attempted to shame the sponsors of the speech by disclosing their names and subjecting them to harassment. This suggests a possible response to the disrupters.

Following the Yale disruptions, some judges have announced that they will no longer hire law clerks from Yale. Similar announcements regarding Stanford are likely. In my view, that amounts to collective punishment of the innocent along with guilty. Many law students from these schools do not agree with disrupting speakers, and they should not be denied clerkships.

Instead, the names of the disrupters might be published and made available to potential employers, so they can decide whether they want to hire graduates with such intolerance for diversity of viewpoints.

I made a similar suggestion about publishing the names of Berkeley law students who voted to ban all Zionists—that is, believers in Israel's right to exist—from speaking at fourteen law school clubs, including feminist, Black, and gay organizations.

As one who well remembers McCarthyite "blacklists," I'm uncomfortable about publishing the names of student censors. But if they are proud of their very public efforts to silence speakers with whom they disagree, they should be proud to have their names published so that potential employers can have relevant information before they make hiring decisions.

That would be far better than judges and other employers refusing to hire ANY students from the offending schools.

Law schools are supposed to teach advocacy skills and a commitment to the rule of law.

They should have and enforce vigorous free speech policies. They should not have deans, like Steinbach, who are part of the problem, rather than part of the solution.

Stanford should apologize to Judge Duncan for the dean's actions and inactions. He observed that in his view, "This was a set up. She was working with the students." Stanford should discipline any students who violated its speech policies. Most importantly, it should foster values of diversity of viewpoints, rather than merely diversity of race and ethnicity. Perhaps the law school should appoint a new dean of "diversity of opinions, tolerance for other views, and free speech."

Stanford Law Disruptions Were Orchestrated by the National Lawyers Guild

It turns out that the disruption by several dozen Stanford University law school students of a speech to be given by federal judge Kyle Duncan was not a spontaneous exercise of freedom to protest.

It was a well-planned and carefully orchestrated effort to prevent other Stanford students from hearing the judge's conservative views. The disruption was organized by the local chapter of the National Lawyers Guild as part of a nationwide effort to suppress conservative speech. Although not all the participants were associated with the NLG, the main organizers were. The Guild praised "every single person" who participated in the disruption, and called it "Stanford Law School at its best," suggesting it would confront "judicial architects of systems of oppression" with "social consequences for their actions." Here the consequences went beyond "social" to censorial.

Let us understand what the National Lawyers Guild is. Begun in the 1930s as an alternative to the American Bar Association, its original membership consisted of traditional left-wing liberals and Communists. After Nazi Germany and the Soviet Union made the notorious Molotov-Ribbentrop Pact in 1939, most of the liberals resigned. Adolf Berle, a prominent "New Dealer," quit because it had become obvious that the Guild "is not prepared to take any stand which conflicts with the Communist Party line."

When Hitler then broke the pact and invaded the Soviet Union, the Guild changed its policy and rejected Hitler. After Japan attacked the United States in 1941, the Guild "remained silent" rather than oppose the internment of more than a hundred thousand Americans of Japanese descent.

In 1948, the Guild "supported the establishment of the State Israel" because that was the position of the Soviet Union. In 1967, when the Soviet Union began to turn against Israel and increased support for the Palestine Liberation Organization (PLO), so did the Guild. Since that time, the Guild has been a strong supporter of Palestinian terrorism and other efforts to destroy Israel.

The Guild, in addition, refused to support Soviet or Cuban dissidents.

The Guild has never abandoned its Marxist-Leninist provenance. It supports Antifa, which also employs violence to disrupt speakers.

The National Lawyers Guild is not a liberal organization. It does not support civil liberties, due process, or freedom of speech. It is the epitome of "free speech for me but not for thee." It will not be swayed by the argument that hateful, dangerous speech should be tolerated at any cost, and defines such speech broadly to include judicial decisions by Judge Duncan.

Many decent people question whether hateful, offensive, and even speech deemed "dangerous" by some, should be protected. The answer resides in history. Whenever governments are empowered to ban such expression, they use that power expansively, to censor speech critical of their leaders or partisans. The appetite of the censor is voracious. What are seen as legitimate opinions by dissenters are deemed by others—especially those in power—as hateful, offensive, or dangerous. Freedom of speech for all is anything but free. It can be hurtful and risky. But in the end, it is worth the costs.

The National Lawyers Guild seemingly despises America, and in 2020 passed a resolution declaring:

> The United States government is based on and dedicated to preserving white supremacy, hetero-patriarchy, and imperialism . . . US uses its various government agencies to implement its policies and crush political resistance.

It deplores capitalism and the free market: "don't fund capitalism, fund the groups working to dismantle it." And it opposes due process for those with whom it disagrees, for instance, declaring of a "Mass Defense Program" that sends out "legal workers, law students, and lawyers providing legal support for protests":

"We will only show up to actions and in support of movements that directly align with our values."

This is not to say that all the students who participated in the Stanford disruption agree with these positions. Since its inception, the National Lawyers Guild has relied on "useful idiots"—well-meaning left-wingers and liberals who have no idea what the Guild really represents. It disguises its most extreme positions when presenting itself to the public but advertises them to its members. It also hides from the public the fact that despite its name, the membership Guild consists primarily of non-lawyers. When it was truly a lawyers' organization, it was slightly more centrist. And then in the 1970s, the Guild opened its membership to "jailhouse lawyers" (who are not lawyers), legal workers (who are not lawyers), law students (who are not yet lawyers), and anyone else who works with or for lawyers or law firms.

The Guild has more than one hundred chapters in American law schools. Its membership includes many law professors. It apparently plans to organize nationwide disruptions of the kind we have seen at Stanford. The Guild creates the illusion that these disruptions are spontaneous reactions to conservative provocations. They are anything but.

Demonstrations and protests are protected by the First Amendment and by the principles of free speech. Preventing speakers from addressing willing listeners is not. Nor is harassing students who invite conservative speakers, as the National Lawyers Guild has done. They violate not only the rights of the speakers they disrupt, but also of those students who came to hear them. As the late Supreme Court justice Thurgood Marshall observed: "The freedom to speak and the freedom to hear are inseparable; they are two sides of the same coin." These disrupters violated both rights.

Thus far disruptions have occurred at Yale, Stanford, and Georgetown law schools. But you can be sure that they are coming to a law school near you. The NLG will not be satisfied until no conservative speaker is allowed to speak at any law school. That is its objective, and it may well succeed, because cowardly administrators—especially deans of diversity, in order to avoid the embarrassment of what happened at Stanford, Yale and Georgetown—will try to make sure that conservative speakers are not invited. They understand that it is much harder to object to the less visible non-invitation of conservative speakers than to publicly disrupting them.

We who support freedom of speech for all sides must organize as well. We cannot count on the American Civil Liberties Union anymore: its silence supports the censorship of the National Lawyers Guild. Our voices must be heard against censorship-by-disruption, by non-invitation, or by any other improper means.

Why Newsmax Has a Stronger Case Than Fox

Fox's decision to settle is incomprehensible—and may hurt the First Amendment.

Dominion did not lose three-quarters of a billion dollars from Fox's alleged defamation. It's unlikely they actually lost very much at all; indeed, they probably gained considerable credibility and additional business. This was especially so since the judge made findings favorable to Dominion's professionalism. Had the case gone to verdict, and had Fox lost, the network probably would have been required to pay a relatively small amount of damages—certainly nothing approaching the amount for which they settled.

Moreover, there was a substantial chance that Fox could have won this suit, either at trial or on appeal. Dominion had a heavy burden to demonstrate that Fox was guilty of actual malice; that is, a reckless disregard for the truth. The trial judge denied—in my view erroneously—Fox its constitutional right under the Seventh Amendment to challenge Dominion's narrative. He essentially found as a matter of fact that Fox had lied—an issue that should have been left to the jury. Even so, Dominion may not have been able to meet the high standard required to prove actual malice.

Finally, two justices of the Supreme Court have raised questions about the actual malice standard—and this case might very well have made its way to the high court. Once before the justices, virtually any outcome would have been possible.

Accordingly, from a purely rational cost-benefit analysis, this settle-ment—which gave Dominion an enormous windfall—is incomprehen-sible. No good lawyer, evaluating the trial and appellate prospects and the lack of actual damages, would have recommended such a settle-ment. Something else must have been at play—and part of the reason for the settlement is almost certainly to prevent the public from learn-ing the actual reason why Fox settled.

Some infer that, despite the fact that much of its dirty laundry had already been spread out for all to see in the early discovery phase of the case, there was even dirtier laundry that might have been uncovered had the case gone forward and had the special master been allowed to rummage through more emails and other communications. We may never know the real reasons why Fox threw in the towel.

We may also never know the precise impact this settlement may have on freedom of speech. Among the most pernicious forms of cen-sorship is self-censorship, which tends to be invisible. Media companies such as Fox may be chilled by the prospect of further lawsuits. Indeed, other lawsuits are still pending against Fox and other media outlets. They may self-censor out of caution.

It is often forgotten that freedom of speech is a two-sided coin. One side is the right of the speaker, such as Fox, to express controver-sial and unpopular views. The other side is the right of the viewer and listener to see and hear those views. When the speaker self-censors, the listener is generally not even aware that they have been denied a basic freedom. I know, from personal experience, about several situations where media have censored First Amendment–protected material out of fear of expensive lawsuits. Fox is not the only media outlet that has been sued by Dominion. Others have too, including Newsmax.

I frequently appear as an unpaid guest on Fox and as a paid legal expert on Newsmax. In both instances, I speak only for myself and not for the networks, as I also do in my column. I am also suing CNN for having doctored the tape of my appearance before the United States Senate so as to make it appear that I said the opposite of what I actually said. So I am not an unbiased observer with regard to these lawsuits.

With that said, as an advocate of maximum freedom of speech for more than sixty years, I fear for the First Amendment. The one-sided settlement made by Fox may, on balance, have served its interests. It certainly fattened Dominion's bottom line, but it was not good for the First Amendment and for the rights of Americans to hear the diversity of views on important subjects of public interest.

I believe that the 2020 election was essentially fair and produced the right result. Accordingly, I think that Fox presented the views of guests and commentators that were false. Newsmax was different. It reported a diversity of viewpoints, but without embracing allegations that turned out to be false. In my view, Newsmax has a stronger case than Fox, both as a matter of facts and law. I don't know whether Newsmax will litigate. I hope it does and I hope it wins.

It is interesting to note that these cases could not have been brought against internet platforms that are protected from defamation action by a federal statute designed to encourage maximum diversity of viewpoints on the internet. No such protection is accorded to other media companies. Congress is reconsidering the internet exemption and may limit it. And the courts may well rethink media defamation law in general.

So, stay tuned. The law of defamation, as constrained by the First Amendment, is very much in play. The Fox settlement may have an impact on how the law develops over time. What that impact may be is anyone's guess.

Could "Journalists" Sink Any Lower: Beware of Alex Novell

Journalists are supposed to be governed by rules of ethics, but too many of them will do anything, violate any rule, break any trust, lie to any source, in order to get a career-building story. Most journalists comply with their ethical obligations, but the ones who do not cause understandable distrust among the general public.

Recently, a young man named Alex Novell emailed me saying: "I'm a graduate student at NYU working on a documentary film about the history of the Taglit-Birthright program." He asked me for "an interview with you as it would provide expert commentary for the film." I agreed first, because I like to encourage students who are doing interesting projects; second, I assumed, as he indeed led me to assume, that he was a current student New York University and that his project was part of his studies under the supervision of the school; and third, I care deeply about Birthright and its impact on American students and, having worked with the program, deeply respect it.

Novell began the interview by asking several relevant questions about Birthright. Then suddenly, as the interview was about to come to an end, he threw out the following accusatory question: How much did you pay the woman who accused you to change her story? I told him that I paid her nothing, but he persisted on the subject. I answered all of his questions and asked him why he used Birthright as a pretext to ask me about the false accusation. We then had an exchange of emails in which he denied that he ever represented that he was a current student, claiming—falsely—that he said that he had "graduated from NYU." He admitted that if he had represented himself as a current student working on a NYU-sponsored project, that "would have been false." But that is exactly what he did write me: "I'm a graduate student at NYU working on a documentary film." Not "I'm a former graduate student with no current connection to NYU." He was deliberately deceptive and did make false statements.

I then told him that, since he obtained the interview by fraud, he no longer had permission to use my recorded answers, and did not sign any release.

To be clear: I stand by all my answers. I told the truth about the false accusation. I did nothing wrong and have nothing to hide. In fact, the woman who I have long said falsely accused me recently admitted that she may have misidentified me, confusing me with someone else. Indeed, I might well have agreed to be interviewed about the false accusation if he had been honest in asking instead of deceptive.

I later learned that he was in fact making a "documentary" in which he tries to justify the use of fraudulent pretexts by journalists to "get" people with whose views they disagree. The only thing worse than using deception to create a story, is to try to justify such reprehensible tactics.

This is not Sacha Baron Cohen, a comic actor who uses pretext for humorous purposes. This is a person who claims to be a journalist, who is employing fraud to interview people he does not like. Apparently, he plans to call other people as well, presumably those like me who support Israel. He apparently believes that because I defend Israel, he is justified in defrauding me.

This then, is a warning to other people who support Israel to be aware that this fraudulent and pretend "journalist" is out there ready to employ sleazy tactics unworthy of real journalists. No one should ever agree to be interviewed by Novell. And NYU should be aware that its good name is being misused and tarnished by Novell's unethical misrepresentations.

Novell has now tried to shift blame to me, saying that I should have checked him out on Google before agreeing to be interviewed. So I did, and I found nothing that would have alerted me to his fraudulent intentions and action. This is why I am writing this op-ed: so that anyone Novell seeks to interview in the future, will be able to learn about his sordid history.

Harvard's "Council on Academic Freedom"

The fact that more than one hundred Harvard University professors have now joined together in a council on academic freedom is both good news and bad news. The purpose of the group, organized by my colleague and friend Steven Pinker, is to ensure that freedom of speech and academic freedom survive at Harvard. It is good that so many professors signed on to it so quickly. It is bad that it is even needed at a place like Harvard whose motto, Veritas, means truth. But "truth" can be a double-edged sword, especially at a university.

The "truth" can sometimes be the enemy of freedom. When people believe they, and only they, have access to THE TRUTH, they see little need for debate, dialogue, dissent, and disagreement. Indeed, they regard such contrary views as heresy. That has been the way of many religions over the years as well as numerous ideologies such as Communism and fascism. Universities should not recognize any particular truth or promote any specific narrative.

The role of universities is to teach students how to think, not what to think. The process of discovering, examining, and criticizing ever-changing truths is the proper role of higher education, not inculcating currently accepted verities. That is not education; that is propaganda.

Ideological warriors, however, who at today's universities are generally on the "hard left," want their institutions to promote particular truths and narratives and to reject others. Sometimes this is done overtly, more often subtly. The reality is that at many universities, including Harvard, certain views are unacceptable. Both teachers and students know what they are and often self-censor to avoid being stigmatized. It is not getting better; it is getting worse.

Although several media highlighted the fact that one hundred faculty members joined this newly created council on academic freedom, the real headline is that so many faculty members refused or declined to participate in an organization whose goal is to promote free speech.

Some radical professors and students even oppose the organization, presumably because they do not support its goals of free speech and academic freedom. These include many former civil libertarians and liberals who have now joined the ranks of the guardians of political correctness.

This problem is not unique to Harvard, as evidenced by recent events at Stanford, Yale, Georgetown, University of Pennsylvania, and other elite institutions where speakers have been shouted down or subject to discipline for expressing politically incorrect views outside of the classroom.

When I first came to Harvard in 1964, the political correctness of the day tilted to the right. My liberal-civil libertarian views were suspect among many of the conservative faculty. Letters from alumni objected to my "unsound" views influencing students. Although no one tried to censor me. I was advised that my "unsound" views would hurt my obtaining tenure. (They did not.)

Today many of my views are also regarded as politically incorrect and unsound, but this time it is by the extreme left. The difference is that today's censors have tried to silence and cancel me, as well as others who espouse centrist, liberal, and civil libertarian positions—and certainly if they express conservative or, God forbid, pro-Trump views! That is why this council on academic freedom is so important, and that is why it is so disappointing that so many former liberals and civil libertarians have declined to join it.

It is good that the new free speech council is politically quite diverse, including professors with a wide range of political and ideological views. The shared perspective is in favor of freedom of speech and academic freedom for all views, no matter how unpopular. The goal is to protect the expression of all views and to protect those who are threatened or sanctioned for expressing them. It is also to promote the widest diversity of views on campus.

Freedom of speech, due process, the right to counsel, and other fundamental liberties are in peril in today's deeply divided society in which everyone must choose a side. Picking the wrong side, particularly in academia and the media, can endanger one's prospects. Remaining silent is often the safest course, so self-censorship has become a widespread tactic among individuals who do not support the political correctness of the day.

The new council alone will not reverse the national trend toward groupthink and political correctness, but it promises to play an active role in protecting freedom from those who claim a monopoly on knowing Veritas. It is an honor to be an active member.

History Is a Lot More Complicated Than City Council's Statue-Haters Can Admit

New York's City Council, having already removed the statue of Thomas Jefferson from City Hall, now wants to take down *all* statuary of George Washington and Christopher Columbus.

(Is the city of Washington and the district in which it is located next?)

This is part of a campaign to get rid of monuments honoring anyone who owned enslaved people or profited from slavery.

It also includes anyone who "participated in systematic crimes against indigenous people or other crimes against humanity."

It does not require a balancing of these sins and crimes against the good deeds and virtues of those honored.

George Washington did benefit from slavery, although he emancipated his own slaves upon his death.

But what he accomplished for other people changed the face of America for the better.

There probably wouldn't have been a United States of America were it not for Gen. Washington.

He demanded equal rights for those of all religious persuasions, sending letters to the leaders of various denominations.

"The citizens of the United States of America have a right to applaud themselves for having given to mankind examples of an enlarged and liberal policy: a policy worthy of imitation. All possess alike liberty of conscience and immunities of citizenship," he wrote to the Jews of Newport, RI.

"It is now no more that toleration is spoken of, as if it was by the indulgence of one class of people, that another enjoyed the exercise of their inherent natural rights. For happily the government of the United States, which gives to bigotry no sanction, to persecution no assistance, requires only that they who live under its protection should demean themselves as good citizens in giving it on all occasions their effectual support."

This was the first time in history a nation's leader proclaimed equal rights for its Jewish citizens.

Certainly, that and his other good deeds should be part of any calculus in evaluating America's first president.

On the other side of the scale are black leaders such as Malcolm X, who did considerable good in energizing African American citizens but whose long history of blatant antisemitism continues to have a negative impact today on black and other radicals.

Should the names of streets honoring *him* be changed?

There must be a single standard of evaluation when it comes to taking down monuments and street names, difficult as it would be to agree on any principled standard.

Consider, for example, President Franklin Delano Roosevelt, who has an island named after him.

He did a great many good things, but his failures were monumental and costly.

They include maintaining racial segregation in our armed forces while thousands of young African Americans were sent into battle defending democracy.

He closed the doors to Jewish immigration before and during the Holocaust, deliberately making it difficult for Jewish refugees even to fill the unused "quotas" authorized by law.

He is personally responsible for the deaths of many Jews who could have been saved had Roosevelt simply followed the law rather than pandered to the antisemites in Congress and the State Department.

History is filled with these complexities.

Thomas Jefferson's views on slavery were complex. Abraham Lincoln's views on the rights of African Americans were likewise complicated.

Woodrow Wilson was a man of peace but a virulent racist.

We have no objection to one of the alternatives the City Council proposes: adding an "explanatory plaque" to any monument not taken down, explaining both the misdeeds and the good deeds of the historical figure—so long as the explanation is historically accurate, fair, and nuanced.

But radicals determined to shape the narrative in accordance with their particular ideologies don't want accuracy, fairness, and nuance.

Nor can academic historians necessarily be trusted. Too many of them use and abuse history to promote their ideological, political, and racial agendas.

Let the marketplace of ideas determine the legacies of past historical figures.

Websites should be provided near the monuments in which conflicting views could be shared and debated.

That is the American way, especially since even the explorer after whom our continent is named had a complex legacy!

The City Council should be uniting New Yorkers and Americans around critical issues of crime, fentanyl abuse, immigration, and the economy—it should not be focused on divisive issues of the past.

The Epstein Documents Reveal How I Was Framed—but I'm Still Being Canceled

The unsealing of thousands of documents relating to Jeffrey Epstein[3] raises fundamental issues regarding the role of courts and the media in dealing with sexual misconduct[4] accusations.

---

3   Olivia Land and Nikki Mascali Roarty, "All the A-listers named in the newly unsealed Jeffrey Epstein documents," *New York Post*, January 4, 2024, https://nypost.com/2024/01/04/news/all-the-a-listers-named-in-the-new-jeffrey-epstein-documents/.

4   Alan Dershowitz, "Exonerated: Why I fought to clear my name in Jeffrey Epstein allegation," *New York Post*, November 9, 2022, https://nypost.com/2022/11/09/exonerated-why-i-fought-to-clear-my-name-in-jeffrey-epstein-allegation/.

The disclosure, ordered by a federal judge, made headlines around the world because the material contains the names of—and sometimes accusations against—prominent people. But some documents *exonerate* individuals, including me, who were wrongly accused—which the media have largely ignored.

From the day I was falsely accused of Epstein-related sexual misconduct in 2014, I demanded the release of all relevant documents because I had nothing to hide, and I was confident full disclosure would prove my absolute innocence.

The unsealing has indeed shown exactly how I was framed nearly ten years ago and why my accuser, Virginia Giuffre, eventually acknowledged she may have mistakenly identified me.

One media site, TMZ, reviewed all the unsealed documents and headlined its account "Victim Told to Name-Drop Dershowitz to Sell Her Book."[5] It reported that Sharon Churcher, a British tabloid journalist, urged Giuffre in 2011 to include me in her book proposal, despite the absence of any evidence I did anything wrong, because I'm famous and represented high-profile clients.

In an email, Giuffre told Churcher she had a ghostwriter to tell her story about being victimized by Epstein, saying, "I wanted to put the names of those a–holes, oops I meant to say, pedo's, that J. E. sent me to."

"Don't forget Alan Dershowitz," Churcher replied. "J. E. buddy and lawyer—good name for your pitch as he repped Claus van Bulow and a movie was made about that case."

She acknowledged there was "no proof" I did anything wrong but said "you probably met him when he was hanging [out] w JE."

(The truth is, I never met or saw her.)

Following this smoking-gun email exchange, Giuffre did include me in her book proposal but as someone she *saw* with Epstein but with whom she *did not* have sex. Only after retaining contingency-fee

---

5   TMZ Exclusive, "Victim Told to Name-Drop Dershowitz to Sell Her Book, According to Emails," TMZ, January 4, 2024, https://www.tmz.com/2024/01/04/jeffrey-epstein-victim-virginia-giuffre-emails-alan-dershowitz-sell-book-bill-clinton-vanity-fair/.

lawyers in 2014 did she "remember" she had sex with me, apparently confusing me with another person she saw with Epstein.

Without giving me an opportunity to disprove the false accusations by my travel and other records, the lawyers put them in a public filing. The federal judge in the case sanctioned the lawyers for accusing me and struck all reference to me from the pleadings, but the damage had already been done—the false accusation was published around the world, causing me enormous harm.

To her credit, my accuser now recognizes she may have misidentified me, and she has dropped all legal claims against me.

This is what she said November 7, 2022:

> I was very young at the time, it was a very stressful and traumatic environment, and Mr. Dershowitz has from the beginning consistently denied these allegations. I now recognize I may have made a mistake in identifying Mr. Dershowitz.

And Churcher acknowledged in a now-disclosed recorded interview that she knows that I was falsely accused. Other evidence—including recordings, emails, and FBI files that have not yet been unsealed or unredacted—also confirms my innocence. My lawyers have moved for the release of all relevant evidence but thus far without success.

This episode demonstrates the importance of full disclosure of evidence and the dangers of suppressing material that may help the public decide on issues of innocence or guilt. Only some of the material sealed in the *Giuffre v. Maxwell* case has been made available to the public.

The time has come—indeed, is long overdue—for all the evidence in that case to be unsealed and unredacted so it can be considered in the open marketplace of ideas and facts.

Notwithstanding the conclusive evidence of my innocence the released documents provide, I am still being canceled by several institutions. A large synagogue in Miami, for example, had asked me to speak about Israel and anti-Semitism but canceled the speech because I was "on the list." It didn't matter that I was on the list because the evidence proved I'm innocent; the mere fact I am on an Epstein list was enough to get me canceled.

This is reminiscent of the 1940s and '50s, when Senator Joseph McCarthy would hold up a list of alleged Communists, and those named on it would lose their jobs, regardless of the evidence or lack thereof.

The new McCarthyism is just as sinister.

CHAPTER 4

Can the Supreme Court Constrain the New McCarthyism?

The Supreme Court has long served as a check on abuses and excesses of the other branches. The following essays address the important question of who checks the Supreme Court.

The House Can Help Find the Supreme Court Leaker

The marshal doesn't have subpoena power, but the Judiciary Committee does.

The marshal of the Supreme Court seems to have come up empty in her investigation of who leaked Justice Samuel Alito's draft opinion in *Dobbs v. Jackson Women's Health Organization*. But there may yet be a way of finding out who did it—if the House Judiciary Committee is willing to play hardball with the press.

After the marshal's report came out, Donald Trump offered the following advice on his social-media site: "Go to the reporter and ask who he/she is. If no answer is given, throw anyone in jail until an answer is given. . . . It won't be long before the name of this slime will be revealed!"

The marshal's office has no such authority, and there's unlikely to be a criminal investigation in connection with the leak. But the

Judiciary Committee could subpoena the *Politico* reporters who broke the story.

They would surely refuse to reveal the source, and the committee would have to petition a court to compel the disclosure. Under federal law, journalists don't have an absolute privilege to keep their sources secret, as Judith Miller can attest. As a *New York Times* reporter, Ms. Miller spent eighty-five days in jail in 2005 for refusing to divulge a source in a leak investigation involving the identity of a former covert Central Intelligence Agency officer. Other journalists have been compelled to reveal their sources when courts decided the governmental interest in disclosure outweighed the journalistic interest in protection.

What are the countervailing interests in this potential case? In general, the public has a great interest in sources revealing, and the media publishing, secrets about official misconduct or questionable actions that the government seeks to suppress. The Pentagon Papers and some of what was published by WikiLeaks may fit into this category. (I provided legal counsel to Alaska Senator Mike Gravel and WikiLeaks founder Julian Assange in those cases.)

But what legitimate objective was served by the disclosure of a draft Supreme Court opinion weeks before it was issued? I can think of several illegitimate goals, from improperly influencing justices to inflaming public opinion. After the leak but before Dobbs was decided, a man was arrested near Justice Brett Kavanaugh's house and charged with attempted murder. He has pleaded not guilty.

Even if no legitimate purpose was served by this particular leak, some would argue that compelling journalists to reveal their sources might discourage other sources from disclosing important information about government misconduct.

Another argument is that compulsion would be futile, since all decent journalists would go to jail rather than give up a source. Maybe. But some reporters have complied with court orders. Ms. Miller was eventually persuaded to testify by her source, I. Lewis Libby.

In any event, either of these arguments would amount to an absolute privilege that would deny the courts the power to compel reporters to reveal their sources.

A fair weighing by a court would conclude that this is a close case. Since Congress has never enacted a shield law, neither side has a presumption in its favor. But the argument for compelled disclosure is strong because the source didn't seek to expose any wrongdoing by the government, only the usual workings of the Supreme Court and a decision that would have become public within weeks. A court could conclude that the public's right to know who the leaker was outweighs its interest in learning the outcome of a court ruling in advance.

Has the Supreme Court Given Up on Finding the Leaker?

Following the Supreme Court's released findings of the investigation into who leaked the draft decision overruling *Roe v. Wade*, the matter seems to be closed. There has been no public disclosure of any further efforts to identify the malefactor.

This is an unsatisfactory resolution to one of the most serious breaches of confidentiality in American history.

Let us not underestimate the seriousness of this leak. It apparently encouraged a potential assassin to try to murder Justice Brett Kavanaugh in an effort to change the outcome of the case. It could easily have succeeded in doing so.

The failure to discover the leaker will encourage others to engage in actions which they believe are well-intentioned civil disobedience even if it does not involve the disclosure of governmental wrongdoing. The mystery of who leaked this draft decision must be solved.

The investigation done by the Supreme Court was destined to fail. It was put in the hands of the Court's marshal, whose job it is to protect the justices and to assure order in the Supreme Court building. The office of the marshal is not equipped to conduct difficult investigations.

The matter should have been turned over to the FBI or a special counsel appointed by the Justice Department, as was done with the unauthorized possession of classified material by President Joe Biden and former president Donald Trump.

Let us be clear about one thing: the improper disclosure of the Supreme Court draft opinion in this case was at least as serious a breach as the Biden or Trump violations. Neither Biden nor Trump disclosed any classified material or actually endangered the security of the

United States. They were dangerous because of the potential improper disclosure, whereas the Supreme Court leak involved an actual disclosure that impacted the High Court in numerous negative ways.

Trump criticized the Supreme Court investigation: he argued that the reporter who published the draft opinion should have been subpoenaed and threatened with imprisonment if he or she did not disclose the source. The reporter would undoubtedly claim that such compulsion would violate the journalist-source privilege that exists in many jurisdictions. It is not an absolute privilege, as evidenced by the fact that journalists, most famously, as noted earlier, Judith Miller of the *New York Times*, actually spent time in prison for refusing to comply with judicial orders to disclose her source. Subpoenaing a journalist and threatening her with imprisonment should be an absolute last resort.

Would it be justified in this case? Perhaps. The likelihood is that, like Miller, the journalist who received and published the draft opinion would refuse to disclose its source, although no one ever knows what impact the threat of imprisonment would have on a given journalist.

The journalist was not at fault for publishing the draft opinion. It was highly newsworthy, and like the Pentagon Papers and other confidential materials that have been published, the journalist receiving them has an obligation of disclosure to the public.

The same cannot be said about the Supreme Court employee who violated the commitment to confidentiality by improperly disclosing a document that was supposed to be kept secret until the decision was rendered by the justices. If the source or sources are finally identified, they will probably defend their actions on the basis of a higher good. But noble ends to not justify improper or unethical means, especially if the disclosure might well have threatened innocent lives.

So do not allow the investigation to end with the report of failure. Thus far the entire matter has been relegated to the judicial branch because that is the one most directly affected. All Americans are the victims of this breach, and both the executive and legislative branches have default roles to play if the Supreme Court cannot do the job properly.

Despite the fact that disclosure in and of itself may not be a crime, it may involve criminal conduct either before, during, or after the disclosure itself. If the leaker lied to a law enforcement person—including the Supreme Court marshal—that might be a crime. The FBI certainly has jurisdiction to investigate whether a crime has been committed.

Congress, too, may have an appropriate role in assuring that this breach does not recur. The report issued by the investigators faulted the security at the High Court. That problem will not be easy to solve because law clerks work on drafts and often take them home. The investigation also disclosed that several law clerks told their wives or partners about the decision.

When I was a law clerk in the Supreme Court sixty years ago, each justice had only two law clerks and there were far fewer personnel in the institution. The first two months, the doors of the Supreme Court were open to anyone. A visitor could simply knock at the justices' door and ask for an appointment. Then in the third month, President John F. Kennedy was assassinated.

After the assassination, nearly everything changed. Security was enhanced, barriers were erected, and access to the justices was severely limited. Nothing, however, was done to protect the secrecy of draft opinions and it seems that little or nothing has been done since.

It will not be cost-free to impose restrictions on law clerks' access to draft opinions and their handling of them. Even so, this cost, provoked by the current breach, may be worth incurring in order to protect future disclosures.

Is Prayer in School Constitutional?

New York City Mayor Eric Adams, whom I generally admire, has advocated reintroducing prayer in public schools. The suggestion, though doubtless well-meant, is nevertheless unconstitutional. The First Amendment of the United States Constitution reads: "Congress shall make no law respecting an establishment of religion..." That means any religion, all religions. It does not matter which.

The First Amendment poses no barrier to his personal preference. This is what Mayor Adams said: "Don't tell me about no separation of church and state."

Well Mayor Adams, I am going to tell you about separation of church and state. It was a great idea espoused by Thomas Jefferson, James Madison, and the brilliant writers of our Constitution. It was based on the writing of Rhode Island minister Roger Williams, who saw it as protecting the church from the corrupting influence of the State. Please read not only the First Amendment but also the dozens of court cases that have applied it to prohibit religious prayer in public schools. You have the right to believe that the "Church is the heart." So keep going to church, but do not compel young students to pray to your God or to any God.

Adams also suggested a false choice between prayer in the schools and guns in schools: "When we took prayers out of schools, guns came into schools." There is no evidence to support this questionable theory of causation. Neither prayers nor guns belong in schools.

Adams may not be able to "separate [his] belief" from his actions as mayor. But the Constitution requires that mayors, as public officials, do just that. He claims that "the policies we make as an administration are rooted in the mayor's belief in his creator." In other words, those citizens of New York—and there are many of them—who do not necessarily believe in "his" creator, are not included in his policies.

We are divided enough today along racial, ethnic, gender, ideological, and partisan lines. Now Mayor Adams wants to divide us further along religious lines. History has proved that there is no such thing as "interdenominational" prayer, because all religions are different, and those individuals with no religion are not included. Mayor Adams did not inform us whose prayer he would include: Should it be Protestant, Catholic, Jewish, Muslim, Buddhist? What about the child who was brought up as an atheist or agnostic? Or the religious student who does not believe in public prayer? When it comes to religion, there can be no consensus. Nor should there be.

When "non-denominational prayer" was introduced in Boston several decades ago, fights erupted in the classroom. When a young Jewish woman, who refused to recite a Christian prayer, was shamed and disciplined, I had to come to her defense. When my mother was a public school student in the Williamsburg section of Brooklyn, her Catholic teacher made her memorize parts of the Latin Mass, which she was always able to recite. The teacher honestly thought she was instilling Americanism into these children of immigrants. But Americanism requires compliance with the United States Constitution.

All around the nation, public schools are becoming platforms for propaganda. Students are being told what to think, rather than being taught how to think, critically and analytically. Personal and political views about race, gender, ideology—and now religion—are replacing (or at least supplementing) math, science, and objective history. Many on the right want religion, but not sex or race ideology, to be taught in public schools. Many on the left want sex and race ideology, but not religion. Both are wrong. Neither belongs in taxpayer-supported public schools.

Mayor Adams's call for unconstitutional prayer is merely the tip of a very deep and dangerous iceberg that afflicts both the left and the right. Tragically, it also afflicts the center, as reflected by the demand being made by Mayor Adams, who himself is a centrist.

Too many Americans, like Mayor Adams, are prepared to ignore or defy the Constitution when it serves their political interests. He says: "Don't tell me about no separation of church and state." Others say: "Don't tell me about the Fifth Amendment, or the Fourth Amendment, or the First Amendment"—or the impeachment clause of the Constitution. "We want to get our way, and the Constitution be damned."

So instead of starting each school day with a prayer, why don't we start each school day with the recitation of the First Amendment? Then the teacher can explain why prayer is a private matter—for the home, the church, or the mind. It is not the job of the teacher to inculcate his or her religious views—or those of Mayor Adams.

How Is the Supreme Court Going to Get Out of the Corner into Which It Painted Itself in Respect to Abortion?
Will they turn to logic, experience, or politics?

If there is no constitutional right to abortion—as the Supreme Court held in reversing *Roe v. Wade*—then it follows that states are free to ban all abortion pills, regardless of the timing or circumstances of the pregnancy.

Yet there is widespread public support, even among Republicans, for the right of a woman or girl to terminate early pregnancies. Will a majority of the justices take the Dobbs case to its logical conclusion and allow states to ban the "morning after," the "week after," or the "month after" pill? If not, where will they draw the constitutional line and on what basis?

Most Americans have mixed views regarding abortion. They oppose it near the end of pregnancy when the fetus is viable, except when the health of the mother is in danger. They favor it at the beginning of the pregnancy.

The dispute among non-extremists focuses on the middle terms. But the efforts of the justices over the past half century to draw clear lines based on the Constitution have drawn criticism from all sides. There is scant reason to think that future efforts at temporal compromise will fare much better, but non-principled line drawing may be the only way out of the no-win box the justices have made for themselves.

Moreover, line drawing seems more appropriate to legislatures and administrative agencies than to courts, thus lending weight to the argument that the Supreme Court should leave it to the states to decide when abortion should be permitted.

Last week's case did not involve state legislation. It involved FDA approval and the alleged unsafety of the pill. Soon, though, the high court will be confronted with a state law that prohibits some or all early abortions, even using drugs that pose no danger to the woman.

We have a clear idea how Justice Clarence Thomas would vote and a pretty good idea about Justice Samuel Alito, both of whom dissented from last week's unsigned decision to allow the drug at issue to continue to be prescribed at least temporarily.

We also know that Justices Elena Kagan, Sonia Sotomayor, and Ketanji Brown Jackson will vote to strike down any such ban. Chief Justice Roberts will probably join them with regard to early pregnancy, though that is not certain.

It is even less certain how President Trump's three appointees—Justices Neil Gorsuch, Brett Kavanaugh, and Amy Coney Barrett—will vote, although the logic of their votes and opinions in Dobbs should lead them to uphold any and all state bans on even the earliest of abortions. As Justice Oliver Wendell Holmes Jr. once observed: "The life of the law has not been logic." He said it has been "experience." Many today think it's politics.

The Court's decision to engage in judicial activism by overruling Roe, instead of merely upholding the Mississippi law that prohibited most abortions after fifteen weeks, was bad politically for Republicans, who paid a price in the election that followed. It would be much worse for Republicans if the Republican justices made it impossible for young women to end all early pregnancies, regardless of the circumstances.

Although judges are not supposed to take into account the political implications of their constitutional decisions, many do. It is possible that despite the logic of Dobbs, some of the justices who went along with the ill-advised breadth of that decision will figure out ways, illogical as they may be, not to allow states to ban the earliest pregnancies under all circumstances. It is also possible that the majority may feel compelled to follow the logic of Dobbs and uphold draconian state laws banning all abortion pills.

It is conceivable, of course, that Scotus will be spared the necessity of announcing such an extreme and politically unpopular decision—if no state were to legislate such a broad ban. Zealous advocates of the claimed constitutional "right to life" from the moment of conception, are likely to prevail somewhere. And equally zealous advocates of the "right to choose" are certain to challenge the ban.

Nor could the justices easily duck such a challenge. So we will see whether "logic," "experience," or "politics" prevails among the justices in the deeply and ideologically divided Supreme Court.

Justice Alito Says He May Know Who the Leaker Is!

Justice Samuel Alito has told the *Wall Street Journal* that he may know who leaked his draft opinion overruling *Roe v. Wade*, but that he lacks sufficient evidence to accuse the suspect in public. That is commendable, but it doesn't tell us whether he shared his suspicions, on a confidential basis, with the marshal's office which the chief justice assigned to conduct the investigation. That office concluded that it could not determine by "a preponderance of the evidence" who the culprit is.

But Alito may have enough information to satisfy the lower standard of "probable cause." That standard would justify focusing the investigation on the specific suspect and requiring him or her to sign an affidavit, undergo a lie detector, and submit to a more intrusive search.

Alito's information might also incline the Justice Department or Congress to conduct its own investigations with far greater resources than are available to the marshal's office. These include granting the suspect and/or other possible witnesses use immunity and compelling them to testify fully. They also include subpoenaing the *Politico* journalists who published the leaked opinion. They would certainly invoke the journalist/source privilege, but that privilege is not absolute under federal law. Moreover, the leaker here was not a whistleblower: he or she was not disclosing government corruption or misconduct; the only corruption and misconduct was engaged in by the leaker.

An important purpose of the privilege is to encourage disclosure of corruption in government. The type of leak done here must be discouraged, not encouraged. It was calculated to interfere with the proper workings of the Supreme Court. It was also dangerous: it may have led to the attempted assassination of Justice Brett Kavanagh, who was seen as a swing vote. It is imperative that the leaker be identified and held accountable.

This was not merely a leak of secret information. It was almost certainly part of a plan to corruptly change a Supreme Court opinion by improper means. The leaker probably was well-intentioned: he or she believed—as I do—that overruling *Roe v. Wade* would have a terrible impact on pregnant women. But the means chosen by the leaker—early disclosure of the draft opinion with the goal of putting external pressure on possible swing justices to change their votes—is utterly improper under the rule of law and the rules of the Supreme Court.

Determining the source of the leak may be difficult but it is not impossible. The likely suspects number under one hundred. Alito said he was certain it was not a justice. The only other people who could have given an accurate and complete draft opinion were the law clerks, printers, and the small number of other SCOTUS employees who had access to it. The most likely suspects are law clerks for the dissenting justices. These are only a few handfuls of people.

Moreover, it is likely that some law clerks who were not themselves the leakers know or have a pretty good idea who the culprit may be. He or she may well be seen as a hero to some—a civil disobedient who was willing to risk discipline in the hope of preventing a greater evil. But civil disobedients should be willing to accept the consequences of their lawlessness, which this one has been unwilling to do.

There is a growing suspicion that the inability to catch the leaker may reflect ambivalence by some about the willingness to undergo the trauma of an accusation and public accounting. They may believe that the damage has been done and that anything more will only cause recriminations and further damage to the high court as an institution.

Alito almost certainly does not share that view. If he did, he would not have said what he said to *The Journal*, which he had to know would ignite interest in an issue that was dying a slow death. Indeed, he may well share the view that more can be done if there is the will to do it, and that his interview should make it more difficult to continue to do nothing.

I hope that is the case, because the status quo is untenable. The culprit must be identified and brought to justice, not only to deter further leaks, but to refute the growing belief that the lack of progress in the investigation may reflect if not an actual cover-up—at least an unwillingness to uncover a painful truth.

Are Universities Preparing to Circumvent Supreme Court Decision Banning Affirmative Action?

The Supreme Court is weighing whether to prohibit the use of race as a criterion for admissions. If that occurs, many universities will likely seek ways to circumvent the decision to continue the racial quotas now in place.

Although all universities deny having quotas, many have numerical "targets" or "goals" that in practice amount to quotas. These quotas are both floors and ceilings: they are floors for applicants of color and ceilings for Asian-Americans.

Already some universities are beginning the process of circumvention by eliminating objective criteria such as test scores. Without test scores, admissions officers can substitute subjective factors as surrogates for race. It was alleged in the current Supreme Court cases that this is precisely what is being done with some highly qualified Asian American applicants, who are being turned down based on vague criteria that are widely thought to smack of racial bias.

"Diversity, inclusion, and equity" are the current surrogates. They are defined narrowly to emphasize race, rather than intellectual, economic, religious, and other diversifying factors that are highly relevant to universities' academic missions.

Under current policies in many universities, a wealthy Black applicant from a prominent family who attended a fancy prep school is favored over a first generation Asian-American who's had to work while attending public school. This so precisely because there are numerical quotas that don't distinguish based on individual factors.

It is also because it is easier for admissions officers to consider something as simple as race—just look at the checked box—than to evaluate each individual based on a variety of relevant factors. It was also easier to consider test scores and grades, but emphasizing such criteria makes it more difficult to reach the racial quotas or targets.

So, the tactic is to eliminate or minimize test scores and to employ criteria that mirror race without explicitly running afoul of any Supreme Court ruling and without reducing the number of admitted minority applicants.

Many universities have considerable experience going back many years in such circumvention, since they have been doing it for more than a century with Jewish and Catholic applicants. Elite schools such as Harvard, Yale, Wellesley, Stanford, and Princeton denied employing religious quotas, but everyone knew the precise numbers that turned out every year.

They knew how to manipulate criteria such as "character," "manners" and "compatibility," which the negatively targeted groups were deemed to lack, to limit the number of undesirables. They didn't fool anyone, but in those days, they didn't have to, because the law did not protect applicants who had been discriminated against.

Soon it will, and so the schools will have to be more subtle and less transparent. As my former colleague Lawrence Tribe put it: "Universities as intelligent as Harvard will find ways of dealing with the decision without radically altering their composition. But they will have to be more subtle than they have been thus far."

I leave it the reader to interpret Tribe's remark. But it sounds to me that he is advocating a process that leaves the racial quotas or targets essentially intact, while being less transparent about employing race as a criterion to achieve those quotas.

What kind of message does it send to our future leaders, now studying at universities, when prominent professors and administrators try to circumvent Supreme Court decisions, even to achieve praiseworthy ends?

This is different from the way southern universities sought to circumvent desegregation decisions in the 1950s and '60s. They created subterfuges for discriminating against African American applicants. Current university administrators are seeking subterfuges for discriminating in favor of such applicants—at the expense of other applicants.

But although the ends are very different, the means are quite similar.

This is yet another example of ends believed to be desirable justifying means that are not. We see that today in many contexts, such as the selective weaponization of the criminal justice system to target political enemies. It's done subtly and without fingerprints.

But it eats away at constitutional protections. Those of us who care about constitutional means as well as ends will be watching and holding circumventors to account, regardless of their good motives. As Justice Brandeis aptly observed: "The greatest dangers to liberty lurk in insidious encroachment by men of zeal, well-meaning but without understanding."

The Supreme Court Moves Us One Step Closer to a Color-Blind Society

After decades of vacillation, the Supreme Court of the United States has finally and firmly declared that the Constitution does not permit publicly funded universities to consider race, as such, in its admission processes. This is a decision that many, including this author, have been advocating since the 1970s, when my first law review article

appeared, calling for affirmative action to be based on non-racial criteria and individual accomplishments.

The Supreme Court has been moving in this direction for some
time now, but it has until now allowed loopholes the size of university
football stadiums. These loopholes were exploited by universities to
enforce quota systems whereby approximately the same percentage of
minority applicants would be admitted every year. The results of these
quotas impacted most heavily on one of the most discriminated against
groups in American history—Asian Americans. The plaintiffs in the
Harvard case were such Americans. It will be interesting to see how
their numbers are affected by the decision.

Within two hours of the decision, Harvard released a statement and
a video by its new president promising compliance, while also assuring
a continued concern for diversity and other criteria which often serve
as covers for racial quotas. It remains to be seen what Harvard and
other schools believe constitutes compliance.

The majority decision, written by Chief Justice John Roberts, still
allows for some consideration of race, so long as it is individualized. It
permits universities to consider student essays that focus on an applicant's race, so long as she or he relate their race to individual disadvantage, inspiration, or other vague criteria. Harvard highlighted that part
of the decision in its statement and will surely employ it to the greatest
extent possible in order to maintain current percentages.

Even if universities manage to circumvent the Court's primary
holding that race alone cannot be considered, the 6-3 decision, written by the Court's centrist leader, announces an important principle
of Constitutional law that had been in doubt since the advent of race-
based affirmative action. The opinion explains in detail why taking
race, as such, into account—whether to advantage or disadvantage an
applicant—is inconsistent with the history and policies underlying the
Fourteenth Amendment's equal protection clause.

The opinion rejected the argument that the post–Civil War
Amendments were designed only to protect African Americans who had
just emerged from the horrors of slavery. The opinion also rejected the
argument that race alone can be taken into consideration in an effort to
increase equality, diversity or other values that universities are entitled to

preserve. It makes the important point that using race as such necessarily stereotypes and reduces individuals to being part of racial groups.

Although this decision was split along current conservative-liberal lines, with the court's three liberals dissenting, it actually reflects traditional liberalism. Justice William Douglas, perhaps the most liberal justice in Supreme Court history, advocated precisely this race-neutral approach when affirmative action was first introduced. He was right then, and his liberal, color-blind approach has now been vindicated.

A simple example demonstrates why employing race as a criterion is both unconstitutional and immoral. As the Supreme Court correctly pointed out, admission to elite universities is a zero-sum game: for every student or group that is given preference, another is disadvantaged.

So consider this zero-sum choice: a Black applicant comes from a wealthy and well-educated family; his mother is a federal judge and his father runs a billion-dollar hedge fund; they both went to elite high schools and universities; they live in an affluent neighborhood with excellent schools; they receive top-notch health care (I know such people). A white applicant grew up in a rural Midwestern area; his mother died of a fentanyl overdose when he was six; his father, an alcoholic, abandoned the family shortly before that; he went to mediocre public schools, but he struggled to achieve high grades and test scores.

Before today's decision, a publicly funded university could give preference to the privileged black applicant over the unprivileged white applicant, even if the white applicant had higher numbers and better recommendations. That is simply wrong. And now it is also illegal.

Under the Supreme Court's new decision, all applicants must be treated as individuals. Of course, individuals belong to groups—racial, religious, gender, etc. These groups may have a profound influence on the individual and individual applicants are entitled to use their group association as part of their total profile. But universities are not allowed to make decisions based solely on skin color (which itself is often a continuum).

It will be fascinating to observe how universities respond to this decision. So stay tuned.

The quest for a color-blind society based on Martin Luther King Jr.'s dream is still a long way off. This decision brings us a giant step closer to achieving it.

Alito Is Wrong: Congress Can Impose Ethics Rules on the Supreme Court

In his informative interview with the *Wall Street Journal*, Justice Samuel Alito made some compelling points. He was correct in claiming the right to defend himself and the court against politically motivated accusations. But he was wrong in asserting that Congress lacks the power to compel the justices to enact and implement rules regulating their ethics.

Alito's argument goes something like this: He correctly points out that "Congress did not create the Supreme Court"—the Constitution did. He is also correct that there is "no provision in the Constitution [that gives Congress] the authority to regulate the Supreme Court."

The fallacy in his argument is his failure to consider the history following the adoption of our Constitution. Over the years since our founding, Congress has in fact regulated the Supreme Court in numerous ways: it has changed the number of justices, their salary, and the location and premises of the high court. And of course, it may impeach a justice if it finds that he or she committed treason, bribery, or other high crimes and misdemeanors. Although the Constitution lays out the mandatory jurisdiction of the Supreme Court, Congress has played a role in regulating even that important aspect of the Supreme Court's work.

Alito correctly points out that no specific provision of the Constitution deals with the role of Congress in regulating the ethics of the justices, but he fails to note that no provision of the Constitution explicitly authorizes the Supreme Court to overrule actions of Congress and other branches of the government. Yet they have been doing so since *Marbury v. Madison* in 1803 and its progeny.

Alito may be making an extremely broad claim, namely that the powers of Congress and the Supreme Court are limited by the explicit grants of authority enumerated in Articles 1 and 3 of the Constitution. He admits that his "is a controversial view," but it may be even more controversial than it sounds. It may challenge the very concept of judicial review, because of the absence of any provision in the constitution explicitly authorizing the Supreme Court to strike down legislative or executive actions.

As former Chief Justice John Marshall said in justifying his expansive view of constitutional interpretation: "We must never forget that it is a Constitution we are expounding . . . intended to endure for ages to come, and consequently, to be adapted to the various crises of human affairs." A similar argument can be made in favor of the unenumerated power of Congress to regulate the ethics of justices. Indeed, there is more textual support in the Constitution for Congress to regulate the ethics of justices than there is for justices to pass judgment on the laws of Congress. Article 3 provides that "the judges both of the Supreme and inferior courts shall hold their offices during good behavior, and shall, at stated times receive for their services a compensation . . ." It also says that the Supreme Court's appellate jurisdiction in the few cases other than where it has original jurisdiction is subject to "such exceptions [and] regulations as the Congress shall make."

These provisions strongly imply that Congress has the power to regulate good behavior, including ethical behavior, along with the power to set the amount of compensation and the appellate jurisdiction.

To be fair to Alito's controversial argument, the framers of the Constitution did not focus on the precise issue of Congress' power to regulate the ethics of justices, whereas Alexander Hamilton and some others did discuss judicial review, without explicitly providing for it in the Constitution. The fact that it was discussed and omitted cuts both ways, as does the fact that regulating the ethics of justices was not mentioned.

Our system of governance is based on the separation of powers and checks and balances. The judiciary is an independent branch but it—like the other branches—is subject to checks. Unlike the legislative and executive branches, the judicial branch is not subject to the ultimate check in any democracy, namely periodic elections. This makes it even more important that justices be subject to the legislative check of compelled ethical rules and the executive check of prosecution for violation of these rules.

The underlying purpose of checks and balances is to assure accountability and to prevent any branch or institution of government from operating above the law. It would turn that purpose on its head if the Supreme Court could exempt itself from being bound by the kind of ethics rules that bind the elected branches.

How Does the Supreme Court Look Through the Prism of Classical Liberalism?

Imagine if a man and a woman decided to marry and tried to hire a caterer. The caterer asks, "Are either of you divorced?" When the woman said she had a brief marriage and amicable divorce ten years earlier, the caterer says that her own religion prohibited her from in any way participating in the marriage of a divorced person.

Would the Supreme Court have upheld that claim in the face of a statute that prohibited discrimination based on marital status? What if the couple that sought to get married consisted of a white man and the Black woman, and the caterer refused on the grounds that her religion prohibited interracial marriage?

There are two profound issues raised by these questions. First, does the Supreme Court decision extend beyond artistic endeavors such as that claim by the web designer who won her case today? Second, whether claimed religious justifications have to be somehow valid in the eyes of a court. Could a court distinguish between mainstream Catholic views against divorce and extremist religious views that justify racial segregation?

In the case decided today by the Supreme Court, there was a direct clash between the First Amendment and anti-discrimination laws. There can be little doubt that the First Amendment prevents the state from coercing anyone, religious or otherwise, from expressing views with which they disagree. And creating a website is, at least in the view of the plaintiff, the expression of a constitutionally protected viewpoint.

Would the same conclusion flow, however, if the web maker wanted to express the view that interracial marriage is prohibited by the Bible? The answer to that question must be yes, since the First Amendment doesn't discriminate among viewpoints.

As Chief Justice Rehnquist once put it: "Under the First Amendment there is no such thing as a false idea. However pernicious an opinion may seem, we depend for its correction not on the conscience of judges and juries but on the competition of other ideas."

That is just as true of religious opinions as it is political, philosophical, and personal ones. What if no artistic expression is at issue? For example, what if a family-owned hotel refused to rent rooms to Blacks, Jews, Muslims, or Atheists on the basis of their religious views? The Supreme Court didn't reach that case, but lower courts will surely be asked to extend the decision to non-artistic objections.

Supreme Court decisions tend to take on a life of their own, especially since the justices review very few cases and tend not to follow up on their decisions in their immediate aftermath. Thus, lower courts have relatively free rein to interpret the often-ambiguous rulings by which they are technically bound but realistically free to expand or contract.

This will surely be the case with two of the major decisions decided in the final days of the Court's session: one involving gay marriage; and the other involving the use of race in university admissions. In both cases the court left open the possibility that their rulings will be interpreted quite differently by various lower courts.

The broad messages of both opinions are clear: the religious exception decision is part of a growing trend at the high court toward emphasizing the free exercise clause of the First Amendment at the expense of the non-Establishment Clause. The trend had been the opposite during the 1960s and 1970s. Yet now it is clear that religion will generally win.

The second discernible trend is away from the use of race in decisions made by state actors. This trend has been obvious now for several decades, as the Supreme Court vacillated over whether and how race can be used in various contexts.

It is likely that this trend will continue, as universities try to figure out how they can maintain their racial quotas—and they are quotas, despite fervent denials—without explicitly employing race as a criterion.

There was a third decision decided today, the final day of the court's season, that also represents an important trend. The Court struck down President Biden's order granting relief to students who had academic loans. This trend represents a movement away from executive authority and toward legislative authority.

Congress will now have to be clearer and more explicit when it authorizes the President or any executive agency to exercise powers that are constitutionally reserved to the legislature.

Although these decisions, and several other important ones released over the past months, have generally been decided along what the press calls liberal-conservative lines, they don't reflect the difference between classic liberalism and classic conservatism.

Classic liberalism would favor the decision prohibiting the use of race, even though the three "liberals" dissented. Classic liberalism might also support the preference for legislative over executive power. And finally, classic liberalism would at least be conflicted over compelling a religious objector to violate his or her principles.

The Liberal Warren Court Could Have Written the Supreme Court's Recent "Conservative" Opinions

The three contentious decisions announced near the end of the Supreme Court's recent term regarding Blacks and affirmative action, gays and the First Amendment, and student loan forgiveness—all could have been rendered by the liberal Warren court of the 1960s.

President Biden criticized the current Supreme Court as not being "normal"—by which he apparently meant not like previous High Courts. The historical record does not support that conclusion.

I clerked on the Supreme Court during its most liberal term, 1963-1964. I feel sure that at least five of its members, including its liberal chief justice, Earl Warren, and Associate Justices William Douglas, Hugo Black, and Arthur Goldberg (for whom I clerked) would have supported the results, if not all the reasoning, in these three cases. So would some of the moderates, such as Justices Potter Stewart, John Harlan, and Tom Clark.

On Black preferences in admission, the liberal view back then was that race as such could not constitutionally be taken into account by a state actor. Douglas, perhaps the court's most liberal jurist, expressed this view clearly in his separate opinion in the case of *DeFunis v. Odegaard* written in 1974.

Douglas and other liberal jurists believed that economic and other non-racial factors could be taken into account, but not race itself. Stewart, a moderate, explicitly agreed with that position.

On the issue of whether the government could compel a web or cake maker to express views with which she disagrees, the liberal view was that the First Amendment generally trumps public accommodation laws.

This would have been regarded as a close case by liberal justices, but I believe they would have come down, as many civil libertarians today have come down, on the side of the First Amendment. This decision, too, represents the liberal mainstream.

Finally, on the decision regarding student loans, the liberal view has generally been to prefer that the legislative, rather than the executive, branch make fundamental decisions regarding the expenditure of government funds.

Liberal justices would have probably sided with the current court in concluding that Congress must be crystal clear in allocating legislative functions to executive bureaucrats.

In all three cases, the liberal justices of the 1960s would have been unhappy with the actual consequences of these three cases on political and ideological grounds. They would personally have favored the admission of more Blacks to universities, the protection of gays, and the forgiveness of student loans.

Yet they would have subordinated their political and ideological views to what they regarded as the mandates of the Constitution. Back in the day, both liberal and conservative justices often joined decisions in which their constitutional views clashed with their political ones. In general, they favored the Constitution.

This has now changed considerably. Today, most justices tend to elevate their political and ideological views over enduring constitutional values. This is true of both liberals and conservatives, and indeed each side claims they are doing it to offset the partisanship of the other side.

The end result of this change has been to weaken the constitution and to delegitimize the court in the minds of many objective observers. The current justices are far more result-oriented than their predecessors. And support and criticism for their decisions are result-oriented as well.

Too few today care about neutral principles that favor neither party nor any ideology. They demand results and they demand them now. It doesn't matter to them whether these good outcomes are the result of legislative, executive, or judicial decisions.

What seems to matter more are their personal and political views on whether more Blacks are admitted, more gays are protected, and more students are assisted. This may be understandable but it is inconsistent with the role of judges.

The reason why unelected, lifetime-appointed judges are given power to overrule the decisions made by the elected legislative and executive branches, is that the Supreme Court is supposed to decide issues based on enduring nonpartisan principles that are rooted in the language and meaning of the Constitution.

The Supreme Court is not supposed to be a super-legislature or executive, authorized to overrule decisions with which they disagree politically or ideologically. The politicization of the Supreme Court undercuts the unique functions of the judiciary.

It is not enough to say that each side is reacting to the overreaching of the other side. Two constitutional wrongs make a constitutional fight, not a right. They do not serve larger interests of American citizens in the rule of law.

The cause of this politicization of the judiciary lies primarily in the process by which justices (and other judges) are currently nominated and confirmed. There was a time when the main criteria for appointment was the judicial temperament and legal ability they exhibited.

Today, anticipated outcomes come first. How will the justice vote on abortion, gun control, and other agenda-driven issues? The quality of their opinions is secondary.

The only cure lies in the appointment process. Presidents and the Senate must return to a time reflected by President Hoover's appointment of Benjamin Cardozo to replace Justice Oliver Wendell Holmes.

Hoover asked his attorney general to prepare a list of the ten most qualified judges in America. The list included Cardozo, but he was at the very bottom. Hoover told the attorney general that it was a great list, but it was upside down.

He then appointed Cardozo despite his being a Democrat from a state that already had more than one justice. Cardozo served with distinction, never allowing his partisan or ideological views to prevail over the Constitution.

It may be wishful thinking to believe we could ever return to those days, but all Americans would benefit if current presidents and senators followed Hoover's non-partisan lead in appointing justices.

The alternative is an increasingly partisan Court that will continue to be perceived as just another political branch of government, but without the legitimacy of having been elected.

Courts Are Playing Too Much of a Role in the Coming Election

Alexander Hamilton described the judiciary as "the least dangerous branch," because it has the power of neither the sword nor the purse. It was supposed to play an important but limited role in our governance, as part of the system of checks and balances, but in recent years—especially since *Bush v. Gore* in 2000—the courts have begun to play far too important roles in determining the outcome of elections. This certainly seems to be the case today, in the run-up to the 2024 presidential election.

Some radical Democrats are trying to use the courts to deny President Trump the right to appear on state ballots. This will probably fail, but not without causing considerable confusion in the early primaries. If it were to succeed, it might well divide the country beyond repair, as millions of Americans would be denied the right to vote for the candidate of their choice. The Fourteenth Amendment is being distorted by partisans to achieve partisan results.

Then there are the criminal cases against Trump in New York, Georgia, Florida, and the District of Columbia. Whether intended or not, these cases threaten to have a significant impact on the coming presidential election. In the future, have no doubt that partisans on the other side will try to manipulate the Fourteenth Amendment to achieve their political results. The end result would be a direct attack on democracy.

It is likely, though not certain, that—before the election—Mr. Trump will be convicted in some of these cases. Yet any reversal of the convictions that might happen on appeal would probably not occur until after the election. The thumb of the judiciary would therefore be on the electoral scale.

There is also the issue of presidential immunity which is currently on appeal and may end up before the Supreme Court. That case will determine whether and to what extent Mr. Trump can be tried for his alleged role in the January 6 events and other challenges to the 2020 election.

These cases are likely to have an impact on Mr. Trump's electoral strategy. They will keep him off the trail during the height of the election season, because criminal defendants are generally required to be present during their trials. The trials end in the late afternoon and Mr. Trump will surely campaign as he is leaving the courthouse, as well as before he enters it.

There will be other legal proceedings as well that may impact the 2024 election. These include the trials and tribulations of President Biden's son Hunter, whose cases will garner attention during the electoral season.

Elections should not be influenced so significantly by court cases. Never before in our history has the judiciary played so central a role in an election. It makes more sense for voters to cast their ballots on issues relating to the economy, foreign policy, immigration, abortion, and other matters that affect them and their families.

It's contrary to the spirit of our elections for the focus to be on legal and constitutional issues, many of which are difficult to understand, thus making it easier for politicians to use sound bites instead of thoughtful arguments.

What, though, is the alternative? If a presidential candidate, or the son of the incumbent, has arguably engaged in criminal conduct, investigations are in order, and if the evidence supports it, prosecutions. Yet it's wrong for prosecutors to use the criminal justice system to achieve political ends.

Criminal prosecutions should not be brought against candidates running for office, unless the evidence is overwhelming. Most crimes have statutes of limitations which would allow deferring any prosecution until after the election. Prosecutorial discretion should be exercised with sensitivity toward the potential impact on elections.

We live in an age where every aspect of government, especially the criminal justice system, has become weaponized by both sides to achieve partisan political goals. This trend does not serve the interest of the American public, but it will be difficult to stop it or even slow it down, since tit-for-tat retaliation has also become an important part of this partisan warfare.

Let us at least understand that the framers of our Constitution did not intend the judicial branch to play so large a role in the political process of electing our president.

Chapter 5

International McCarthyism: Israel, Anti-Semitism, and the World

---

Introduction

On October 7, 2023, Hamas terrorists invaded Israel and murdered, raped, burned, and beheaded approximately twelve hundred Israelis, mostly civilians. They also kidnapped more than two hundred Israelis, also mostly civilians.

Within one day—well before Israeli soldiers entered Gaza in response—hard-left anti-Israel extremists praised the Hamas barbarism, categorizing it as legitimate military action and blaming the deaths "entirely" on Israel.

As soon as I learned about the October 7 attack, I began to write about the barbarism, and the support for it by hard-left demonizers of Israel. Predictably, I was condemned and accused of "McCarthyism."

In one of my first articles, published in the *New York Law Journal*, I castigated the National Lawyers Guild for defending the Hamas savagery as an entirely justified "military action." The NLG demanded the release of all Palestinian prisoners—including convicted murderers—without saying a word about the Israeli hostages. I also criticized other organizations and individuals—especially lawyers' groups—that praised Hamas and blamed its victims.

I argued that if a lawyer belongs to the National Lawyers Guild, or other legal organizations that support Hamas, clients should be entitled to ask them whether they support the barbaric acts committed by that terror group on October 7, as the NLG apparently did. Some will probably say they were unaware that their organization supported the Hamas atrocities. Others may say they support Hamas—despite its designation as a terror group to whom it is criminal to provide material support—but not these specific acts. While still others—like the NLG—will try to justify the atrocities as appropriate military responses to an occupation.

Clients have the right to know which of these (or other) positions a lawyer selected to represent them espouses. Many clients will not want to be represented by a lawyer who believes that the rapes and beheadings of civilians, including children, are appropriate military actions. Others may.

In any event, clients are entitled to have the information to help make the decision.

Students and lawyers have a First Amendment right to espouse outrageous and immoral views, without fear of punishment by the government. But private clients also have a right to evaluate their potential lawyers on the basis of how they exercise that right.

A leading NLG activist, Ellen Yaroshefsky, responded to my article without disclosing her long and intense association with the NLG. She called my proposal "McCarthyism revisited," which is at least ironic in that she then demanded that Harvard investigate me "as to the content of his ethics course" and take "action" against me for what I taught my students—a true revisiting of McCarthyism.

At the time of these accusations and counter accusations, I was writing this book whose subtitle is "Why the New McCarthyism Is More Dangerous Than the Old." So I was obliged to respond to her accusation that I was guilty of McCarthyism.

Here is what I wrote:

November 15, 2023
In her letter about my recent op-ed, Ellen Yaroshefsky demands that Harvard investigate me and the courses I teach, and—"consider action against"—me for my op-ed and then, giving a new definition to chutzpah, she accuses me of McCarthyism.

The thrust of my article is that the National Lawyers Guild, on the day after the October 7 massacres and before Israel entered Gaza, praised the Hamas rapes, beheadings, and kidnappings as entirely justified "military actions." The Guild demanded the release of all Palestinian prisoners, including those convicted of mass murders, but didn't say a single word about the innocent hostages being held by Hamas. It demands that "normalizations" with Israel be denied. My article criticized the Guild for its support of terrorism and its insensitivity toward the Israeli victims.

Without disclosing that she herself is an active member of the National Lawyers Guild, she claimed that it was I acting unethically.

She also repeatedly misstated the facts and chronology, claiming that I criticized the guild for "advocating a cease-fire." But my criticism came before there was any fire to cease. My op-ed was not about the Guild's later one-sided demand for a cease-fire but rather about the Guild's earlier defense and glorification of the mass murderers Hamas perpetrated on October 7. Nor was it about Palestinian self-determination, which I support. I have been an advocate of the two-state solution since 1970. My op-ed was entirely about lawyers who openly supported the Hamas atrocities.

I have conferred with several ethics experts who agree with me that a lawyer who supports such barbarities—much like a racist lawyer who supports lynching or a sexist lawyer who supports rape—should not be assigned to a client without full disclosure of their outrageous views. The client may decide to retain the lawyer despite these views, but that is the lawyer's choice, and the information necessary to make it should not be deliberately withheld from the client by the law firm.

I would be happy to debate that important and current issue with Ms. Yaroshefsky without name calling. In that debate, I would insist that she state the facts correctly and that she disclosed her status as a leading member of the National Lawyers Guild. She did not respond to my invitation to debate.

Following that exchange, I continue to write and speak about the Hamas barbarism and Israel's military response to the ongoing attacks against its civilians. Much of my writing deals with issues relating to the main subjects of this book—woke culture, including the new bureaucracies built around "diversity, equity, and inclusion" (DEI) and "intersectionality." It also focuses on freedom of expression, due process, and the double standards applied to Israel, its supporters, and its critics. Hence it is appropriate that the final chapter of this book deals with the impact of "woke" culture on Israel.

University Students and Professors Support Hamas Murderers and Rapists

Student groups at Harvard, Yale, City University of New York, and other major institutions of learning have issued statements in support of the Hamas murderers and rapists. Hundreds of students at Harvard issued the following statement: "We the undersigned student organizations hold the Israeli regime entirely responsible for all unfolding violence . . . the apartheid regime is the only one to blame." Similar statements were issued by student groups around the country. Many faculty members and administrators support—indeed encourage—such bigotry. These statements were issued before a single Israeli soldier entered Gaza.

This should not be surprising in light of the demonizing propaganda that has flooded university campuses for decades. Speakers such as Norman Finkelstein have become among the most popular supporters of Hamas's genocidal goals. While Israeli babies, women, and elderly civilians were being butchered, this despicable bigot and Holocaust minimizer published the following: "If we honor the Jews who revolted in the Warsaw Ghetto—then moral consistency commands that we honor the heroic resistance in Gaza. I, for one, will never begrudge—on the contrary, it warms every fiber of my soul—the scenes of Gaza's smiling children as their arrogant Jewish supremacist oppressors have, finally, been humbled."

The comparison is obscene. In the Warsaw uprising, brave civilians rose up against well-armed Nazi soldiers who were trying to kill them. The only murders and rapes were by the stormtroopers. In Israel, the murderers and rapists were the Hamas butchers who Finkelstein supports.

Despite, perhaps because of, these outrageous immoral and historically inaccurate defamations, Finkelstein will continue to be invited to speak to large audiences at our major universities, while pro-Israel speakers—even those like me who support a two-state peaceful solution—will continue to be banned.

It is outrageous that hard-left woke progressives who claim to support women's rights are in the forefront of defending rapists who parade their bleeding victims in front of supporters.

Many of the Israelis who were murdered at the peace concert and at nearby kibbutzim supported a two-state solution and the rights of innocent Palestinians. This doesn't matter to the genocidal Hamas murderers. All that matters is that the victims were Jews—Israeli Jews, American Jews, British Jews. The goal of these murderers is not a two-state solution or a peaceful resolution of the Middle East conflict. It is the murder of Israel's population and of Jews around the world who support the only nation-state of the Jewish people. It is bigotry pure and simple, and anyone who supports it deserves the most extreme condemnation in the court of public opinion.

The most troubling aspect of these university statements in support of rapists and murderers is that many who signed them will be among our future leaders. The universities that admitted and teach them have historically turned out future members of Congress, presidents, economic leaders, journalists, and others who will determine the fate of our children and grandchildren. These universities have failed our future.

Much of the blame lies with the faculty and administration of elite universities, which have taken strong views against racism, sexism, homophobia, and other forms of bigotry, while remaining silent about the oldest prejudice: anti-Semitism, which today disguises itself as anti-Zionism. Jews and Zionists are not included among minorities who deserve protection.

Among the Harvard groups most prominently blaming Israel for these rapes and murders is "Amnesty International at Harvard." That group is the Harvard affiliate of the Nobel Prize–winning international organization that claims to be in favor of peace and non-violence. I don't know whether the Harvard affiliate represents the views of its parent organization, but if it does not, then Amnesty International must immediately disassociate itself from these abhorrent anti-peace and pro-violence views. Indeed, Harvard University, with which these groups boast an association, must also immediately disassociate itself from them.

None of these major universities would allow a Ku Klux Klan or other anti-Black, anti-gay, anti-woman organization to be associated with the university. Whatever these universities would do with regard to such other bigoted groups, they must do with regard to these bigoted groups. This is not about politics. This is about supporting murderers and rapists of Jews. These bigots must not be allowed to hide behind political claims.

When a single African American named George Floyd was brutally and unjustifiably murdered by police, this caused a major "reckoning" at American universities and other institutions. Billions of dollars and other resources were redirected at remedying anti-Black bigotry. The time has come for a new reckoning—a reckoning by American universities with their tolerance and even encouragement of anti-Semitism and anti-Zionism.

Campus Anti-Semitism Has Become Systemic Due to "Diversity, Equity, and Inclusion"

Two major changes in universities have contributed significantly to the dramatic rise of anti-Semitism on college campuses.

The first is the creation of large bureaucracies whose purpose is to propagandize students in favor of a particular ideology: diversity, equity, and inclusion. The second is the formation of special departments and programs designed to promote the ideologies of particular identity groups, such as Blacks, women, gays, Muslims, Native Americans, and Jews.

The multibillion-dollar DEI bureaucracy has become a central contributor to anti-Jewish attitudes on campuses. The effect, if not the intent, of this ideological bureaucracy is to marginalize Jews.

The first component of DEI is diversity, but its definition of diversity is limited to skin color and other aspects of identity politics. It explicitly excludes diversity of opinions, ideas, and ideology. The effect is the university looks more diverse, but actually is less diverse in the most important aspect of education, namely ideas. This genre of diversity lowers the number of Jewish students and faculty.

Jews do not conform to diversity in terms of identity politics, even if they do for other aspects of diversity. In fact, the number and percentage of Jews at top-tier universities have declined since the introduction of DEI.[1]

The second element is equity, which is precisely the opposite of equality. Equality is reflected in Martin Luther King Jr.'s dream that someday his children will be judged not by the color of their skin, but by the content of their character. Equity demands that people be judged by the color of their skin and other immutable characteristics. Jews thrive on equality and meritocracy. They suffer from the artificial and easily manipulable concept of equity.

Finally, there is the stated goal of inclusion. As former Harvard president Lawrence Summers has noted, DEI inclusion in most bureaucracies explicitly excludes Jews.[2] When inclusion becomes a justification for exclusion, the entire concept must be questioned.

In addition to discrimination against Jews, DEI also discriminates against dissenting views. On many campuses, applicants for admission and jobs must signify approval of DEI. Those of us who fundamentally disagree with the goals and means of DEI are threatened with exclusion if we follow our consciences.

The second development that has plagued universities over the past several decades has been the creation of special departments and programs that pander to specific identity groups. The result has been a massive increase of antisemitism emanating from these identity departments. Many of these departments have voted to boycott and divest from Israel. Others have invited only anti-Israel and anti-Semitic speakers, refusing to allow pro-Israel and anti-DEI speakers to express their contrary ideas to students.

This includes several Jewish Studies departments, which have followed the woke progressive line of being hypercritical of Israel and Zionism.

---

1   Sara Weissman, "Jewish Student Enrollment Is Down at Many Ivies," *Inside Higher Ed*, May 8, 2023, https://www.insidehighered.com/news/admissions/2023/05/08/jewish-student-enrollment-down-many-ivies.

2   Larry Summers, "Reflections on Antisemitism and the University," larrysummers.com, https://larrysummers.com/2023/11/13/reflections-on-antisemitism-and-the-university/.

Universities should teach about all identities with the same critical eye they apply to other subjects. Academia should not have special departments, many of which are nothing more than uncritical cheering squads for particular identities.

The end result of DEI and specialized departments has been to institutionalize anti-Semitism at many universities. There have always been anti-Semites among university faculty, administrators, and students, but these two developments have turned sporadic individual Jew hatred into systemic anti-Semitism.

Just as the George Floyd case encouraged a "reckoning" with systemic racism, the recent increase in anti-Semitism requires universities to engage in a reckoning about how these two developments have contributed to the singling out of Jews and Zionists for discrimination and prejudice on many campuses.

DEI bureaucracies and identity departments have turned identity politics on campus into a zero-sum game. Particular groups benefit at the expense of other groups. Identities are pitted against each other. The result has been for students and faculty to be valued less as individuals and more as members of groups. And some groups on campus are privileged more than other groups. In this hierarchical ranking, Jews are the least privileged—ironically because they are seen as the most privileged by society in general. This encourages anti-Semitism.

A related cause is that the woke-progressive mindset deplores meritocracy as a criterion for success. And Jews have historically thrived within meritocracy.

There used to be systemic racism, sexism, and homophobia in many university admission and hiring decisions. Such systemic prejudice no longer exists. To the contrary, at most of today's universities, we have systemic anti-racism, anti-sexism and anti-homophobia.

But this systemic change has contributed to the growing antisemitism on many university campuses. This blight will only get worse unless changes are made in DEI and special academic departments based on identity.

For Universities Facing Lawsuits Over Anti-Semitism, First Amendment Offers Uncertain Defense

Violence and threats against Jewish students have become so rampant on many American campuses as to create a hostile and unsafe environment. University administrators face difficult challenges—legal, educational, moral, and financial—in trying to deal with this growing concern.

Recently, the secretary of education, Miguel Cardona, warned schools receiving federal aid that if they are insensitive to anti-Semitism and Islamophobia on their campus, they could lose federal funding. Harvard, on whose faculty I served for sixty years, is among them, and I am prepared to become a whistleblower and witness against my school.

At the same time, I and other lawyers have been called by numerous parents of Jewish students who are contemplating lawsuits against colleges to which they are paying tuition for their children. They report that Jewish students are experiencing hostile environments and threats to their safety.

They point to events such as that which occurred at Harvard, where a group of anti-Israel students surrounded a Jewish student, harassing him, blocking his exit, and reportedly throwing him to the ground. They cite threats against Jewish fraternity houses, kosher kitchens, and other campus institutions frequented by Jewish students.

There are claims of grade discrimination by professors against Israeli students or students who express pro-Israel views. Although Mr. Cardona echoed the Biden administration in joining together anti-Semitism and Islamophobia as equal dangers on campus, it is obvious that the major hostilities today are directed at Jewish and Zionist students rather than Islamic or Palestinian Arab students. Indeed, some, though not all, of the threats have come from Islamic and Arab students.

Anti-Semitic and Islamophobic hate speech are all protected by the First Amendment, with several exceptions. Incitement to immediate violence and harassment are not protected. Nor is providing material support for designated terrorist groups such as Hamas and Hezbollah. This includes financial contributions that are intended to fall into the hands of a terrorist group.

There is an important legal difference between actions taken by the Department of Education, which is a governmental agency, and those taken by private individuals who bring lawsuits against universities. The government is prohibited from taking any action that compels either a public or a private university to restrict protected free speech.

This does not preclude a private citizen from bringing a lawsuit against either a public or a private university for creating or tolerating a hostile environment toward its Jewish students or for failing to satisfy its contractual obligation to protect them from harassment or threats of violence. Suits have already been filed against NYU, Harvard, and the University of California at Berkeley, and more are coming.

A public university may be able to defend its refusal to ban protected speech under its own First Amendment obligations. A private university can also claim to be acting in the spirit of the First Amendment, but such a claim might not constitute a complete defense to a breach of contract suit that alleges that a private university ignored its obligation to its students to provide a safe environment.

There are no binding precedents on these complex issues, and the courts will have to balance conflicting rights—to free speech and to a safe environment. Universities will not be able to defend against the claim that they are applying a double standard to Jews as contrasted with other minorities.

It is crystal clear that such a double standard exists at most universities. No university would tolerate a Ku Klux Klan club that publicly stated that, say, the lynching of African Americans was justified. Nor would it tolerate public statements that gay or transgender students who were attacked deserved it because of their lifestyles.

These are all examples of constitutionally protected speech that no university would tolerate. Yet Harvard refused to condemn student groups that published letters blaming the Hamas atrocities of October 7 "entirely" on Israel. Other universities have remained silent in the face of rabidly anti-Semitic posters such as the one demanding that the world be "clean" of Jews.

The First Amendment requires all government institutions to remain neutral when it comes to the content of ideas. As Chief Justice Rehnquist put it in 1990: "Under the First Amendment there is no such thing as a false idea." This means no university that is public or accepts federal funding can seek to distinguish between Jews and other minorities, on the grounds that Jews are somehow "privileged."

They must apply precisely the same standard to anti-Jewish or anti-Israel provocations as they would or do to anti-Black, anti-feminist, or anti-gay speech. It is doubtful that any university today meets that test. To the contrary, the diversity, equity, and inclusion bureaucracies at many universities expressly exclude Jews.

As a former president of Harvard, Secretary Summers, recently put it: "[w]ith few exceptions, those most directly charged with confronting prejudice—Offices of Diversity, Equity, and Inclusion—have failed to stand with Israeli and Jewish students confronting the oldest prejudice of them all."

So, if a lawsuit can establish that a given university—private or public—created or tolerates a hostile environment against Jewish students that it would not tolerate against other minority students, that lawsuit might well prevail, even against a First Amendment defense.

Not-So-Hidden Agenda Behind "Pro-Palestinian" Protests: The End of Israel and Support for Hamas

Every single demonstration I have seen also features signs calling for the end of Israel as a genocidal, apartheid, colonialist state.

The protests against Israel around the world purport to be demanding a ceasefire, but that is not their real agenda. The not-so-hidden agenda is a demand for the end of Israel and support for Hamas. The protests began the day after the Hamas massacres of twelve hundred Israelis and the kidnapping of more than two hundred.

The early protests supported the massacres and called for the Mideast to be "free" and "clean" of the Jews who live in Israel proper. Those protests against Israel began before the Israeli army responded to the Hamas atrocities and so they were not motivated by any concern for Palestinian civilians. They supported the murder of Israeli civilians.

Now that Israel is responding, there are new signs and chants demanding a ceasefire that would benefit Hamas. But every single demonstration I have seen also features signs calling for the end of

Israel as a genocidal, apartheid, colonialist state. Demonstrators also tear down posters with the pictures and names of Israeli children who were kidnapped by Hamas and are being held as hostages. That, too, is not about helping Palestinian civilians.

So don't be fooled by so-called "pro-Palestine" or pro-ceasefire protests. The few people who actually join these protests out of such beneficent motives are being used to support the real goals of the organizers: namely the destruction of Israel, the strengthening of Hamas, and the recurrence of the barbarism of October 7.

The reality is that an imposed ceasefire will not save civilian lives. To the contrary, it will cost many more lives in the long run by incentivizing Hamas to repeat the cycle it has perpetuated for decades: kill Israeli civilians; hide Hamas rockets, commanders, and tunnels among Palestinian civilians, hoping that Israel, despite its effort to minimize civilian casualties, will kill some children who are being used as human shields; parade the children in front of television cameras, thereby causing outrage against Israel; force Israel into a ceasefire; and then repeat the process after Hamas rearms and reorganizes.

Leaders of Hamas have already bragged that the slaughters of October 7 were only the beginning. That they will be repeated as long as they benefit from it, as they will if a ceasefire is imposed.

Good people who care about stopping this apparently endless cycle of civilian deaths caused by Hamas should be protesting against the ceasefire and in favor of the total destruction of Hamas. Such a result would be "pro-Palestinian," because Hamas has caused more damage and harm to the Palestinian people than Israel. So anyone who is truly pro-peace, pro-Palestinian and pro-civilian should be encouraging Israel to finish what Hamas started, by eliminating that terrorist organization from the Gaza Strip.

It may seem counterintuitive to oppose a ceasefire in the interest of reducing civilian casualties, and that is part of the Hamas strategy. It understands that people are more influenced by pictures of dead babies than by logic and experience. They also understand that most people do not think in the long term. Instead, they look for short-term Band-Aids such as ceasefires. But applying a Band-Aid instead of a disinfectant may result in infections.

So the next time you see a demonstration in the local streets, on the university campus, or on television, read the signs carefully. Even if you misguidedly support a ceasefire, don't join the demonstration unless you also support Hamas, the end of Israel, and the slaughter and kidnapping of Israeli civilians. Don't be fooled by the anodyne covers that hide the malicious goals of the protests. Don't allow yourself and your good name to be misused by bad people with evil intentions.

These worldwide protests—ill-intentioned as some may be—are having an impact on the policy of many nations, most especially the United States. Israelis, who are generally highly critical of their government, are not falling for the deceptive nature of these efforts.

They know that Hamas seeks to destroy Israel and to do to the millions of Israeli Jews what they already did to twelve hundred of them. But much of the rest of the world naively assumes that joining a call for a ceasefire is being a do-gooder. It is not. Anyone who joins these protests, whatever their personal views, becomes a do-badder encouraging anti-Semitism and barbarism.

Corporate Media Is Eagerly Gobbling Up Hamas's Casualty Narrative

When a hostage is accidentally killed by a soldier or policeman who is trying to kill the hostage-taker, who is guilty of the murder? That's the question to understand as the press gets it wrong in Gaza.

The *New York Times* has published a distorted and internally inconsistent "analysis" of casualties allegedly inflicted by Israel on civilians in Gaza.[3]

Under a headline about "civilians" killed by Israel, they cite the total number of deaths reported by the Hamas-controlled Gaza health authorities as gospel, and then hide a one-sentence disclaimer that these Hamas generated figures do not even purport to "separate the deaths of civilians and combatants." Nor do they identify how many

---

3   Lauren Letherby, "Gaza Civilians, Under Israeli Barrage, Are Being Killed at Historic Pace," *New York Times*, November 25, 2023, https://www.nytimes.com /2023/11/25/world/middleeast/israel-gaza-death-toll.html.

of those who they count as "civilians" are actually Hamas collaborators who allow their homes to be used to hide rockets, tunnels, or terrorists.

They seek to justify these glaring omissions by uncritically repeating the undocumented and absurd Hamas claims that more than three-quarters of Gazans allegedly killed are women and children—again failing to distinguish between these two very different categories or to indicate how many of the "children" are fourteen-, fifteen-, sixteen- or seventeen-year-old Hamas child soldiers and terrorists.

Nor does the *Times* separate out the many Gazans who have been killed by misfired terrorist rockets launched from Gaza at Israeli targets—as many as 15 to 20 percent of terrorist rockets land in Gaza.[4]

Most significantly, the figures cited by the *Times* do not identify the number of Hamas human shields who were deliberately placed in harm's way by Hamas commanders and terrorists. Every one of these human shields killed are the legal, moral, and political responsibility of Hamas, not Israel.

The law is clear that when a hostage is accidentally killed by a soldier or policeman who is trying to kill the hostage-taker, it is the hostage-taker and not the soldier or policeman who is guilty of the murder, even though the bullet that killed the hostage was fired by the innocent soldier or policeman.

The same is true of the use of human shields: those who placed the shield in harm's way are guilty, not those who were trying to kill the combatants.

In order to claim that the civilian casualties in Gaza are greater than in other recent wars, the *Times* focused on the Russia-Ukraine conflict. But there is no valid comparison—it's oranges and bicycles.

The Russians have been deliberately targeting Ukrainian civilians. Ukrainian soldiers are not hiding among civilians. Ukrainian leaders are not using their own civilians as human shields. Every Ukrainian civilian killed by Russian weapons is the fault of Russia alone.

---

4   "What Everyone Needs to Know About Hamas' Lie About a Rocket Strike on a Gaza Hospital," AJC/Global Voice, October 23, 2023, https://www.ajc.org/new s/what-everyone-needs-to-know-about-hamas-lie-about-a-rocket-strike-on-a-gaza-hospital.

The same is true of civilian casualties in other wars cited by the *Times*: no group in the history of modern warfare has used human shields as extensively and deliberately as Hamas.

It is highly misleading, therefore, to compare the number of civilian deaths among human shields in Gaza with the numbers of civilian deaths in other wars in which human shields were not used at all or were used only sparingly.

The fact that the *Times* would offer such absurd and irrelevant "comparisons" reflects its extreme bias against Israel and—along with its other examples of journalistic malpractice—discredits its entire deeply flawed analysis.

The sad reality, not reported by the *Times*, is that Hamas actually wants Israel to kill people who appear to be civilians, precisely to encourage the press to do what the *Times* is doing: blame Israel for every death, especially among children and women.

This is part of what Hamas itself calls its "CNN strategy"—a strategy it has been successfully pursuing for years. It is as simple as it is cynical: begin by murdering as many Israeli civilians as possible—firing rockets, using terror tunnels, and crossing the fence, as was done on October 7.

Then, Hamas hides the rockets, tunnels, and terrorists among civilians, knowing that Israel will have to try to prevent recurrence by attacking the military targets that are hiding behind human shields; parade the dead human shields, especially children, in front of the press and expect the world to blame these deaths on Israel; repeat this strategy again and again, as long as the media cooperates by uncritically playing its assigned role.

In light of the false and prejudicial reporting by the *Times*, this deadly strategy can be given a new name: the "*New York Times* Strategy."

By distorting and misreporting the number of actually innocent civilians whose deaths are the fault of Israel, the *Times* and other press play into the hands of Hamas and encourage it and other terrorist groups to expand the use of human shields and to increase the number of civilians—both Palestinian and Israeli—who are killed as part of this deadly but successful strategy.

The Media Ignore Hamas's Long, Deliberate Strategy to Increase Civilian Deaths

Hamas has a calculated policy of doing everything to increase deaths among the civilians of Gaza.[5]

Besides deliberately using civilians as human shields,[6] it denies them the opportunity to use the vast complex of tunnels-shelters it has built to protect its terrorists and its valuable hostages.

Israel, on the other hand, has spent hundreds of millions of dollars constructing shelters for its civilians, as well as prioritizing the development of the Iron Dome designed to protect Israeli civilians from Hamas rockets.

It should come as no surprise, therefore, that despite Hamas's desire to kill as many civilians as possible and Israel's desire to kill as few civilians as possible, the number of Gazan civilians killed exceeds the number of Israeli civilians killed in this conflict. But you wouldn't understand this from reading the *New York Times'* Sunday front-page "analysis" of comparative death figures because the Gray Lady fails to provide the reasons for the disparity.

Nor does it disclose that not all Gazan "civilians" are innocent.[7] Many are complicit with Hamas in numerous ways. Some "civilians" even participated in the October 7 massacres, crossing the broken fence and raping and murdering innocent Israeli civilians. Others allow their home to be used to hide rockets, tunnel entrances, and fighters.

There are, of course, entirely innocent civilians—even among the 70 percent who approve of the massacres. Babies and young children cannot be blamed for the sins of their parents, though sixteen- and seventeen-year-old terrorists, whom the media count as children, are clearly

---

5   Post Staff, Alexandria Sillo, and Olivia Land, "Israel-Hamas war live updates: Gaza Strip 'in the midst of a near-total internet blackout': reports," *New York Post*, December 4, 2023, https://nypost.com/2023/11/27/news/israel-hamas -war-live-updates-of-hostage-release-and-temporary-cease-fire/.

6   Natalie Ecanow, "Hamas officials admit its strategy is to use Palestinian civilians as human shields," *New York Post*, November 1, 2023, https://nypost.com/2023/11/01/opinion /hamas-officials-admit-its-strategy-is-to-use-palestinian-civilians-as-human-shields/.

7   Douglas Murray, "On the ground inside Gaza, where Israel is trying to save civilians from Hamas," *New York Post*, November 15, 2023, https://nypost.com/2023/11/15 /opinion/on-the-ground-inside-gaza-where-israel-is-trying-to-save-civilians-from-hamas/.

legitimate military targets. As are female terrorists the media describe simply as "women," suggesting all women are innocent civilians.

Indeed, the *Times* notes "officials in the Hamas-run Gaza Strip do not separate the deaths of civilians and combatants." But the credulous paper uses "the roughly 10,000 women and children reported killed in Gaza as an approximate—though conservative—measure of civilian deaths."

When a political entity like Hamas attacks and declares war on another political entity like Israel, it knows full well the attacked nation will respond militarily. It understands that in the process, civilians will die. That is the nature of all wars.

Millions of German and Japanese civilians died along with Russians, Poles, and other civilians in World War II. War is hell, and those who start wars willfully inflict hellish consequences on their own civilians as well as others. The difference is that some warring nations go to great lengths to protect both their own civilians and those of their enemies.

Israel is such a nation. Others, like Hamas, go to great lengths to maximize civilian casualties on both sides. Hamas has had a policy of maximizing civilian casualties since its inception as a terrorist group. Its leaders themselves call it the CNN strategy. We have been writing about it for decades, but we call it the "dead-baby strategy." And it works—with the complicity of many media.

It's as simple as it is effective: Kill as many Israeli civilians as possible; then hide the killers and their weapons among civilians, including babies; hope and expect some babies will die, despite Israel's efforts to avoid civilian casualties; as soon as a baby dies, display its body to the media, which will blame it on Israel; Israel will then be pressured into a ceasefire that will strengthen Hamas and allow it to kill more civilians.[8]

It's a proven formula for success, so why stop?

Or as the shampoo ad puts it: "Wash, rinse, repeat"—kill their civilians, hide behind your civilians, repeat, and repeat. The only way

8 Ronny Reyes, "Israel-Hamas truce to be extended for two more days, officials say," *New York Post*, November 27, 2023, https://nypost.com/2023/11/27/news/israel-hamas-truce-to-be-extended-for-two-more-days/.

to stop this cynical cycle of civilian deaths is for the media to accept responsibility for their complicity.

Every time a dead civilian is shown or described, the media must provide the context of why these civilians are dying: Hamas's deliberate use of human shields; Hamas's deliberate refusal to provide shelter for its citizens; the complicity of many Gaza "civilians" with Hamas; the inevitability of collateral civilian deaths after an unprovoked attack; the great efforts to which Israel goes to reduce civilian deaths; the unreliability of Hamas-provided data; the long history of Hamas using and repeating the "dead-baby strategy."

Until and unless the media start telling the whole truth about Hamas's culpability, its murder of civilians will continue.

National Lawyers Guild Supports Hamas Rapes and Murders

Within a day of the brutal massacre of Israeli babies, women, the elderly, and others, the National Lawyers Guild issued a statement in support of the mass murderers. The National Lawyers Guild is a group of hard-left lawyers, students, and legal workers. It has branches in law schools throughout the country and has many members, especially among law students.

It began as a liberal organization before World War II and included many legal luminaries, including Jews. But it was quickly taken over by the Communist Party, and it supported the Hitler–Stalin Pact of 1939. As a result of its support for Hitler, many liberal members quit. However, committed Communists who always follow the party line remained members. Following World War II, the National Lawyers Guild again attracted some liberals who saw it as an alternative to the conservative American Bar Association. But then in the 1970s, it was taken over by radical leftists, including some members of the Communist Party. It was no longer a home for liberals.

In 1948, the Guild followed the lead of the Soviet Union in supporting the establishment of Israel. But when the Soviet Union and the Communist Party turned against Israel in the 1960s, the Guild followed suit in opposing Israel and supporting Palestinian terrorists. Nonetheless, some liberals, including Jews, remained members. It remains to be seen whether it will lose the support of Jewish liberals, following the events of October 7, 2023.

It is important to note that the lengthy statement by the Lawyers Guild in support of Hamas and in opposition to Israel was issued before Israel responded to the Hamas attack. It was posted on October 8, while bodies were still being recovered from the south of Israel.

The statement begins by emphasizing "the legitimacy of the right of the Palestinian people to resist the legal military occupation, apartheid, and ethnic cleansing . . . as well as Israel's perpetration of its atrocities." It described the rapes, beheadings, murders, and kidnappings committed by Hamas as "the recent military actions carried out by Palestinian resistance . . ." It urged the public to support resistance to Israel's occupation "by all available means including armed struggle." It criticized those who had condemned Hamas's barbarity. It accused Israel of genocide and demanded that Hamas be removed from the United States list of foreign terrorist organizations. It demanded that Israel be held legally accountable for the defense of its citizens. It claimed that Israel's goal is to "annihilate" the Palestinians, and it demanded the release of every single Palestinian prisoner—including those convicted of mass murder. It did not call for the release of the hostages held by Hamas, and it opposed efforts of any country to "normalize relations with Israel." It said not a single word in condemnation of the rapes, beheadings, and kidnappings of Israeli babies, children, and women.

I am not aware of any law school in which the National Lawyers Guild has a chapter condemning or even criticizing this statement. Indeed, it has gone largely unnoticed in the law school community. But this statement was not produced from thin air or by artificial intelligence, it was written and circulated by specific leaders of the National Lawyers Guild, including students at America's leading universities.

Students who support this outrageously anti-Semitic, anti-American, and anti-humanitarian statement are currently being given job offers by America's leading law firms, by government agencies, by hedge funds, and by other potential employers. I am sure that these employers are unaware that they may be hiring lawyers who support the rapes and beheading of Jewish women and children. Full transparency, which lies at the core of the marketplace of ideas protected by the First Amendment, demands that the name of every member of the National Lawyers Guild who supports this statement be made public, so that potential employers know who they are hiring. Few clients would be willing to be represented by lawyers who have advocated the rape, beheading, murder, and kidnapping of Jewish civilians.

If there were groups of law students at any law school that advocated the lynching of African Americans, the raping of women, or the killing of gay and transgender people, the National Lawyers Guild would be the first to demand that the names of the students supporting such atrocities be made public. Now the shoe is on the other foot, and it is the Guild that is supporting such barbarity.

Publicizing the names and law schools of students who support Hamas violence against civilians is not "doxxing." It does not disclose private information about their home addresses, their sexual preferences, or anything else other than their names. These students have identified themselves as members of the National Lawyers Guild. They are adults and are responsible for their actions and inactions.

Publishing their names serves the interest of truth and transparency. And so, I intend to publish—on my website, my podcast, and in my op-eds—the names of any student who signed or supported the bigoted statement of the National Lawyers Guild.

Doctors Without Borders Acts Like a Hamas Front

Doctors Without Borders (DWB) holds itself out to be a politically neutral medical provider that cares about all people equally. That was its pretend pose when it won the Nobel Peace Prize.[9] In actuality, it was always a hard-left group that played politics with medicine. But recent events have exposed the depths of its bigotry and destroyed its fraudulent claims of neutrality.

Since October 7, it has become a full-time front for Hamas barbarity and a declared enemy of Israel and of the Israeli victims and hostages. It has also become a medical megaphone for Hamas lies.

---

9   "The Nobel Peace Prize 1999," NobelPrize.org, https://www.nobelprize.org/prizes /peace/1999/summary/.

The head of the Gaza unit of DWB was recently interviewed by CNN. After parroting Hamas lies about Israel allegedly targeting doctors, journalists, and children, she was confronted by the reporter with a truth: "Hamas uses human shields." This was her mendacious response: "No, we don't." Not "no they don't," but no "we don't." The "we" obviously referred to the organization she was speaking for, namely Hamas, whose lies she was communicating. But she was also speaking for Doctors Without Borders, for whom she works.

Her lies about human shields have long been disproven by hard evidence. As a NATO report in 2019 documented:

> Hamas, an Islamist militant group and the de facto governing authority of the Gaza Strip, has been using human shields in conflicts with Israel since 2007. . . . The strategic logic of human shields has two components. It is based on an awareness of Israel's desire to minimize collateral damage, and of Western public opinion's sensitivity towards civilian casualties. If the IDF uses lethal force and causes an increase in civilian casualties, Hamas can utilize that as a lawfare tool: it can accuse Israel of committing war crimes, which could result in the imposition of a wide array of sanctions.
>
> Alternatively, if the IDF limits its use of military force in Gaza to avoid collateral damage, Hamas will be less susceptible to Israeli attacks, and thereby able to protect its assets while continuing to fight.[10]

By denying this reality, DWB encourages Hamas to persist in its double war crimes: using Palestinian civilians to help it target Israeli civilians.

Another DWB leader demanded that Israel accept a unilateral ceasefire, without saying a word about the remaining hostages or the victims of murder and rape on October 7. Because they are doctors, they have enhanced credibility for their bigoted and mendacious claims on behalf of Hamas.

---

10 James Pamment et al, "Hybrid Threats: Hamas' use of human shields in Gaza," NATO Strategic Communications Centre of Excellence, June 6, 2019, https://stratcomcoe.org/publications/hybrid-threats-hamas-use-of-human-shields-in-gaza/87.

The same is true for UNICEF and UNRWA, which operate under the UN aegis, but rarely deviate from the Hamas line. These one-sided organizations have also demanded a unilateral ceasefire by Israel without demanding the return of all the hostages as a precondition. Nor have they focused their attention on the twelve hundred Israelis, including children, who were murdered, raped, beheaded, and kidnapped. Or on the Hamas promise that it will repeat these atrocities.

A UN Watch report documented celebrations by UNRWA of the Hamas massacres. And it has now been learned that hostages have been hidden by UN employees to prevent their rescue by Israel. Also, hundreds of the murderers and rapists attended UNRWA schools, which have become propaganda mills for Hamas.

These anti-Semitic groups are funded by the US government and tax-deductible charitable contributions. These payments are based on the false assumption that the organizations are neutral and serve all people equally on humanitarian bases. But they don't. In the Israel/Hamas conflict, they serve only Hamas. In fact, the partisan assistance they provide Hamas may well be criminal. US law makes it a felony to provide "material support" to designated terrorist organizations like Hamas.

Whether criminal or merely immoral, these bigoted organizations are helping Hamas do its dirty work. And they are hurting Israel and the Israeli victims and hostages. They are also hurting Gaza civilians by denying that Hamas uses them as human shields and encouraging Hamas to continue to use hospitals and schools to harbor terrorists.

They do not deserve American financial support or the charitable contributions of decent people. Indeed, they should be condemned in the court of public opinion and perhaps in the courts of law.

The time has come for the media to conduct thorough investigations of these organizations. Congress too should investigate their receipt of direct and tax-deductible funds and the manner in which these dollars are spent.

Because they have undeserved reputations for neutrality and integrity, there is a disincentive to probe their workings. But the truth is that they do much harm along with some good, and donors have the right to know the whole truth.

Hamas Is Murdering Palestinian Babies in Gaza Hospitals

Media outlets around the world are showing dead and dying Palestinian babies in hospitals—but what they are not showing is who murdered these babies.

The answer is clear. American intelligence has now revealed that Hamas has built its command centers and its tunnels underneath hospitals.[11] It has also revealed that Hamas has been stealing fuel intended for hospital generators.[12]

Babies are now dying because Hamas has stolen the fuel to run these generators. Babies are also dying because Hamas is using them as human shields to protect its murderous terrorists.

Yet much of the media and the international community continue to point the finger of blame at Israel for these dead babies. That only encourages Hamas to continue to use its decades-long "dead baby strategy," which works because the media continues to show the dead babies without explaining the truth about who killed them.

The time has come—indeed it is long overdue—for the media outlets to start telling the truth. But they won't, in part because they prefer bloody images of dead babies over thoughtful analysis of the root causes of these tragic deaths. "If it bleeds, it leads," and if the bleeding comes from babies, it leads even more powerfully.

The main cause of these deaths is Hamas strategy, and a secondary cause is the role of the media in implementing the Hamas strategy. A third group that bears some responsibility for the dead Palestinian babies is comprised of Gazan doctors, United Nations personnel, and other supposed do-gooders.

Representatives for these groups appear regularly on television categorically denying that there is any Hamas presence in or beneath the

---

11 Jake Tapper, "Hamas has command node under Al-Shifa hospital, US official says," CNN, November 13, 2023, https://www.cnn.com/2023/11/13/politics/al-shifa-hospital-us-intelligence/index.html.

12 Anna Schecter, "Hamas is hoarding vast amounts of fuel as Gaza hospitals run low, U.S. officials say," NBC News, November 1, 2023, https://www.nbcnews.com/news/investigations/hamas-hoarding-vast-amounts-fuel-gaza-hospitals-run-low-us-officials-s-rcna122977.

hospitals. One such doctor recently said that, in the ten years he has worked at the hospital, he has never seen a Hamas terrorist.[13]

The reality is that Hamas could not operate in and around the hospitals without the knowledge and complicity of hospital administrators, doctors, and the UN. These organizations have undeserved credibility with the media because of their titles, but the reality is that they toe the Hamas line and repeat its propaganda.

Babies—both Palestinian and Israeli—will continue to die as long as the cynical Hamas strategy is successful, as it has been for decades. The world is turning against Israel and in favor of Hamas as the terror group causes the deaths of more and more Palestinian babies.

The only way to break this cycle is for the media and the international community to expose and condemn it as a clear violation of the laws of war, which expressly prohibit the use of hospitals and patients to protect terrorists. Yet this gross and highly visible violation is not condemned by the United Nations, the International Criminal Court, nor other credible organizations.

Israel, on the other hand, is repeatedly condemned for attacking terrorists who hide in hospitals and use patients as shields. Under international law, any hospital that is used for military purposes loses its status as a protected medical facility.[14] Israel must still make reasonable efforts to avoid hurting patients, as it is doing. It has offered to evacuate patients to field hospitals and hospital ships, but Hamas tries to prevent patients from moving because they're needed to shield their terrorists.

Israel has now produced videos of the military bases underneath the hospitals,[15] as well as of Hamas terrorists stealing fuel that was

---

13 Al Jazeera English, "'Never seen it': Norwegian doctor disputes Hamas in hospitals," YouTube video, https://www.youtube.com/watch?v=sohETs7AVLk.

14 "The protection of hospitals during armed conflicts: What the law says," International Committee of the Red Cross, November 2, 2023, https://www.icrc .org/en/document/protection-hospitals-during-armed-conflicts-what-law-says.

15 Nic Robertson et al, "Israel shows alleged Hamas 'armory' under children's hospital in Gaza. Local health officials dismiss the claims," CNN, November 14, 2023, https://www.cnn.com/2023/11/14/middleeast/israel-alleges-hamas-armory-under -hospital-in-gaza-hnk-intl/index.html.

intended for medical use.[16] It has also shown videos of an armed Hamas terrorist walking into a hospital with a rocket launcher clearly visible on his shoulder.[17] But these images are largely ignored by viewers and commentators in favor of the more dramatic images of the dead babies. That too is part of the Hamas strategy.

So next time you see a dead Palestinian baby on TV, shed a tear for that innocent victim. But point the finger of guilt at Hamas, not Israel, if you don't want to see more dead babies murdered by Hamas.

Palestinians Share Hamas Guilt

At the end of the Second World War, many Germans who actively supported Adolf Hitler and the Nazis acted as if they actually had nothing to do with genocide inflicted on the Jews. They pretended that Hitler and a few handfuls of Nazis had suddenly come down from Mars and had taken over the bodies and souls of ordinary, innocent, and decent German people.

In his masterful book, *Hitler's Willing Executioners*, Daniel Goldhagen destroyed that myth and proved conclusively that Hitler and the Nazis had widespread support among ordinary Germans, and that many, if not most, of them were aware of Hitler's final solution.

This historical reality did not necessarily justify the deliberate killing of German civilians by Great Britain and the United States in Dresden and other German cities, but it made the civilian adult "victims" of these bombings somewhat less sympathetic, and it made it easier to blame their deaths on the Nazis who started the war with widespread civilian support, if not enthusiasm.

A similar mythology is already emerging around the atrocities committed by Hamas against Israeli civilians. Government officials, the media, academics, and others pretend as if there is a sharp distinction between Hamas and the ordinary decent civilians of Gaza.

---

16 @AvivaKlompas, X, November 12, 2023, https://twitter.com/AvivaKlompas/status/1723742748811894802.

17 "IDF releases footage of Hamas firing RPG from Gaza City hospital," i24NewsTV, November 13, 2024, https://www.i24news.tv/en/news/israel-at-war/1699881898-idf-releases-footage-of-hamas-firing-rpg-from-gaza-city-hospital.

How many times have you heard the claim that the adult citizens of Gaza are not in any way responsible for the horrendous crimes of Hamas? Or that Israel is imposing "collective punishment" on the innocent civilians of Gaza? The reality is far more nuanced and complex.

As in Nazi Germany, Hamas was elected by the citizens of Gaza in the last election, in 2006.[18] Today, they would likely still be reelected by an overwhelming majority.[19] Indeed, support for Hamas has increased dramatically since the massacres of October 7,[20] which were wildly cheered by many civilians.[21]

Recall the recording of the young terrorist who bragged to his father that he had just murdered ten Jews "with my own hands," and the proud father congratulating his mass murdering son on his holy "accomplishment."[22] Is the father an innocent civilian who deserves our sympathy?

Hamas, itself, refuses to distinguish between combatants and civilians.[23] First, Hamas boasts that it has the widespread support of the vast majority of Gazans. Second, it uses alleged civilians as human

---

18 Ishaan Tharoor, "The election that led to Hamas taking over Gaza," *Washington Post*, October 24, 2023, https://www.washingtonpost.com/world/2023/10/24/gaza-election-hamas-2006-palestine-israel/.

19 Danielle Greyman-Kellard, "Palestinians in Gaza, West Bank strongly support Hamas, October 7 attack," *Jerusalem Post*, November 17, 2023, https://www.jpost.com/arab-israeli-conflict/article-773791.

20 ToI Staff, "Poll: 75% of New Yorkers say antisemitism up since October 7," *Times of Israel*, https://www.msn.com/en-us/news/world/poll-75-of-new-yorkers-say-antisemitism-up-since-october-7/ar-AA1keSV4.

21 Al Jazeera Network, "Palestinians In Gaza And The West Bank Celebrate On October 7, Hand Out Sweets, Fire Guns In The Air, Following Hamas's Invasion And Massacre Of Israeli Civilians In The Gaza Envelope," MEMRI.org, October 7, 2023, https://www.memri.org/tv/palestinians-gaza-west-bank-celebrate-october-seven-massacre-hand-out-sweets-fire-guns.

22 Carrie Keller-Lynn, "IDF shows foreign press Hamas bodycam videos, photos of murder, torture, decapitation," *The Times of Israel*, October 23, 2023, https://www.timesofisrael.com/idf-shows-foreign-press-raw-hamas-bodycam-videos-of-murder-torture-decapitation/.

23 Robert Goldman, "How the 'laws of war' apply to the conflict between Israel and Hamas," *The Conversation*, October 15, 2023, https://theconversation.com/how-the-laws-of-war-apply-to-the-conflict-between-israel-and-hamas-215493.

shields and declares them to be martyrs if they are then killed.[24],[25] At least some of these martyrs willingly served as shields for Hamas combatants. Third, when the Hamas-controlled health authorities release their phony statistics on deaths, they refuse to distinguish between combatants and civilians.

When they provide numbers of Gazans who they claim have been killed, they hide the fact that many of these Gazans are either combatants or are complicit in Hamas crimes by willingly allowing their homes to be used for the storage and firing of rockets.

Hamas fully understands that the line between combatants and Gazan civilians is often an artificial one, and they use it as both a sword and a shield in the public relations war.

When Hamas deliberately attacked Israeli civilians, they knew full well that Israel would have to respond, that Hamas would use civilians as human shields, and that despite Israeli efforts to avoid civilian casualties, some Palestinians would become "collateral" damage—that is, be killed or wounded when Israel took military action necessary to prevent a recurrence of the massacres of October 7.

Hamas is thus responsible—morally, legally, and politically—for the civilian deaths that were the predictable and indeed intended result of the October 7 attack. These civilian deaths were intended to shift the focus away from the Hamas barbarities and toward the collateral damage resulting from Israeli self-defense measures.

The adult civilians of Gaza who encouraged, supported, rewarded, and cheered on the massacres of Israelis also bear some moral and political, if not strictly legal, responsibility.

This leaves the children. It must first be determined what constitutes a "child" in the enumeration of Hamas. They count anyone under nineteen. It also depends of course on the way children are used. When it comes to recruiting child soldiers, Hamas considers thirteen-, fourteen- and

---

24 Jason Willick, "We can't ignore the truth that Hamas uses human shields," *Washington Post*, November 14, 2023, https://www.washingtonpost.com/opinions/2023/11/14/hamas-human-shields-tactic/.

25 TalkTV, "'Compelling Evidence of Human Shield Tactics' British Colonel Analyses Latest Hamas Footage," YouTube video, November 20, 2023, https://www.youtube.com/watch?v=sajDZX_YRfw.

fifteen- year-olds as sufficiently mature to become terrorists. But when it comes to publishing inflated figures about the dead, suddenly every seventeen-and-a-half-year-old mass murdering terrorist is counted among the poor "children" mercilessly killed by the bloodthirsty Israelis.

Also, every mass murdering woman, regardless of age, is separately listed, as if to suggest that their sex automatically makes them innocent civilians. And the media and others willingly fall for these cynical bait-and-switches.

Let the Hamas authorities at least separate the terrorist combatants—including women and children—from the total numbers allegedly killed. They should also separate out the Gazans who were killed by errant terrorist rockets, as well as civilians who were killed by Hamas trying to go south pursuant to Israeli safety instructions.

It is highly likely that a list of purely innocent civilians who deserve our sympathy—babies, very young children, non-supporters of Hamas—would be a fraction of the inflated numbers uncritically and often provocatively regurgitated by the media.

US May Prevent Israel from Defeating Hamas

Secretary of Defense Austin recently issued the following warning to Israel: "You know, I learned a thing or two about urban warfare from my time fighting in Iraq and leading the campaign to defeat ISIS. Like Hamas, ISIS was deeply embedded in urban areas. And the international coalition against ISIS worked hard to protect civilians and create humanitarian corridors, even during the toughest battles. So the lesson is not that you *can* win in an urban warfare by protecting civilians. The lesson is that you can *only* win in urban warfare by protecting civilians. You see, in this kind of a fight, the center of gravity is the civilian population. And if you drive them into the arms of the enemy, you replace a tactical victory with a strategic defeat."

That ill-advised admonition reflects a basic misunderstanding of the relationship between Hamas and most Gazans. Recent polls show overwhelming support by Gazans not only for Hamas but also for its barbarities of October 7. The sad reality is that the civilian population of Gaza is already in the "arms of the enemy." They are part of the problem, not the solution.

The only way to get these "civilians" out of the arms of Hamas is to show them that atrocities committed by Hamas will hurt the civilians of Gaza as well as the terrorists of Hamas. This message is obviously not intended for infants and young children, who are completely innocent, but it does include most adults, men and women alike, many of whom not only cheer for Hamas but are complicit in their terrorism by allowing themselves to be used as human shields and their homes and mosques to be used as hiding places for weapons and commanders.

When the allies killed hundreds of thousands of German and Japanese civilians during World War II, this did not drive the surviving civilians into the arms of the enemy. To the contrary, the show of strength and the total victory of the allies drove most of them into the arms of the victors who promised them a better life—and delivered through Marshall Plan in Germany and the rebuilding of Japan. Not even the bombings of Hiroshima, Nagasaki, Tokyo, and Dresden drove the civilians into the arms of the military evildoers who provoked the allied response.

The lesson of the total war and unconditional surrender that ended World War II is far more relevant to Gaza than the experiences in Iraq. Moreover, Iraq was not a success for the United States. Many civilians were killed and much of Iraq is currently in the arms of Iran. Not exactly a model to be followed by Israel. So, Secretary Austen, well-meaning as he is, should be careful about the advice he offers.

Israel should continue to try to prevent civilian casualties while aggressively pursuing its legitimate military goals: the complete destruction of Hamas's ability to terrorize Israeli civilians, and the return of all the hostages. The world—and especially the US—should understand that when Hamas undertook the barbarous attack on Israel with the help, support, and approval of many Gazans, they sentenced their civilian population to disastrous consequences, just at the Germans and Japanese did when they started World War II. They then compounded these consequences by using civilians as human shields. The inevitable collateral consequences to civilians—especially young children—should be blamed on Hamas. Israeli soldiers should not be required to sacrifice their lives and to forgo an Israeli victory to protect the citizens of Gaza from self-inflicted wounds caused by Hamas. Moreover, the greatest beneficiaries of the total defeat of Hamas would be the civilians of

Gaza, even if they don't currently realize it. The same was true for the civilians of Germany and Japan.

Israel is doing more than any military in history to try to minimize the civilian casualties that are caused by Hamas. They should not be asked by the US to do more, if doing more would defeat their legitimate military goals. To sacrifice victory in order to placate the civilians of Gaza—or to reduce criticism of Israel from the biased international community, academia, or the media—would be wrong both morally and strategically.

How You Can Tell an Anti-Semite from an Anti-Zionist

From the beginning of political Zionism in the nineteenth century, there have always been anti-Zionists, even among Jews. Some were religiously opposed to the establishment of a Jewish state; others were politically opposed; still others were culturally opposed. There was Arab and Muslim opposition to any Jewish political entity in the region.

That was then. Since that time, the vast majority of decent people have supported the right of the Jewish people to self-determination, in the form of Israel as the legitimate nation state of the Jewish people. When Israel declared independence in 1948, it was recognized by all the major western nations including the United States and the Soviet Union. The left, both internationally and in the United States, strongly supported Israel and Zionism. Only the Arab and Muslim nations along with their allies opposed Zionism.

Everything changed when the Soviet Union, anxious to build relationships with oil-rich Arab dictatorships, turned against Israel. This change was accompanied by strong opposition to Israel and Zionism by Communist parties and their surrogates throughout the world.

Today there are anti-Zionists who favor a secular binational state—which almost no Israelis or Palestinians support. Some modern-day, hard-left, anti-Zionists hate Israel because of its close association with the United States, which they regard as the bastion of imperialism, colonialism, and capitalism. But the sad reality is that most anti-Zionists today are motivated by a hatred of the Jewish people—by a contemporary variation on classical antisemitism.

It is not always easy to distinguish anti-Zionists from anti-Semites, but there are some criteria that may be helpful.

The first is whether those who claim to be only anti-Zionists and not anti-Semites apply a single standard of demonization to countries other than the nation state of the Jewish people. Or do they single out only Israel? Do they protest the lack of statehood for the Kurds and the occupation of Kurdish land by Turkey, Syria, and Iraq? What about the Uyghurs in China? The mass killings of civilians in Darfur? The Russian invasion and murder of Ukrainian civilians? The many other occupations and denials of human rights around the world? If not, then why only Israel? Is it because it is the nation state of the Jewish people? The burden of justification is on the selective demonizers.

Related to the above is whether the demonizers also condemned Hamas for its mass murderers, rapes, and kidnappings of October 7, or only criticized Israel for its military reaction to the Hamas massacres. Organizations like the National Lawyers Guild condemned Israel and praised Hamas the day after the massacres, well before Israeli soldiers entered Gaza. Many student groups at Harvard and other elite universities blamed Israel for the murders, rapes, and kidnappings.

Another criterion is whether they call for the release of the Israeli hostages taken and held in violation of the laws of war. Many groups and individuals have demanded the release of all Hamas prisoners, including mass murderers, while remaining silent about or even justifying what Hamas has done including the kidnappings.

Then there is the explicit hatred of all Jews, in addition to all Israelis. Susan Sarandon, Alice Walker, and the late Bishop Desmond Tutu have been among the most prominent among these bigots but not the most outrageous. Sarandon called for Jews to be scared, while others called for them to be gassed. Still others have assaulted Jewish students, shouted down Zionist speakers, and engaged in violent demonstrations. They have called for Israel to be free of Jews from "the river to the sea," and for the world to be "cleansed" of all Jews.

There have been no calls for a two-state solution. To the contrary, nearly all the protests demand the end of Israel.

The bottom line is that it is impossible to understand the massive hatred shown against Israel since October 7 without pointing to the reality that Israel is the Jew among nations and has therefore become the focus of the current Jew hatred.

Some of the young people who have contributed to this hatred are probably unaware of the sordid history of anti-Semitism of which they have now become complicit. That is no excuse, but it may explain why so many uninformed Jewish students who know little or nothing about the complexities of the Middle East have become useful idiots and are caught up in the anti-Semitic frenzy that is spreading around the world.

University students have historically been on the forefront of many hate movements such as Nazism, Communism, and Islamism of the kind that brought the mullahs to power. Some have later regretted their involvement in such causes when their evils became manifest, but their early involvement gave credibility to these horrors. Many of the young woke progressives who support Hamas today deliberately blind themselves to the reality that this terrorist group also murders gays, feminists, and dissenters, and that those who support it have the blood of these murdered people on their hands. Those gays, feminists, and progressives who are aware of Hamas's widespread bigotry seem to hate Jews more than they support the groups with whom they identify.

Bigotry often starts against the Jews, but it rarely ends there. Those who today are joining the hatred against Jews and Zionists may soon become the targets of spreading hatred.

I'm an Identity "Doxxer"—And Proud of It!

The propriety of identifying by name the students and faculty who have signed anti-Semitic statements or engaged in anti-Semitic actions is currently being debated. Opponents of this practice call it "doxxing," as if that term ends the debate. But doxxing is a meaninglessly broad concept that must be deconstructed in order to give it any reasonable interpretation.

The condemnation of doxxers was first directed at those who published the home addresses and private telephone numbers of individuals with whose politics they disagreed. It occasionally included providing the names of children and the locations of their schools. Some doxxing involved disclosing the sexual preferences and other private information that were thought to be embarrassing. A few advocated violence against the disclosed individuals. But until the recent Israel-Hamas war, the accusation of doxxing has not generally been directed at those who have merely identified individuals who participated in anti-Semitic, anti-Israel, or other bigoted activities.

The debate thus far has been over whether any kind of doxxing is ever permissible. Indeed, efforts have been made to get universities to ban all doxxing, and some schools have created special offices to deal with the dangers of doxxing to students.

Yet certain doxxing is protected by the First Amendment. It would be unconstitutional for government-supported institutions to prevent the publication by some students (or the media) of information about other students. The Constitution cuts both ways on this issue. It protects the protests, while also protecting disclosure by the doxxers.

Beyond the constitutional issues are concerns about the ethical propriety of various kinds of doxxing. Little attention has been paid to the factors that might distinguish acceptable from unacceptable doxxing. Here are such some factors.

The nature of what is disclosed: Does it go beyond mere identification of the individuals and the organizations to which they belong? There is a considerable difference between disclosing the identity of protestors and providing private information, such as addresses, phone numbers, names of children, and sexual orientation. Though most such disclosure may be protected by the law, some deserve opprobrium.

A related distinction is between doxxing that poses a realistic threat of violence and those that endanger career prospects, such as university admission, jobs, or a political future. The case for not disclosing the former is more compelling than the case for not disclosing the latter.

A third factor might be the role of government in either compelling or prohibiting disclosure. During the Civil Rights movement some states compelled disclosure of the membership lists of organizations such as the NAACP. Now there are efforts by some to get the government to prohibit disclosure of the names of protestors. Others argue that the government should remain neutral: neither compelling nor prohibiting disclosure.

There are certain factors that should probably not be taken into account in deciding whether disclosure is ethically permissible. One such is the content of the advocacy. The same rule should apply to disclosing the names of neo-Nazis, sexists, and homophobes, on the one hand, as disclosure of the names of anti-Semites and anti-Zionists, on the other. The criteria should be content neutral. Yet some who would disclose the identity of the former seek to prevent disclosure of the latter.

Disclosure should not depend on the consequences to the person disclosed, except if it involves violence. Whether the disclosure will result in loss of job opportunities, rejections by universities, or even deportation should not generally determine whether disclosure is ethical. How the disclosure should be dealt with is up to other institutions. In a recent case, MIT refused to impose public discipline on students who violated the rules of the university for fear that they might be deported. That should not be the concern of those deciding whether to disclose.

Applying these criteria to the current situation, I believe it is appropriate to disclose the names of individuals who are active members of organizations that on October 8—before Israeli troops entered Gaza—praised Hamas or blamed Israel for the murders, beheadings, rapes, and kidnappings of civilians. It is also proper to disclose the names of students and faculty who are currently calling for the Middle East to be "free" of Israel and its Jewish population "from the river to the sea." I plan to continue to provide the names and organizational affiliations of such anti-Semites and bigots, just as I would disclose the names of members of the Ku Klux Klan or the Nazi party who praised lynchings, or harassed gays.

If the result of such disclosure is that some law firms or other businesses refuse to hire such bigots, so be it. Individuals, whether students or faculty, should be held accountable for their advocacy.

Pursuant to the marketplace of ideas, there should always be a presumption in favor of full disclosure of all relevant information, including names. This presumption can be overcome by a showing that individuals reasonably fear violence if identified. There is little evidence that anti-Israel students and faculty whose names have been disclosed have been subjected to physical threats. People should be safe from violence, but not from being held accountable for their ideas.

Some pro-Hamas protesters have themselves engaged in violence, threats, harassment, and the denial of free speech. While doing so, they often wear masks and other identity-hiding face coverings. I'm not suggesting that universities should be compelled to identify them, but rather that it is ethical for decent people to try to learn their identities by legitimate means, and to disclose them.

Such disclosure should apply to pro-Israel advocates as well. Their names and organizational affiliations should be made public, and they should bear any legitimate consequences of their advocacy, though all should be protected from physical violence, threats, or harassment. The open marketplace of ideas requires no less.

Woke Cowardice: Wrong University Presidents at the Wrong Time

The forced resignation of the president of the University of Pennsylvania is a good first step in dealing with a far more pervasive problem in higher education.

The three university presidents who disgraced themselves and their universities by their abysmal testimony before the US House Committee on Education and the Workforce represent a far larger concern.

In recent years, many universities have selected as their presidents woke, progressive cowards who pander to the most extreme and most vocal left-wing students and professors. They are the wrong people, at the wrong time, to be leading American educational institutions.

When I first came to Harvard in 1964, university presidents all came from the same cookie cutter. They were white Anglo-Saxon males, who represented the wealthy conservative donors and board members. There were no Jewish university presidents and the then-president of Harvard—Nathan Marsh Pusey—made it clear that no Jew need apply for the presidency or deanships.

Within a decade, following the civil rights movement, matters changed considerably. Several years ago, many of the most elite universities had Jewish presidents and Jewish deans.

Now matters have changed again and many of the new presidents represent the current political correctness reflected by the "diversity, equity, and inclusion" (DEI) bureaucracies. Many also represent, or are sympathetic to, woke progressive movements that today dominate many campuses.

As *Ecclesiastes* observed, "to everything there is a season." This seems to be the season for woke cowardice. Many of the current university presidents also seem to come from a cookie-cutter. They are different from previous university presidents but seem quite similar to each other in their pandering to the DEI and progressive woke constituencies on campus.

The recent spate of rabid anti-Semitism on so many campuses has posed enormous challenges to this new breed of university presidents. For the most part they have failed miserably to meet these challenges, as reflected by the big three who testified so ineptly.

A friend of mine, who was the president of a major university during the "Jewish period," told me that the one characteristic which is not a qualification for being a current university president is "courage." To that, should be added a commitment to principle.

Also at fault for the selection of current university presidents are the boards of directors who select them in an effort to pander to current student and faculty demands for DEI. They have ignored the majority of students and faculty, as well as the majority of alumni and donors. This overlooked and large constituency wants to see academic excellence and political neutrality on behalf of university presidents, deans, and administrators. Most would prefer what has come to be called "the Chicago principles," which require that the university itself stay out of politics.

Only a handful of universities have accepted these principles even in theory. Most universities pick and choose among the political views they publicly espouse. For example, virtually every university condemned the killing of George Floyd by a policeman—but many refused to condemn Hamas's October 7 murder of more than twelve hundred Israelis (and many Americans) and the kidnapping of more than 240 other Israelis. It is this double standard that has opened these administrators to criticism that they are more sensitive to Black lives than to

Jewish lives. They are also insensitive to civil liberties and the rights of those with whom they disagree.

Just as many of these new university presidents were selected for symbolism, so too should they be dismissed for symbolism. What they symbolized during the congressional testimony does a disservice to their students, their faculty, and their alumni. It teaches the wrong lessons to current and future students. It creates divisiveness on campuses that makes Jewish students and faculty fearful for their safety when their university president seems unwilling to apply the same standard to those who advocate genocide against Jews as they surely would against anyone who advocated genocide against Blacks or the raping of women or the shooting of gay and transgender people.

It is not enough that these presidents are constantly forced to apologize for their cowardice because of pressure from the outside. What these universities need now are principled advocates of a single standard, rather than leaders who base their decisions on outside pressures and the need to pander to extremist students, faculty, and administrators.

These are the wrong leaders for today's educational challenges. Those who selected them were employing the wrong criteria. It will not be easy to find the correct replacements who can strike the proper balance between responding to the pervasive anti-Semitism and "cancel culture" on current campuses. One thing is clear: they should be selected on the basis of relevant, individual meritocratic criteria—not the cookie-cutter criteria of the DEI bureaucracies.

Accusing Israel of "Genocide" Reflects, at Best, Ignorance of the Term's Meaning and, at Worst, Complicity with Hamas Terrorists

The latest in a long history of blood libels against the Jewish people is the recent lie that its nation-state is deliberately committing genocide against the civilians of Gaza.

The meaning of genocide is the intentional killing of a racial or ethnic group. The term was coined by a Polish-Jewish lawyer in 1944 to describe the Holocaust, which involved the deliberate murder of every Jew the Nazis could get their hands on.

Since that time, there have been genocides in Cambodia, Rwanda, Darfur, and other places.

Israel's military efforts to defend itself against a recurrence of the mass murders and kidnappings of October 7 do not even come close to constituting genocide or crimes against humanity. To the contrary, Israel has done more to protect the civilian population of Gaza than any country in the history of warfare.

This is especially so since it is Hamas that has caused the killing of so many civilians by using them as human shields, by stealing their food, medicine, and fuel, and by refusing to provide shelters for ordinary citizens.

On a broader perspective, the Muslim population of Gaza has expanded considerably since Israel's occupation that began in 1967 and ended in 2005. The only loss of population has been among Christian Arabs, many of whom have been forced to flee as a result of Islamic persecution.

Even after it ended its occupation, Israel has treated numerous sick Gazans and provided relatively high-paying jobs to thousands of Gazans. Hardly what a nation intending to commit genocide would do.

The United States did not commit genocide in Iraq or Afghanistan, despite the many thousands of civilians who became collateral damage during its wars against ISIS and Al Qaeda. Nor did other Western countries that have fought urban wars, such as France in Algeria and Great Britain in the Middle East.

Hamas knew that by crossing into Israel and murdering, raping, and kidnapping its civilians, it was signing a death warrant for many Gazan civilians whom Hamas intended to use as human shields.

The accusation of genocide against Israel is particularly malicious, since it was actual genocide against Jewish people by the Nazis that led to the coining of the term. In that respect, accusing Israel of genocide is a form of Holocaust denial.

Young people who hear the genocide libel against Israel and see that there are no gas chambers in Gaza may conclude that there were no gas chambers in Nazi-occupied Poland. And by equating legitimate self-defense measures with the building of gas chambers, these false accusers are diminishing the power of the term genocide.

There is no credible evidence that Israel has ever intentionally targeted innocent civilians in their legitimate efforts to kill Hamas commanders, destroy their tunnels, and disable their rockets. Why would they? They achieve no benefit from the death of innocent civilians. To the contrary, they are hurt in the court of public opinion.

It can be argued, of course, that Israel should try harder to reduce the ratio of civilians to terrorists killed. It has been estimated that approximately two civilians have been killed for every terrorist who has met his just fate.

It is impossible to know the exact figures, because the definition of a civilian is controversial in Gaza where many people from the age of fifteen onward actively facilitate Hamas terrorism. Also, many of those killed were the victims of errant rockets fired by terrorist groups from Gaza but landing near Gaza civilians.

Yet even if the ratio were ten civilians to one terrorist, as it has been for other countries fighting urban terrorism, that too would not constitute the crime of genocide.

Israel's efforts to minimize civilian casualties by sending ground troops instead of relying exclusively on aerial bombing—as they did at the beginning of the war—cost many lives among IDF soldiers.

Although Israel never deliberately kills civilians, those who use the term genocide against Israel are deliberately misusing that word as a political weapon. They know that Israel increased its control over the borders of Gaza only after Hamas took over and began to fire rockets and dig terror tunnels to kill Israeli civilians.

They know that Israel has no intention of intentionally wiping out the civilian population of Gaza. They know that the population has increased. They know that medical care and jobs have long been provided by Israel. And they know that Israel would never have entered Gaza if not for the brutal attacks of October 7.

The university students and others who falsely accuse Israel of genocide are complicit in Hamas's terrorism. They may not know the real facts, just as many of them have no idea about which river and which sea are referenced in the slogan "Free Palestine from the river to the sea." They may not know the definition of genocide or the history of the Holocaust.

The ignorance of many of these protesters and sloganeers is unbounded, but no one who has any sense of history can credibly claim that Israel is committing genocide. The truth is that the false accusation of genocide is yet another blood libel against the Jewish people.

The Hard Left Has Finally Discovered Free Speech

Some of the same hard leftists who have been on the forefront in denying free speech rights to those deemed politically incorrect have now begun to champion the First Amendment in defense of those who advocate the killing of Jews.

Among the worst offenders is Harvard's President Claudine Gay, who for years—both as dean of the faculty and as president of Harvard—has championed the idea that it is more important for students to feel safe, and not have their ideas challenged, than for free expression to be allowed on campus. The bureaucracy through which this notion operates is diversity, equity, and inclusion (DEI), which punishes microaggressions and other forms of speech that certain students claim makes them feel unsafe. The entire woke progressive movement rests on restricting expression that alienates or upsets protected minorities.

In her disastrous testimony in front of Congress, President Gay swore under oath that we at Harvard "embrace a commitment to free expression." If only that were so. For years now, Harvard has been suppressing expression deemed by some to be politically incorrect, as reflected by its last-place ranking[26] among American universities in protecting free speech by the Foundation for Individual Rights and Expression. Lectures have been canceled because of content some deemed offensive. Students have been reprimanded for microaggressions. Acceptances have been rescinded for allegedly racist or sexist speech engaged in by high school students. A former president—Lawrence Summers—was forced to resign over comments about women in engineering. An atmosphere of intimidation has permeated the campus. Freedom of expression was dying a slow death at the university, whose motto is "Veritas" but whose actions have suggested "Pravda."

---

26 Sean Stevens, "Harvard gets worst score ever in FIRE's College Free Speech Rankings," *Fire*, September 6, 2023, https://www.thefire.org/news/harvard-gets-worst-score-ever-fires-college-free-speech-rankings#:~:text=Last%20year%2C%20it%20ranked%20170,an%20%5C.

Then suddenly, following the barbarous Hamas attacks of October 7 and the flurry of antisemitic rhetoric immediately following them, the same groups that denied free speech to those who criticize minorities protected by DEI have discovered the First Amendment as a protection for those who are calling for the death of Jews.

"Free speech for me, but not for thee" has been the unspoken mantra of the hard Left. Or, more specifically, "freedom of speech to make Jews feel unsafe but not to make favored minorities uncomfortable."

There are two principled responses universities may take to this unequal application of freedom of expression. The first, and the one which I personally prefer, is to allow total free speech consistent with the First Amendment on all campuses. This would permit advocacy, but not incitement, against all and any groups. This pure and equal approach to the First Amendment is what the Supreme Court has demanded of the government in most circumstances. It allowed Nazis to march in Skokie, Illinois, and Communists to advocate the overthrow of the government. It does not allow direct and immediate incitement to violence. The line between advocacy and incitement has been a difficult one to draw since the Supreme Court mandated that distinction. But it is the law, in theory if not always in practice.

The First Amendment is not directly applicable to private universities and other non-governmental organizations. Universities remain free to impose speech codes and other limitations on free expression that they feel enhance the learning experience and the safety of students. Public universities have greater restrictions, but they too have some flexibility in adapting the First Amendment to the special needs of educational institutions.

If private universities, such as Harvard, MIT, and Penn decide not to adhere to the standards of the First Amendment and impose limitations on free speech, they should do so equally and without preference for some groups over others. Few universities, if any, satisfy that criteria. Most prefer certain minorities over others, as well as certain political views over others.

If Harvard had a history of applying a single standard, its president would have had an easy time answering the question of whether Harvard's rules prohibit the advocacy of genocide against the Jews. Here's what she would have been able to say: "Under the standards Harvard has applied in the past, there is no doubt that calling for genocide against the Jews is a clear violation of Harvard rules." But she refused to acknowledge the truth—that Harvard has not embraced "a commitment to free expression" equally for all of its students and faculty.

It can be hoped that perhaps the Harvard Corporation's decision to fire President Gay will actually result in a change in its policies toward free speech. Perhaps Harvard will finally "embrace a commitment to free expression" for all. This may be wishful thinking, especially in light of the continuing influence of the DEI bureaucracy over who can say what about whom, without fear of university reprisal. But it is the right thing to do.

Claudine Gay's Double Standard on Freedom of Speech Renders Her Unfit to Lead Harvard

Yet she is only part of a deeper problem at Harvard in particular and higher education in general.

When Claudine Gay was appointed president of Harvard, many of us expressed concern about her dismal record on civil liberties. As dean of the faculty, she was responsible for the firing—she called it non-rehiring—of Professor Ronald Sullivan, who had served, along with his wife as co-dean (it used to be called "master") of Winthrop House, until he agreed to represent disgraced mogul Harvey Weinstein.

Several students then said that Mr. Sullivan's role as co-dean made them feel unsafe. Despite the absurdity of the claim—Mr. Sullivan had previously represented a double murderer without complaint—Ms. Gay agreed that the students had a right to feel safe and decided not to reappoint Mr. Sullivan and his wife.

Ms. Gay said that he had failed to give a satisfactory explanation for his one-month-long representation of an accused rapist—as if representing an accused rapist requires any explanation other than the Sixth Amendment right to counsel. She also said he had failed in his "pastoral" role in making the students feel safe.

As dean she was also a supporter of the diversity, equity, and inclusion bureaucracies that are at the forefront of enforcing rules against so-called micro-aggressions and other violations of free expression. Students and faculty walked on eggshells to avoid offending protected groups, including Black and gay and transgender students.

It was no surprise to me that Harvard was ranked dead last among major universities in supporting free speech. It repeatedly placed concern for the feelings of certain students above concern for freedom of expression. The situation became so bad that a group of faculty banded together to establish the Harvard Council on Academic Freedom, which I joined.

Ms. Gay was not part of that effort to protect free speech. To the contrary, her appointment as president was an important stimulus to creating a group dedicated to the defense of free speech.

Then came the barbarisms of October 7, Israel's response, the proliferation of anti-Semitism, Ms. Gay's disastrous congressional testimony, and the near-universal criticism of it. Suddenly Gay discovered the First Amendment and freedom of speech.

Indeed, she became its champion, when it involved hate speech against Jews and their nation-state. Even macro-aggressions against Jews—like calls for the genocide of Jews—became a matter of "context." In the past, even the most trivial microaggressions did not require context. The diversity, equity, and inclusion bureaucracy saw to that.

It was this combination of lack of concern for free speech when it was directed against protected minorities and a sudden concern for free speech when directed against Jews that manifests a discriminatory double standard that angered so many students and alumni.

The time was ripe for her to step down. She has failed as a protector of students, as an education leader, and as a spokeswoman for Harvard. She has lost the faith of many alumni. She was the wrong person, at the wrong time, in the wrong job.

Yet she is only part of a deeper problem at Harvard in particular and higher education in general. The deeper problem is the systemic emphasis on race, gender, sexual preference, and identity politics and education. This emphasis is manifested by the diversity, equity, and inclusion bureaucracy, the proliferation of special identity departments and programs, as well as race-based affirmative action, which persists despite the Supreme Court decision outlawing it.

President Gay was the personification of these problems. Indeed, her appointment as president cannot be explained except by reference to these developments. She was appointed because she symbolized diversity, equity, and inclusion. Now she symbolizes its failure. She had to go if higher education is to be saved from the extremists who now dominate it.

Several hundred Harvard professors came to Ms. Gay's defense, arguing that the decision whether to fire her should not be based on pressure from alumni or politicians. Yet they have not addressed the compelling substantive reasons behind the widespread call for her termination.

Alumni and student views have always been taken into account as part of Harvard's decision-making processes. These views should be debated on their merits. In my view, the merits strongly favored the resignation of Ms. Gay because of what she has done and not done in imposing a double standard on Harvard's actions.

Dismantle, Discredit, and Utterly Destroy the Orwellian DEI Groupthink That Put Her There

University of Pennsylvania President Liz Magill and Harvard's President Claudine Gay have resigned because they articulated and enforced a double standard of free speech to the detriment of Jewish students.

"See no evil, hear no evil, speak no evil." How better to describe these university presidents?

America watched in disbelief as these three sat before a Congressional committee this week and declined to call for the disciplining of demonstrators on their campuses, who chant for the mass murder of Jews.

"I will ask you one more time," an exasperated Rep. Elise Stefanki told Harvard University President Claudine Gay in the hearing. "Does calling for the genocide of Jews violate Harvard's rules of bullying and harassment? Yes or no?" she asked.

"Antisemitic rhetoric when it crosses into conduct, that amounts to bullying, harassment, intimidation, that is actionable conduct, and we do take action," responded Gay in language suggesting authority but devoid of any real meaning.

"So the answer is yes?" pressed Stefanik. "That calling for the geno-cide of Jews violates Harvard Code of Conduct. Correct?"

"Again, it depends on the context," replied Gay.

"It does not depend on the context. The answer is yes," the con-gresswoman exploded, "and this is why you should resign."

I couldn't agree more. These university leaders failed a basic test of moral clarity when they couldn't bring themselves to uphold the same standard for Jewish students that they would for any other group on campus.

Am I—someone who first began teaching at Harvard sixty years ago—ashamed of the institution? Yes.

Am I surprised by this outrage? No, not in the least.

Magill, Gay, and Kornbluth are not leaders in education. They are politicians. Even when they talk the talk, they rarely walk the walk.

The job of a university president is to serve their constituents, raise money, and keep their campuses quiet. So, they coddle the loudest voices in the student body, the faculty and, of course, the donors.

When financier Ross Stevens threatened to withdraw his $100 million gift to the University of Pennsylvania if Magill was not fired, she stepped down. And now, bowing to similar pressure, after attempting to defend her testimony in a statement on Wednesday, President Gay has issued a full apology.

"I am sorry," Gay told *The Harvard Crimson* on Friday. "Words matter."

Well, too little, too late. These are not principled people.

Even before Tuesday's hearing, the US Department of Education launched an investigation into Harvard for allegedly failing to ade-quately respond to anti-Semitic harassment on campus. I would hap-pily offer the agency my testimony as to the institution's sordid record of discrimination. But the truth is that no firings or federal probe, while necessary, will be sufficient to restore fairness at Harvard.

What Gay, Magill, Kornbluth and their dozens of lawyers and advisers don't recognize is that campus anti-Semitism is the result of policies they still support.

In Rabbi David Wolpe's resignation from the university's Antisemitism Advisory Group on Thursday he wrote, "The system at Harvard along with the ideology that grips far too many of the students and faculty, the ideology that works only along axes of oppression and places Jews as oppressors and therefore intrinsically evil, is itself evil."

Rabbi Wolpe is correct. And this "evil" ideology goes by the acronym DEI—Diversity, Equity, and Inclusion.

In the aftermath of the appalling murder of George Floyd, Harvard, and so many American institutions, rushed to reckon with their histories. Hundreds of millions of dollars were spent hiring hard-left, woke, progressive bureaucrats steeped in the culture of identity politics. Some universities mandated that professors take loyalty oaths to DEI, attend compulsory sensitivity sessions, and actively censor opposing points of view.

We now see that the result was nothing short of Orwellian.

As for "diversity," there is little tolerance for speech that is critical of DEI, a sure sign of its intellectual weakness.

"Equity," as it turns out, is the opposite of equality, despite it being a similar sounding word. For while equality demands individuals be judged on their merit, "equity" only favors those that belong to select identity groups.

And perhaps most hypocritical and dangerous of all—this ideology of "inclusion," as Rabbi Wolpe observes, excludes Jews.

Never forget that Harvard admittedly failed to explicitly condemn Hamas or quickly denounce a student group letter that held Israel, "entirely responsible" for the October 7 terrorist massacre.

This is the DEI worldview. Today it looks down on Jews. Who will be next?

What is needed now is the courage to stand up to an evil ideology infecting our institutions.

The DEI bureaucracy must be dismantled, discredited, and utterly destroyed.

Harvard Crimson refuses to Publish Letter Critical of President Gay

Criticism of President Gay, especially about her double standard of free speech, is being stifled at Harvard, while it is increasing around the world. As an example, *The Harvard Crimson* has refused to publish a letter I wrote critical of President Gay's testimony in Congress. Here is the story: On December 12, the *Crimson* published an article by law professor Charles Fried providing a legalistic defense of her claim that those who call for genocide against Jews cannot be disciplined without considering "the context."[27]

Here is my response:

The problem with Charles Fried's defense of President Gay's "context matters" statement, is that he fails to acknowledge that for Gay context apparently matters only for genocidal threats against Jews. Context does not matter for micro-aggressions against Blacks, gays, and other minorities protected by the diversity, equity, inclusion bureaucracy that she has long championed.

Under the DEI regime, admissions have been withdrawn, lectures canceled, and students admonished—at Harvard, Penn, MIT, and other universities—for their speech—without regard to the context in which they were said.[28]

Fried fails to see the broader context of the double standard employed by so many universities—including Harvard—against Jews and other minorities that are excluded by DEI.

Yes, context matters, and in this broader context Gay was wrong to brag to Congress about Harvard's commitment to free expression, without also telling them that Harvard's selective application of free speech standards earned it a last place rating for free speech by

---

27 Charles Fried, "President Gay Was Right: Context Matters," *The Harvard Crimson*, Dec. 12, 2023, available at https://www.thecrimson.com/article/2023/12/12/fried -free-speech-context/.2

28 At Harvard, a lecture invitation was rescinded against a woman who said that there were only two genders and an acceptance rescinded for a high school student who made a racist comment.
    See Caroline Downey, "Feminist Philosopher Disinvited from Speaking at Harvard Over Trans Views," *National Review*, Apr. 25, 2022, available at https: //www.nationalreview.com/news/feminist-philosopher-disinvited-from-speaking -at-harvard-over-trans-views/; and Anya Kamenetz, "Harvard Rescinds Offer to Parkland Survivor After Discovery of Racist Comments," *NPR*, Jun. 18, 2019, available at https://www.npr.org/2019/06/18/733809263/harvard-rescinds-offer-to -parkland-survivor-after-discovery-of-racist-comments.

FIRE.[29] It is in that context that Gay's new and selective double standard for protecting the free speech of Jew haters should be evaluated.

It is to be hoped that Gay's new contextual standard will in the future be universally applied to *all* speech at Harvard, and that the DEI bureaucracy will henceforth be denied the power to censor and cancel expression that is directed against protected minorities.

Despite my forward-looking and positive conclusion, the chairperson of the editorial board wrote that "they are not interested in publishing it." I think this is the first time in my sixty-five years of writing letters to the editor that one has been turned down. And this one is from a professor who has been on the Harvard faculty for sixty years and has published numerous articles and letters in the *Crimson*.

It is a telling irony that the same editorial board that reassured its readers that "free speech is [its] guiding principle" refuses to publish a letter calling for less censorship and viewpoint discrimination on campus.[30] That seems to be reflective of Harvard's double-standard approach to free speech: contextual free speech for the enemies of Jews and their state; censorship for supporters of Israel and critics of Harvard.

By refusing to publish my short reply to Professor Fried, it was not my free speech that was denied. It was the right of *Crimson* readers to hear all sides of a controversial issue—because the *Crimson* decided to shut down the marketplace of ideas. When the media refuses to publish legitimate criticism of the institution it covers, the checks on the biases of that institution are weakened.

The marketplace of ideas should be open to all relevant voices—alumnae, students, potential students, dissenting faculty, and others.

Nor has the faculty served as an effective check. Many signed uncritical letters of support for President Gay, demanding that corporations

29 Sean Stevens, "Harvard Gets Worst Score in FIRE's College Free Speech Rankings," *FIRE*, Sep. 6, 2023, available at https://www.thefire.org/news/harvard-gets-worst-score-ever-fires-college-free-speech-rankings.

30 The Crimson Editorial Board, "Harvard and President Gay Must Not Yield," *The Harvard Crimson*, Dec. 12, 2023, available at https://www.thecrimson.com/article/2023/12/12/editorial-gay-harvard-partisan-attacks/.

ignore "outside forces," including alumnae contributors. But they did not respond to the substantive criticism of these contributors and others about the double standard being applied by President Gay to attacks on Jews.

In light of this pervasive double standard, it is not surprising that so many Jewish students feel that Harvard does not value and protect them.

In recent years, the *Crimson* has become the megaphone for anti-Israel and anti-Semitic extremism on campus.[31] It has also become the censor of pro-Israel and balanced views. Last year, for instance, the *Crimson's* editorial board called for the support of the BDS movement against Israel. In its editorial, the *Crimson* explicitly distanced itself from a 2002 editorial, which called divestment too blunt of a tool and the comparison to South Africa apartheid offensive. It wrote, "In the past, our board was skeptical of the movement (if not, generally speaking, of its goals), arguing that BDS as a whole did not 'get at the nuances and particularities of the Israel-Palestine conflict.' We regret and reject that view. It is our categorical imperative to side with and empower the vulnerable and oppressed."[32] It then goes on to paint a false picture that pro-Palestinian viewpoints are being suppressed on campus. The *Crimson* of today writes that, "We have a certain community-wide tendency to dismiss opposing views as inherently offensive and unworthy, straw-manning legitimate arguments and obfuscating difficult but necessary discussions. Yet civil discourse and debate, even when trying, are fundamental steps towards a better reality." Yet it does not seem to apply these standards when it comes to Jews.

Harvard students, faculty, and other readers should make their voices heard in the name of *veritas* and the open marketplace of ideas. Competing Harvard newspapers and media should be established to assure that all reasonable views can be heard. The *Crimson* is part of

---

31 The Crimson Editorial Board, "In Support of Boycott, Divest, Sanctions and a Free Palestine," *The Harvard Crimson*, Apr. 29, 2022, citing "Do Not Divest from Israel," May 8, 2002, available at https://www.thecrimson.com/article/2022/4/29/editorial-bds/; and https://www.thecrimson.com/article/2002/5/8/do-not-divest-from-israel-there/.

32 Ibid.

the problem of growing anti-Semitism at Harvard. It does not serve the Harvard community well in this time of deep divisions and hate.

The marketplace of ideas should be open to all relevant voices—alumnae, students, potential students, dissenting faculty, and others. The *Crimson* and faculty who support President Gay should not have a monopoly on opinions concerning such important issues.

Who Supports Hamas?

The main groups that comprise the bulk of organizers and demonstrators who have supported the Hamas barbarism against Israel are:

1. Radical Islamic groups that, like the Islamic Republic of Iran after the 1979 Revolution, regard Israel as the "Little Satan" and America as the "Big Satan."[33]
2. American revolutionary groups who used to be affiliated with Communism but now call themselves radical socialists or workers parties. Their goal is to overthrow our government, and they attach themselves to every disruptive movement in the hope of garnering support and creating distrust for American democracy.
3. Old-fashioned anti-Semites who hate anything associated with Jews and concoct conspiracy theories that blame "the Jews" for all evils.
4. Useful idiots who have little or no knowledge of the issues but march in lockstep with all "woke," "hard-left," and "anti-colonial" causes on the theory that "if it's left, it must be right."

Recall that these protests began *before* Israel counterattacked against Hamas. They were in full bloom on October 8,[34] even while the bodies of twelve hundred murdered Israelis, including babies burned alive, were still being gathered and counted, and the roughly 240 hostages

---

33 Ze'ev Maghen, "Eradicating the 'Little Satan'" *Wall Street Journal*, January 5, 2009, https://www.wsj.com/articles/SB123093176783149767.

34 Jason Beeferman, "NYC pro-Palestine rally splits Democrats over Israel," *Politico*, October 8, 2023, https://www.politico.com/news/2023/10/08/nyc-palestine-rally -democrats-israel-00120533.

taken by Hamas to Gaza identified.[35] These demonstrations were not against Israeli military actions in Gaza; they had not begun yet. More joined them after that.

The original responses to the Hamas barbarism in the hours and days following the morning of October 7 set the tone and began the organizational actions that followed. Many of the protests that now demand a unilateral ceasefire—including the attempts to shut down Christmas celebrations—are orchestrated by some of the same radical groups that organized the pro-Hamas demonstrations before Israel went into Gaza. Demonstrations and protests by groups such as the Students for Justice in Palestine, Jewish Voice for Peace, or the National Lawyers Guild seem anything but spontaneous[36] and grassroots responses to "Israel's military actions in Gaza." They are not demonstrations against what Israel does; they are protests against what Israel *is*, namely the democratic nation-state of the Jewish people.

To be sure, Israel's legitimate military efforts to destroy Hamas terrorists and the weapons that they have hidden among civilians, and the resulting civilian deaths, have allowed the anti-Israel organizers to recruit more useful idiots who believe they are protesting only against Israeli actions with the chant "from the river to the sea, Palestine will be free." Many of these undereducated and over-propagandized students have no idea what bodies of water they are referring to, or that this chant demands the end of Israel and any Jewish presence in the Middle East. The radical organizers, however, know exactly what that chant and others mean: a demand to "clean" the Middle East of "dirty Jews."

The larger point is that the well-organized and externally funded demonstrations are directed as much against the United States and its values as against Israel and its actions. Without the useful idiot students who join any protest they think is directed against the "colonial"

35 Cassandra Vinograd and Isabel Kershner, "Israel's Attackers Took About 240 Hostages. Here's What to Know About Them," *New York Times*, November 20, 2023, https://www.nytimes.com/article/israel-hostages-hamas-explained.html.

36 Cal Thomas, "We've seen this 'film' before," *The Tribune Democrat*, December 2, 2023, https://www.tribdem.com/news/editorials/columns/cal-thomas-we-ve-seen-this-film-before/article_e9e8a7f2-9062-11ee-9187-ef555d675176.html.

and "oppressor" targets of "intersectionality," these demonstrations would be relatively small and limited to long-term professional haters of Jews and America.

But these useful idiots make these well-funded and organized protests larger and allow the media to convey the false impression that they are spontaneous. The media insists on calling these protests "pro-Palestinian." Nothing could be further from the truth. When it sounds indelicate to say "pro-Hamas"—a terrorist organization—the signs change to "pro-Palestine." There is nothing to indicate how the Palestinians would actually be helped by the disappearance of Israel and leaving them, like the Iranian people, to the tender mercies of a corrupt, repressive state.

They had voted for Hamas in the first place because they hoped it would be better. Hamas had promised to be better. It was not. Even most of its leaders chose not to live in Gaza: they are now billionaires who, until October 7, had been hiding in five-star hotels in Qatar and Turkey. When they got word that Israel might hold them accountable, they reportedly dispersed.

Where are the calls for anything that would actually help the Palestinians or make their lives better: freedom of speech, equal justice under the law, freedom of the press, better job opportunities, and an end to government corruption and abuse?

The protests are exclusively anti-Israel, anti-American, pro-Hamas, and pro-terrorism. Many of the useful idiots join the protests to support a ceasefire, without realizing that a unilateral ceasefire now would constitute an invitation to Hamas to repeat their barbarism over and over again, as their leaders have promised they would do.[37]

Recall again that the protests against Israel began before there was any fire to cease—that is before Israel responded militarily to the Hamas barbarism. The ceasefire demand was added once Israel counterattacked, as a way to broaden the base of the protest. The radical anti-Israel protesters would not be satisfied with a ceasefire. They want

---

37 *Jerusalem Post* Staff, "'We will repeat October 7 again and again' - Hamas official," *Jerusalem Post*, November 1, 2023, https://www.jpost.com/arab-israeli-conflict /article-771199.

to see the destruction of Israel and the victory of Hamas. Indeed, a recent poll suggested that a majority of young Americans would like to see the end of Israel and its replacement by Hamas.[38]

Hamas, of course, would most likely not be satisfied with merely ending Israel. They want to end all non-Muslim democracies. Already Hamas has sent operatives to parts of Europe, where several were recently caught.[39] There are probably Hamas operatives in the United States, as well.

Most importantly, what if the useful idiots who now march for Hamas in favor of Israel's destruction become a fifth column in America and willingly join Hamas terrorists in targeting Jewish and other institutions in our nation. It was only a half-century ago that young Americans joined the Weather Underground and tried to blow up universities, military recruiting centers, and army bases. If Hamas is not defeated in the Middle East, it is coming to a theater near you.

So when you watch an anti-Israel demonstration on television, please understand who is behind it and what their ultimate goals are, because the next target is American democracy—and you.

Iran Declared War on the United States

Iran has now engaged in a deliberate act of war—*casus belli*—on numerous occasions against the United States. Most recently it was responsible for critically injuring an American soldier.

Since Hamas's October 7 attack on Israel, estimates run as high as one hundred Iranian-backed attacks across the Middle East on US bases, ships, and service personnel. Iran has acted through its surrogates and proxies, including the Houthis, Iraqi militia, Hezbollah, and others.

Under the laws of war, an act of war can be committed by the principal nation itself—which in this case is Iran, or surrogates acting on

---

38 TOI Staff, "Poll: Most young Americans think Israel should be 'ended and given to Hamas,'" *Times of Israel*, December 17, 2023, https://www.timesofisrael.com /poll-most-young-americans-back-ending-israel-many-find-jewish-genocide-calls-okay/.

39 Jessie Gretener et al., "Four suspected members of Hamas arrested in Europe over alleged terrorism plot," CNN, December 15, 2023, https://www.cnn.com/2023/12/14 /europe/hamas-suspects-arrested-terror-plot-europe-intl/index.html.

its behalf—with its approval or support. There can be no doubt, both as a matter of law and military reality, that recent attacks on American troops, including the one that seriously injured a soldier, are attributable to Iran.

Indeed, the United States has so declared and has responded in what it believes is a proportional manner. Critics of the Biden administration believe this response has been insufficient.

Proportionality in responding to military attacks by attacking the attacking nation's military, does not require proportionality.

Under international law, as long as the attacks are directed at military targets, the attacked nation may use overwhelming and disproportionate force in order to deter or punish the attacking army. International law also provides that the counterattack need not be directed specifically at those military targets that were involved in the initial attack. For example, the United States would be entitled to destroy Iran's potential nuclear arsenal in response to the attacks directed at American troops by Iran's proxies.

The question is not one of legality, or even of morality. Iran has essentially declared war on the United States, and the attacked country can respond as it sees fit against Iran's military or its surrogates. The question is purely one of strategy, tactics, and diplomacy. Most importantly, it involves the decision whether to widen the conflict that Iran began against the United States.

Long ago, Iran declared war against Israel, primarily through its surrogates. It helped arm Hamas, Hezbollah, and the Houthis—all of whom engaged in acts of war against Israel.

Israel is now engaged in an entirely justified all-out war with Hamas. Thus far Israel has chosen not to attack Iranian targets directly, except in a limited way against members of Iranian-backed militias in Syria and Lebanon. It has also targeted a leading Iranian commander. But Israel would now be entirely entitled to destroy Iran's nuclear weapons program which is directed against the nation-state of the Jewish people.

There is new reporting from sources close to Atomic Energy observers that Iran is now once again moving toward developing a nuclear arsenal, having allegedly slowed down the process in the recent past. In light of the recent failures of Israeli and American intelligence leading up to October 7, full faith cannot be placed on such reports. The United States and Israel must assume that unless it is stopped, Iran will soon—how soon is always a matter of degree—have a nuclear arsenal.

Imagine how much more dangerous the world will become if Iran could hand off dirty bombs, tactical devices, and other nuclear weapons to its terrorists, proxies, and surrogates. The worst must be assumed, and steps must be taken to prevent cataclysmic scenarios.

This is the right time to take such steps against Iran, because the mullahs have provoked the "big Satan" (the US) and "little Satan" (Israel). Both nations have been their intended targets.

The United States and Israel are now fully justified under the laws of war, and under all reasonable rules of morality, to begin planning a joint attack on Iran's nuclear capacity. Both nations, and especially Israel, have an existential need to prevent Iran from developing or acquiring a nuclear arsenal. It would be far wiser to act too early, as Israel may have done with Iraq, than too late, as we did with North Korea.

The ultimate goal of both American and Israeli foreign and military policy should be a regime change in Iran. The people of Iran want it, the world would benefit from it, and the United States and Israel would be safer if it could be accomplished.

We have tried other policies, such as negotiation, dealmaking, economic sanctions, and other forms of pressure. None have worked. Indeed, the failed American policies have both enriched and emboldened the mullahs. They understand and appreciate only superior force, which we have but are not using.

This may be our Munich moment.

In the run-up to World War II, Western allies, particularly Great Britain and France, sought to negotiate "peace in our time" with Nazi Germany in the hope of avoiding war. They failed, contributing to the deaths of tens of millions of people. Had the Western powers attacked Germany before it became strong enough to capture nearly all of Europe, many lives would have been lost in the beginning, but many more would have been saved in the end.

We must not allow these historical mistakes to be repeated, especially in the nuclear age. Iran must be stopped. It must be stopped now. And it can only be stopped by the United States and Israel acting together, if possible. If not, Israel will almost certainly have to act alone, because it cannot tolerate even the slightest possibility of a nuclear Iran.

October 7 taught Israelis about the consequences of miscalculation, weakness, and unpreparedness. The barbarism of that day was only a microcosm of what Israel—and ultimately the United States—could face if Iran and its proxies were allowed to obtain a nuclear arsenal.

How Grade Inflation Hurts Jews, Asians, and Other Disfavored Minorities

A recent study showed that grade inflation has become rampant at American universities. What used to be C+ has now become an A-, as more than three-fourths of students at elite universities get grades of A or A-.

This grade inflation is a direct result of the diversity, equity, and inclusion bureaucracies and their twin concept of intersectionality. Diversity, equity, and inclusion require that groups—rather than individuals—be treated "equitably," and that preferred groups be advantaged in hiring, admissions, and other benefits.

Jews and other disfavored minorities are thus discriminated against in grading. The only way individuals from disfavored groups can compete against favored groups is by achieving better grades. But if everyone gets the same A grades, the favored groups will get the job and admission benefits.

Grade inflation—which is more prevalent in the social sciences than in the hard sciences—also reflects the subjectivity and propagandistic nature of many of today's courses, in which all ideas are deemed equal (except conservative ones, which students are afraid to articulate.)

This is all part of the DEI attack on meritocracy. DEI demands that individuals be judged by the color of their skin and their identity rather than the content of their character—or their grades. Not that grades should always be determinative, but they are part of any fair meritocratic evaluation process.

Some schools have eliminated grades entirely in the name of equity. Others have achieved similar results by eliminating differences in grading: if everyone gets an A, no one gets an A. It's all part of "equity grading" instead of meritocracy grading.

Blind grading was introduced in many schools to eliminate bias. It worked for women who generally benefited from the blindfold, as they did from screened auditions by orchestras. But it didn't work for some preferred minorities. So DEI now demands that schools begin with the goal of achieving equity grading by any means, including non-blind grading, grade inflation, or grade abolition. Anything to undercut the equality of meritocratic blind grading that didn't achieve the particularistic identity goals of DEI.

Grading should be fair to all. It should eliminate cultural bias and other elements that subtly discriminate against certain groups. But the goal should be real equality, based on hard work, ability, and other relevant criteria, not a trophy for everyone who shows up. Indeed today, some students receive A's even if they don't show up!

The negative impact of equity grading is incalculable. It stifles learning, hard work, and creativity. It fails to prepare students for the competitive world they will inevitably face after they finish being coddled by universities. It threatens to destroy the competitive advantages American universities used to have.

Once some universities accept equity grading, others will be forced to follow, lest their students who are graded fairly suffer in comparison with students whose grades have been inflated by DEI. It's not as if students have gotten better. To the contrary, they have gotten worse. Only their grades have gotten better. That is a combination that assures failure of the educational mission of universities. But you wouldn't know that because the failure is covered up by artificially elevated grades.

It is said that philosophy is often autobiography, and it is true that ideologies are influenced by experience. That is certainly true of me. I am what I am because of tough, fair, grading. I was admitted to Yale Law School from Brooklyn College by the skin of my teeth. Many of my classmates were the scions of wealth and privilege. A Jewish kid from Brooklyn had no chance of completing with them except by working harder and getting better grades. Indeed, even after finishing first in my class, I was turned down by every Wall Street firm, but I was able to secure a Supreme Court clerkship and a Harvard appointment because I achieved a 3.7 average. Today that would put me smack in the middle of the class and without job prospects.

So grade inflation is not victim-free. It benefits some and hurts others. Among those it hurts the most are Jewish, Asian, and other students from groups that are excluded by the "inclusion" criteria of DEI. That amounts to discrimination based on ethnicity and religion. In public universities, that is unconstitutional. In private universities, that is simply wrong and immoral.

Equity grading also hurts those within the groups included by DEI who would have achieved high grades without the benefit of grade inflation. It may benefit some in the short term, but in the long-term, meritocracy is far better and much fairer to most students, than the artificial construct of group equity.

Harvard President Claudine Gay's Exit Is Just the First Step in Saving Our Universities

Over the last several years, many universities have changed their mission from objective, fact-based scholarship to "social justice." But it turns out social justice for some has resulted in social injustice for others. It has been a zero-sum game in which African Americans have benefited at the expense of Asian Americans, Jewish Americans, and other out-of-fashion minorities.

Indeed, the DEI bureaucracy has been a major source of, and stimulus for, the recent increase in antisemitism on campuses.[40] Central to the DEI ideology has been a phony academic construct called "intersectionality," under which the world is divided into oppressors and oppressed, based entirely on identity politics.

The oppressed can do no wrong, while the oppressors can do no right. White males, especially Jewish ones, are accused of being the primary oppressors. It is acceptable therefore to silence and marginalize

---

40 Melissa Koenig, "Feds probe complaints of antisemitism at six more universities, including Stanford and UCLA," *New York Post*, December 14, 2023, https://nypost.com/2023/12/14/news/education-department-investigating -antisemitism-at-six-more-colleges/.

them while giving loud voice to the oppressed. The power of these oppressors, DEI says, is enhanced by meritocracy.

Judging individuals by their hard work and accomplishments, according to the racist underpinnings of identity politics, guarantees the continued empowerment of the oppressors. So meritocracy must go, along with grades and other criteria of individual accomplishment.

Meritocracy must be replaced by equity, which evaluates individuals based on characteristics beyond their control, such as race and sexual identity.

The Harvard Corporation, which made the mistake of appointing President Gay in the first place, comprises largely DEI supporters, as do the boards of many other universities. But Gay's forced resignation demonstrates that these elite boards need not be given the final word.

Universities consist of more than the current faculty, student body, and boards. They are made up of large numbers of alumni as well as future students. And since universities represent our future leadership, the general, public also has a stake in who governs them. So the success of these "outsiders" in forcing Gay's resignation is an important first step in changing the ill-conceived direction in which many of today's universities are heading.

If the process ends with Gay's resignation, nothing much beyond symbolism will have been accomplished. But if it marks the beginning of a fundamental reconsideration of the university's mission, it will have accomplished much. The next, and more important, step must be the complete dismantling of the DEI bureaucracy.

The good news is most of these newly hired bureaucrats do not have tenure and do not have the qualifications to become professors. They can easily be fired, at the savings of hundreds of millions of dollars. The bad news is they have become a powerful force at many universities.

It will take courage and resolve to get rid of them, but it must be done. The DEI mindset must be replaced by the prioritization of meritocracy, broadly defined beyond mere grades but based on hard work and accomplishment. Grades, however, are an important component of any meritocracy, and they must be restored along with other methods of evaluation.

We must return to a time when we all shared Martin Luther King's dream of a society, as well as a university, where people are judged not by the color of their skin but by the content of their character.

The short presidency of Professor Gay may be a turning point in the history of American academia, but only if we take it to the next step and learn the appropriate lessons from her mistakes—and of those who appointed her.

Do Muslim Lives Matter When Killed by Muslims?

When was the last time you saw on TV or in the newspapers a picture of a dead Muslim baby who had been killed by a Muslim? The media simply doesn't show dead Muslim babies killed by Muslims. Is that because there are so few? No! The number of Muslim babies, women, and other civilians killed by fellow Muslims is many times greater than the number of Muslims killed by Israel. But every Muslim whose death can be blamed—either rightly or wrongly—on Israel is displayed by Hamas to the willing media to broadcast these images around the world.

The only exception of which I am aware was when Hamas falsely blamed Israel for the bombing of a parking lot adjacent to a Gaza hospital.[41] The media showed dead Palestinian babies and blamed their deaths on Israel. When it became clear that a misfired Islamic Jihad rocket was to blame, much of the media lost interest—except some Arab media that continued to blame Israel.

We really have no idea how many Muslims have been killed by Israel in Gaza. The Hamas-controlled health bureaucracy issues questionable numbers that don't even purport to distinguish between civilians and combatants. Hypothetically, a majority of the 22,000 allegedly killed Palestinians may have been terrorists.[42]

---

41   "Gaza: Findings on October 17 al-Ahli Hospital Explosion," Human Rights Watch, November 26, 2023, https://www.hrw.org/news/2023/11/26/gaza-findings-october -17-al-ahli-hospital-explosion.

42   Alexander Smith, "As death toll mounts in Gaza, veterans of past negotiations weigh in on possibilities for peace," NBC News, December 31, 2023, https://www.nbcnews.com /news/world/israel-hamas-war-gaza-death-toll-peace-negotiations-veterans -rcna131271.

Hamas does list "children" separately, but does not list their ages. We know however that Hamas considers any person under the age of nineteen to be a "child," even though it actively recruits "children" above the age of twelve or thirteen to become terrorists. So at least some of the "children" who have been killed were active combatants, not civilians.

The same is true of women. Hamas always identifies the dead by gender, as if to suggest that a twenty-five-year-old woman firing a rocket or becoming a suicide bomber must be counted as a civilian.

Now compare the distorted and incomplete Hamas figures to what is known about Muslims who have been killed by Muslims in recent conflicts.

In Yemen alone, some 350,000 deaths[43] have occurred during the civil war started by Iranian proxies. Many of them have been civilians, including almost certainly thousands of babies. But you've never seen any pictures of bleeding Yemeni babies killed by other Yemenis, even though the war has been covered by many media outlets.

The same is true in Darfur where figures range upward of ten thousand dead and many more injured.[44]

In addition, as many as six hundred thousand people have been killed in Syria,[45] including many Palestinian babies and women. Again, no pictures.

If one goes back several decades to what has come to be known as Black September,[46] the Jordanian army killed thousands of Palestinians including many civilians. But their 1970 deaths went largely unphotographed.

---

43 "Yemen war deaths will reach 377,000 by end of the year: UN," Al Jazeera, November 23, 2021, https://www.aljazeera.com/news/2021/11/23/un-yemen-recovery-possible-in-one-generation-if-war-stops-now.

44 Ingrid Formanek, Kareem El Damanhoury, and Sana Noor Haq, "10,000 reported killed in one West Darfur city, as ethnic violence ravages Sudanese region," CNN, July 26, 2023, https://www.cnn.com/2023/07/26/africa/sudan-west-darfur-thousands-killed-intl/index.html.

45 Center for Preventive Action, "Conflict in Syria," Global Conflict Tracker, updated October 17, 2023, https://www.cfr.org/global-conflict-tracker/conflict/conflict-syria.

46 Bruce Riedel, "Fifty Years after 'Black September' in Jordan," *Studies in Intelligence* Vol. 64, No. 2 (June 2020), https://www.cia.gov/static/Black-September-Jordan.pdf.

Today's media has been feasting on pictures of bleeding and dead Palestinian babies, killed and wounded in Gaza. They report Hamas-generated figures without indicating what the comparable figures were when Muslims have been killed and wounded by Muslims in neighboring areas. Statistical comparisons are not as evocative as graphic pictures. But pictures without explanation hide the truth. If it bleeds, it leads—but if it leads, it often distorts reality.

Does a dead Muslim baby matter less if she was killed by a Muslim than by a Jew? Of course not, except to those who would use the deaths of innocent babies as propaganda tools against Israel.

Without making any comparisons, the media also applies a double standard when it comes to the deaths of African Americans in the United States. When George Floyd—a single Black man with a long history of criminality—was brutally killed by a white policeman, that murder became one of the most important stories of the twenty-first century. It resulted in a racial "reckoning," that included major changes in American universities, corporations, and the media itself.

Floyd's life and death mattered, as it should have. But what about the thousands of Black children who are killed every year by Black gang members? Why do their lives seem to matter less to the media—and even to some Black leaders—than the lives of Floyd and the relatively small number of African Americans who are killed every year by white police?

It has become a micro-aggression on some quarters to say that "all lives matter," but no one should be faulted for saying that all Black lives matter, regardless of whether they are taken by the actions of white police or Black gang members.

The same is true of Muslim lives: a Muslim life is no more valuable if taken by an Israeli rocket than by a Muslim rocket. But the media doesn't see it that way.

The International Court of "Injustice" Begins Its Blood Libel Trial against Israel

The blood libel accusation against Israel has now begun in The Hague. The failed nation of South Africa has brought genocide charges against Israel in the International Court of Justice.

What is the International Court of Justice? It is not international, because it excludes judges from certain countries. It is not a real court, because the judges are selected by their countries and many of them simply follow the instructions of those who appointed them. And it has never done justice, because it has long been biased against Israel. It is the United Nations court, and that tells you all you need to know about it. The United Nations has become the megaphone of bigotry and anti-Semitism. As an Israeli diplomat once put it, if Algeria introduced a resolution that the earth is flat and that Israel flattened it, it would win 120 to 27 with 32 abstentions. And you can name the countries in each of the groups before any evidence is presented.

Both the United Nations and its court are shams, especially when it comes to Israel. The facts are clear: Israel has not committed genocide, nor has it violated international law as it defended itself from Hamas barbarity. It is the Hamas charter that calls for genocide against the Jews of Israel, and it is South Africa that is harboring Hamas terrorists and defending its murders and rapes. It should be Hamas that is on trial for attempted genocide and South Africa that is on trial for complicity with Hamas. Instead, the nation-state of the Jewish people is being accused of a blood libel, despite going to great lengths to avoid civilian casualties in its legitimate efforts to destroy Hamas.

There have been too many civilian casualties in Gaza, although no one has any idea how many of the dead and wounded were actually civilians, as distinguished from terrorists and those who assist them. The civilian casualties are the fault of Hamas, first for starting the war by murdering Israeli civilians, and second by hiding their military assets among civilians in an effort to use them as human shields. Hamas apparently even shot at its own citizens to keep them from fleeing to southern Gaza for safety as the Israelis had urged them to.[47]

The evidence is indisputable that Hamas has committed numerous war crimes. First, it attacked Israeli civilians attending a music festival and living in peace. Second, it ordered its terrorists to rape and

---

47 Emanuel Fabian, "IDF releases recording of Gazan saying Hamas shooting at people trying to flee south," *Times of Israel*, October 26, 2023, https://www.timesofisrael .com/liveblog_entry/idf-releases-recording-of-gazan-saying-hamas-shooting-at-people -trying-to-flee-south/.

sexually assault its victims, thus weaponizing sexual assault during wartime. Third, it has fired thousands of rockets at Israeli civilian targets. Fourth, it has built tunnels with exits near Israeli civilian areas, whose purpose it is to murder and kidnap civilians. Fifth, it has deliberately placed its rocket launchers and command centers in civilian areas, in order to induce Israel to cause collateral damage among civilians. Sixth, it has used children and even babies as human shields to prevent Israel from rescuing its hostages. Seventh, it has taken over hospitals, schools, mosques, and other civilian resources and turned them into military assets. Eighth, it has recruited thirteen- and fourteen-year-old boys and girls to become terrorists. Ninth, it has coerced women into becoming suicide bombers targeting Israeli civilians. Tenth, it arranged for civilian workers from Gaza to get jobs in Israel in order to provide them information they used to murder Israeli civilians.

Hamas has praised South Africa for doing its dirty work and bringing the blood libel claim against Israel. Since the death of Nelson Mandela, South Africa has gone downhill as a nation. It has become a corrupt kleptocracy with spiraling crime rates and massive inequality. Both white and Black South Africans are leaving the failed nation in droves. In order to divert attention from its failures toward its own people, it has done what so many anti-Semites have done over the years: it has used Israel and the Jews as scapegoats to deflect attention away from its own failures.

The crime of genocide requires an intent to destroy an entire people, based on ethnicity, race, or religion. It also requires actions, calculated to achieve that goal. Israel has done exactly the opposite in relation to the Arabs and Muslims of Gaza. It ended the occupation in 2005, leaving behind farming equipment and other material resources that could have been used to turn Gaza into Singapore on the Mediterranean. It has provided medical services to Gazans in need of Israel's exceptional resources. It has provided employment for thousands of Gazans with good pay. The end result is that the population of the Gaza Strip has increased dramatically over the years during which Israel has been accused of genocide. These are not the indicia of genocide. What Israel has done has been based on one consideration alone: namely the need to protect its own civilians from efforts by Hamas to conduct genocide against its Jewish civilians.

The very term "genocide" was coined to describe the Nazis' largely successful effort to end the entire Jewish presence in Europe, by the use of gas chambers, shooting pits, and other industrial mechanisms of mass murder. To turn that important word into a weapon against the descendants of the Jews who survived the Nazi genocide is to distort history, morality, and basic decency.

Were the International Court of Justice to falsely conclude that Israel was guilty of genocide, it would destroy whatever remaining credibility that court might have. If that were to happen, the United States and some other nations should and probably would leave the court: it would not deserve the legitimacy afforded by membership of any decent country.

Israel Has Committed No War Crimes—Hamas Has

Critics of Israel have charged the Jewish state with committing atrocities and even "genocide" in its ongoing war with Hamas. The South African government has even brought these charges before the International Court of Justice. The accusations are without merit: Israel has committed no war crimes in seeking to degrade and destroy Hamas in Gaza. Hamas, by contrast, has committed at least four categories of war crimes.

First, Hamas waged an aggressive war against Israel, crossing its border and murdering, raping, and kidnapping civilians. Second, it has targeted civilians with its rockets. Third, it has dressed its terrorists in civilian clothing, thus eliminating the important distinction between combatants and civilians. And fourth, it has used its own civilians as human shields.

Unlike Hamas, which began this war, Israel has acted in self-defense. Under international law it has the right and obligation to defend its citizens by all reasonable and lawful means.

In doing so, the Israel Defense Forces have made extraordinary efforts to target only combatants. Notwithstanding these efforts, Palestinian civilians have been killed, largely because Hamas has deliberately embedded its war machinery among civilians to produce dead bodies to display to the media.

Hamas-controlled health authorities have claimed about twenty-two thousand Palestinians have been killed thus far. But they haven't distinguished between combatants and civilians. Israel claims to have killed approximately seven thousand combatants. Hamas claims that many of those killed were children and women. But they haven't revealed the ages of the dead children, whom the terror group defines as anyone under nineteen. Hamas actively recruits terrorists from the age of thirteen. This brutal strategy, itself a war crime, raises discomfiting questions about Hamas's fatality claims: An eighteen-year-old with an RPG or an assault weapon is as much a combatant as a thirty-year-old.

The same is true of women. Hamas regards women as incapable of performing many roles, but one role many are recruited to perform is that of terrorist and combatant. And so it can't be assumed that all of the women who have been killed were civilians.

Then there are those who have been killed by "friendly fire"—including misfired rockets and bullets fired by Hamas against Palestinians who were trying to flee to safe areas.

Although it is impossible to know for certain how many actually innocent civilians have been killed, the number is certainly far lower than estimates put forward by Hamas and its supporters. Even if it is as high as fourteen thousand, that would produce a ratio of civilians to combatants killed of roughly two-to-one—that is, for every combatant killed, two civilians would have been killed.

If this ratio is close to being true, then Israel's record is far better than that of any other country in the history of modern urban warfare facing comparable enemies and tactics. Typical ratios of civilian to combatant deaths range from three-to-one to ten-to-one, as in the cases of Afghanistan, Iraq, Yemen, and Syria. And those ratios occur in situations where civilians aren't used as human shields.

This brings us to the law of war. The only requirement of proportionality under international law is that when combatants are targeted in areas where civilians are present, the value of the military target must be proportional to the number of anticipated civilian deaths. This highly subjective judgment can't be the basis of a war-crime prosecution, unless the judgment is utterly unreasonable. The two-to-one ratio is not only reasonable, but far better than that achieved by other armed forces facing comparable situations. Thus, were Israel to be prosecuted for violating the principle of proportionality, that would necessarily involve the application of a double standard against the Jewish state.

The charge of genocide made by South Africa is even less persuasive. Real genocides have taken place in the world today, especially in Africa. South Africa has been silent about these neighboring genocides. And it is weakening the term itself by selectively politicizing it against Israel. Gaza has grown in population during the period in which genocide is charged. Israel has provided health care to Gazans in need of Israeli hospitals. It provided high-paying jobs in Israel to thousands of Gazans. These aren't the actions of a nation engaged in genocide.

Genocide is directed against an entire people, not just criminals and terrorists among them. To accuse Israel of genocide is to fail to distinguish between the legitimate military goal of ending a terrorist organization, such as Hamas, and the illegitimate goal of ending the existence of an entire ethnic or religious group.

The term genocide was coined to describe the Nazi effort to rid the world of all Jews. Accusing Israel of genocide is a form of Holocaust denial, since no one even suggests that Israel has extermination camps, gas chambers, or other mechanisms that exemplified the Holocaust. If Israel were to be found guilty of genocide, the very meaning of that horrible crime would be diluted beyond recognition. It would then apply to the US bombing of Hiroshima, the British bombing of Dresden, and the killing of civilians during the Afghan, Iraqi, and Syrian military actions.

Every civilian death in wartime is a tragedy, and Hamas knew it was signing the death warrants of many civilians when it attacked Israel and then hid its war machinery among Gaza's civilian population. The death of a human shield is the legal and moral responsibility of those who deliberately placed civilians in harm's way. Consider the following example: A bank robber starts shooting at customers. When the police arrive, the robber grabs one of the customers and uses her as a human shield. A policeman, in an effort to save the lives of customers, tries to shoot the robber. But the hostage suddenly makes a move, and then the policeman's bullet hits and kills her. Under the law of every nation, it is the hostage taker, not the policeman who is guilty of killing the hostage, even though the bullet that killed her came from the policeman's gun.

It is Hamas and its Iranian patrons that should be on trial, not the victims of Hamas barbarism.

Critics Deploy a Double Standard against Israel in Its Struggle against Hamas

Everyone in the world seems to have an opinion about how Israel should protect itself against future attacks from Hamas. And no matter what Israel does, there are those who will criticize its every action.

When Israel conducted an air war, critics told it to send in ground troops. When the ground troops began to destroy the Hamas military, critics told it to use targeted assassinations against its leaders.

When Israel succeeded in killing some terrorist leaders, the critics doubled down. For some, Israel can do no right, regardless of the provocation. For others, Hamas can do no wrong as long as it is targeting Israelis.

Even the *New York Times* now concedes that Hamas has built its underground military tunnels beneath hospitals, schools, mosques, and other civilian buildings, but when Israel attacks these military targets the critics come out in full force.

The reality is that Hamas and its supporters have placed Israel in an impossible position. It cannot protect its own citizens without endangering the lives of some Gazan civilians that Hamas has deliberately placed in harm's way.

The number of such civilian deaths has actually gone down dramatically in recent days, as Israel has shifted its military tactics and priorities, while the protests against Israel and its supporters have increased.

Most recently, pro-Hamas demonstrators have protested in front of cancer hospitals and Jewish institutions. They have blocked access to bridges, transportation hubs, and streets. They continue to harass people and shout down opposing views. The protesters claim that they are demanding only a ceasefire, but that is patently untrue.

What they really want is to see Israel defeated militarily and Hamas strengthened. Recall that the demonstrations began even before Israel responded militarily to the slaughter and rapes of October 7.

Many of the demonstrators defended these barbarities and blamed them on Israel. They understand that a ceasefire now would constitute a military victory for Hamas and an invitation to repeat its barbaric attacks.

Even now, Hamas rockets are targeting Israeli civilian areas, including cities with their civilian populations. Israel must respond aggressively, as any country would do if faced with comparable threats.

Israel cannot allow the Hamas strategy of inducing civilian deaths by using human shields to endanger its own civilians and soldiers. And it must not be deterred from completing its legitimate military mission by double-standard protests that are designed to deny it the military success to which it is entitled as a matter of law and morality.

The double standard being deployed against Israel is apparent for all to see. There have been no comparable demands for ceasefires, or even for reduction of inevitable civilian casualties, during other comparable wars.

The pro-Hamas protesters are not seeking justice. They are seeking victory for Hamas and defeat for Israel. They are not demanding a two-state solution. They are not even asking for the release of the remaining hostages. Their demand is for a unilateral ceasefire, only by Israel, while Hamas continues to rain rockets and hold hostages.

No one would be fooled by the size and signage of these well-organized and well-funded demonstrations. Their ultimate goal has little to do with the Middle East. The real enemy is the United States, and the real goal is destabilizing our nation. Israel is the immediate focus because of its close alliance with the big devil.

In a recent demonstration, applause broke out when it was announced that an area close to the American embassy had been bombed by Iran. That should surprise no one. Many of the demonstrators support Iran because its enemies are America and Israel.

For the sake of peace in the Middle East and the reduction of civilian deaths in the long run, Israel must be allowed to complete its just mission to destroy the military capabilities of Hamas. So please stop telling Israel how to go about doing what it must do.

Israel, as a vibrant democracy, has enough internal critics who have direct stakes in the outcome of this existential battle. It also has a high sense of morality and legality. It is entirely permissible for outsiders to advise, but not to demand of Israel what no one has ever demanded of other nations facing comparable dangers.

The Civilian Death in Gaza Is Relatively Low

You wouldn't know it from current protests against Israel, but the death toll among civilians in Gaza—even including children and women—is among the lowest in the history of comparable warfare. It has become even lower over the past several months.

According to the *New York Times*, "The number of Gazans dying each day has fallen almost in half since early December,"[48] and it has fallen almost two-thirds since late October. Moreover, the percentage of civilian to combatant causalities has gone down considerably.

In a massive understatement, the *Times* has also reported that these considerable reductions in civilian deaths have been "somewhat overlooked" by the media and critics. "Somewhat"! It has been totally ignored and buried. The *Times* has also opined that Israel's "harshest critics are wrong to accuse it of wanting to maximize civilian deaths."[49]

It is no accident that this reduced civilian death toll has been "somewhat overlooked" by the media and by Israel's critics, including previously by the *New York Times* itself. Israel is subject to a discernible double standard when it comes to its military actions.

Even before the recent dramatic reduction in civilian deaths, Israel's military actions produced far fewer deaths and a far lower ratio of civilian to combatant deaths than in any comparable urban warfare. This is especially significant considering the reality that Hamas deliberately increases civilian deaths by using women and children as human shields and by hiding its military personnel and equipment among

---

48 David Leonhardt, "The Decline of Deaths in Gaza," *New York Times*, January 22, 2024, https://www.nytimes.com/2024/01/22/briefing/israel-gaza-war-death-toll.html.

49 Ibid.

civilians. The current ratio of civilian to combatant is well below two-to-one, which compares very favorably with ratios achieved by other Western democracies in urban warfare.

Critics of Israel almost never cite comparable data from other military encounters. This creates the false impression that the civilian death tolls in Gaza are among the highest in history, when they are in fact among the lowest.

Every actual death of an innocent civilian—especially among babies and very young children—is a tragedy. It is these deaths that are always highlighted by Hamas to the media, but no one knows how many such deaths are actually among this most vulnerable segment of the population, and how many of those are the result of Hamas deliberately using young children as shields.

The Hamas figures for total deaths do not purport to distinguish combatant from what they consider civilian deaths. Nor do they give the ages of the "children" they claim have been killed, though they regard anyone under the age of nineteen as a child, even if they are active combatants who have recruited as fighters from thirteen to nineteen years old. Nor do they count the Gazans who were killed by errant rockets misfired by terrorist launchers, or who were killed by Hamas for refusing its orders not to move to safer locations.

The *Times'* conclusion that the new data suggests that it is "wrong to accuse [Israel] of wanting to maximize civilian deaths"[50] is highly reliant on the false charges of genocide that are being considered by the International Court of Justice.

Nations engaged in genocide do not go to such great lengths in trying to reduce civilian casualties, including placing its own soldiers at heightened risk by employing focused ground forces instead of relying exclusively on air and sea bombardments. The ICJ should immediately reject the genocide charges against Israel and initiate war crime charges against Hamas and Iran, both of which try to increase civilian deaths.

The decreasing civilian death rate among Gazans should also end the campaign to impose a ceasefire on Israel before the IDF completes its legitimate mission to destroy Hamas's military capacity. Successfully

50 Ibid.

completing that mission will save civilian lives in the long run, by reducing Hamas's capacity to keep its promise of repeating the barbarism of October 7 and also by reducing its use of civilian shields.

Israel's conduct in its defensive war started by Hamas has been exemplary. It satisfies all international standards, and its effort to minimize civilian deaths while accomplishing its legitimate goals have generally been successful. There is always a tradeoff between reducing enemy civilian deaths and increasing risks to its own soldiers and civilians. Israel has struck a better balance than most following the unprecedented Hamas barbarisms.

The time has come, indeed it is long overdue, for the world to stop imposing a double standard on the nation-state of the Jewish people. Double standards are a form of bigotry, and when bigotry is addressed to the only nation-state of the Jewish people, it becomes a form of international anti-Semitism against the Jew among nations. It must stop.

This ICJ Compromise Means Israel Will Continue Its Honorable Quest for Justice

Reading the decision of the International Court of Justice in the genocide case brought by South Africa against Israel is like listening to a self-righteous lecture by a law professor written in her ivory tower. Judge Joan Donoghue did the right thing by refusing to enjoin Israel from conducting its military operation against Hamas. Even if the injunction had been issued, Israel would have justifiably ignored it. But the court gave Israel a yellow light to proceed, requiring it to report back in a month on its efforts to prevent its soldiers from committing genocide.

But Israel's soldiers were not committing genocide. They were fighting in the same way that the United States and Great Britain fought urban warfare against terrorist groups. Israeli soldiers, who are among the most moral in the world, do not need to be lectured about not doing something they would never do.

A nation bent on genocide does not put its soldiers at risk by warning the other side about its intended military targets. Nor does it provide humanitarian corridors for the provision of food, medicine, and other necessities of life. The reason there are so many civilian casualties in Gaza is that Hamas deliberately places its own civilians in harm's way by using them as human shields. Notwithstanding newspaper headlines, there have been fewer civilian deaths in Gaza, and a lower ratio of civilian to combatant causalities, than in any modern war in history.

An international community that remained relatively silent in the face of real genocides has no standing to lecture the nation whose people suffered from the worst genocide in world history. Israel should continue to do what it is now doing: attacking Hamas targets, killing Hamas leaders, destroying Hamas tunnels, preventing Hamas rockets from striking Israeli civilians, and winning the war against terrorism. It is Hamas who should be lectured about its multiple war crimes: using hospitals, schools, and mosques to protect its fighters, rockets, and tunnels. But the ICJ did not order Hamas to do or stop doing anything.

The ICJ's decision was written by one of its real judges—an independent jurist who does not take orders from the nation that appointed her. Other judges on the court are simply pawns in their countries' foreign policy. It's surprising therefore that this compromise decision, despite its lecturing tone, was rendered by a court that includes a Hezbollah-appointed judge from Lebanon.

Previous decisions on the court have been entirely political and deserving of no respect. This decision deserves the respect of a thoughtful law review article written by a distinguished professor of international law, but because of the makeup of the so-called court, it does not deserve the respect accorded independent judicial authorities.

Wearing robes does not turn politicians and diplomats into judges. To be a real judge, a lawyer must be completely independent of the government that appointed her or him. The ICJ can never be a real court, as long as the appointment and removal process of its judges remain in the hands of individual countries. The International Criminal Court is somewhat better in this regard, because its judges are not answerable—at least in theory—to their countries of origin. But in practice, many of its judges are in fact beholden to their countries.

International law, and especially the law of war, is largely an academic enterprise. Enforced mechanisms are entirely political and not deserving of the respect accorded real judges.

So let Israel continue in its honorable quest for justice regarding the past atrocities committed by Hamas and the prevention of future atrocities promised by Hamas leaders. When Israel next reports to the court in thirty days, hopefully the war will be winding down and fewer civilians will be killed. Already the number of civilian deaths has decreased dramatically, but the best way to reduce any further would be for the international community to enforce international law that prohibits the use by Hamas of human shields. Unless the ICJ addresses the Hamas war crimes, it will deserve no respect.

The Anti-Israel Bigotry of Many Black Pastors

A large coalition of Black pastors—more than one thousand who minister to hundreds of thousands of parishioners—are protesting President Biden's support for Israel and threatening him with the loss of Black voters in the upcoming election unless he changes course. They see the Palestinians—but not the Israelis—"as part of us," because they are "oppressed people" and "we are oppressed people."[51]

In making this stretched comparison between a foreign population, a majority of whom support Hamas terrorism, and Americans who rely on legal means to combat oppression, these pastors are echoing the dubious mantra of what has come to be known as "intersectionalism." This radical academic construct divides the world into the oppressed and the oppressors. The oppressors can do no right, while the oppressed can do no wrong. As one of the pastors put it: "Black clergy have seen wars, militarism, poverty, and racism all connected."[52]

Under this benighted view, the Israelis, surrounded by hundreds of millions of enemies, are the oppressors, while the Palestinians— supported by most of the Muslim world, the UN, Russia, China, and much of the rest of the international community— are the oppressed.

Even if that view were plausible, which it is not, these pastors have applied an invidious and discriminatory double standard to Israel.

---

51 Maya King, "Black Pastors Pressure Biden to Call for a Cease-Fire in Gaza," *New York Times,* January 28, 2024, https://www.nytimes.com/2024/01/28/us/politics/black-pastors-biden-gaza-israel.html.

52 Ibid

Consider the Black citizens of Sudan, many of whom are oppressed and subject to mass slaughter, by Arabs. According to the *Economist*,

> Genocidal gunmen went from home to home for three days in a refugee camp in Darfur, Sudan, looking for Masalit men and killing them. It was not the first such attack, but by the time they had finished say locals, between 800 and 1,300 members of the Black-African ethnic group had been killed. Unverified videos show streets filled with corpses and terrified people crowded into what appears to be a mass grave, or being beaten by fighters from the mainly Arab Rapid Support Forces (RSF), a paramilitary group, which denied the allegations.[53]

According to Reuters, the Arab killers deliberately selected members of the Masalit tribe because of their darker Black skin, calling them "Anabai," which means "slave."

The Uyghurs of China, the Kurds of Iraq, the Ukrainians, and other groups are at least as "oppressed" as the Palestinians claim to be. Moreover, the Palestinians, unlike these other groups, have turned down offers of statehood on numerous occasions. And they have made terrorism against innocent civilians their tactic of choice.

As one pastor revealingly put it: "The Israel-Gaza war, unlike Iran and Afghanistan has evoked the kind of deep-seated angst among Black people that I have not seen since the Civil Rights Movement."[54] He failed to mention that estimates of civilians killed in these other wars are a large multiple of those killed by Israel in its war against the Hamas murderers.

Why did so few Blacks protest in favor of these oppressed groups? Are they not "part of" the oppressed people? If not, why not? Is it

53 Leaders, "The world is ignoring war, genocide and famine in Sudan," *Economist*, November 16, 2023, https://www.economist.com/leaders/2023/11/16/the-world-is-ignoring-war-genocide-and-famine-in-sudan.

54 Maya King, "Black Pastors Pressure Biden to Call for a Cease-Fire in Gaza," *New York Times*, January 28, 2024, https://www.nytimes.com/2024/01/28/us/politics/black-pastors-biden-gaza-israel.html.

because their oppressors are not Jews, while the alleged oppressors of the Palestinians are Jews?

In 1992, my friend and colleague, Henry Lewis (Skip) Gates, Jr. wrote a groundbreaking article about the historic and contemporary relationship between the Black and Jewish communities. He traced the most recent conflicts back to "Christian anti-Semitism," given the historic importance of Christianity to the Black community. But he laid the primary blame on Black demagogues who were vying for leadership roles in the newly Afrocentric movement.

Professor Gates noted the surprise of many Jews at the "recrudescence of Black anti-Semitism, in view of the historic alliance between the two groups." But he pointed out the "brutal truth" that the "new anti-Semitism arises not in spite of the black-Jewish alliance, but because of it."[55] He explained that the alliance had been formed by a previous generation of Black ministers led by Martin Luther King Jr. The new generation of Afrocentric leaders, including pastors, needed a scapegoat on whom to place the blame for so many Blacks remaining oppressed. Who better to fit that role than the paradigmatic scapegoat of world history—the Jews. Gates noted that Blacks were twice as likely as whites to hold anti-Semitic views, "and that it is among the younger and more educated Blacks that anti-Semitism is most pronounced."

It's now been thirty years since Gates wrote his transformative article, and things have only gotten worse.

Anti-Semitism disguised as double standard singling out the nation state of the Jewish people for condemnation has now become rampant among many African Americans. The Louis Farrakhan brand of undisguised Jew hatred still prevalent among too many people of color, is now becoming more mainstream among radical students as well as conservative Christians of color.

There are still many African Americans who apply a single standard to Israel, even among those who are legitimately critical of some

---

55 Henry Louis Gates Jr., "The new black anti-Semitism is top-down and dangerous," *Baltimore Sun*, July 22, 1992, https://www.baltimoresun.com/1992/07/22/the-new-black-anti-semitism-is-top-down-and-dangerous/.

of that nation's policies, including in Gaza. But the Jewish community—indeed all good people—has the right to demand that all Black leaders, pastors, students, and others apply a single, non-discriminatory standard in relation to the Jewish community and its nation.

Why Don't We Want a War with Iran?
Every discussion about the current Mideast conflict begins with the mandatory mantra, "We don't want war with Iran." Why not? That question is rarely asked.

Iran has declared war on the United States—militarily, legally, diplomatically, morally, and politically. They have engaged in repeated *casus belli* since the mullahs took American hostages in 1979. Since that time, they have used their surrogates to attack American targets. We are entitled to respond militarily, as we are doing. But we are also entitled to go much further and treat them as aggressors who have effectively declared war on us. We are entitled to destroy their capacity to continue to wage war against us and our allies. The policy question is not whether we have a right to wage war against Iran. It is whether it is in our interest to do so.

It would be best if we could achieve all or most of the ends we legitimately seek without employing the costly and dangerous means of all-out war. That is what the Biden administration is seeking to do by attacking some of Iran's proxies without hitting military targets within Iran itself. But can that limited strategy work?

Iran's strategy has long been to use primarily Shia Arab soldiers to do its dirty work, without endangering its own non-Arab soldiers and civilians—a sort of religious colonialism. That is why critics quip that Iran is willing to fight till the last Arab!

The Biden strategy plays into their hands. We are targeting Syrian, Iraqi, and perhaps Yemen Arabs in an effort to deter the non-Arab mullahs of Iran. So far that has not worked. Perhaps the recent escalation of attacks on Iranian proxies will enhance deterrence against Iran. But many experts believe that unless we directly attack the head of the octopus, it will simply grow more tentacles and continue its predation through willing surrogates.

There are, of course, alternatives less than all-out war and more than attacks on proxies. They involve the bombing of military targets inside of Iran. These include Iran's nuclear program, its naval bases and ships, its drone production, its petroleum facilities, and its command centers. All of these could be accomplished from the air and sea without a ground invasion and the loss of American lives an invasion would risk.

Such an escalation could produce many benefits, including the postponement—perhaps even termination—of Iran's acquisition of a nuclear arsenal. It would weaken Iran's growing exports of sophisticated drones. And it would hurt Iran's already suffering economy that is used to export terrorism.

It is impossible to know for certain, whether such a multifaceted attack inside of Iran would weaken or strengthen the mullah's undemocratic hold over the largely secular Iranian people, many of whom would welcome regime change—as would some of Iran's Arab neighbors. One conclusion is clear: in the short term, a US attack on Iran itself would contribute to destabilization in the region. But in the longer term, it might well contribute to stability by reducing the power and influence of the most destabilizing entity in the Mideast, namely Iran.

Israel, too, is at war with Iran. Iran's operatives have targeted Israeli citizens and Jews around the world. It has called Israel a "one bomb state" and has threatened to destroy it with nuclear weapons. Israel, too, has a perfect right to respond to these acts of war. Indeed, it may have no choice but to do so in order to prevent Iran from carrying out its threats of nuclear annihilation.

The Mideast and the world would be a safer place without the current Iranian regime. It would be a far more dangerous place with a nuclear weaponized Iran that could protect its surrogates under a nuclear umbrella.

If Iran can be effectively deterred from pushing its belligerent agenda without an attack within its borders, that would be the best outcome. So, Biden's strategy should be given a chance to work. But if it fails—as history suggests it may—all options must be kept on the table. These include attacks within Iran, even if that means war. That may be the least worst among the many available options.

Pro-Palestinian Pied Pipers Are Leading Your Children to the River and the Sea

Pro-Palestinian, anti-Israel, and anti-American radical extremists are exploiting the abysmal ignorance of many young people about the Israeli-Palestinian conflict. Using the demand for unilateral ceasefire as a cover for their true goal—the total destruction of Israel—they have recruited your children, your friends' children, and other "useful idiots" to join in their anti-Semitic campaign.

The best proof that the demand for a cease-fire is merely a recruitment tool is that the protests began on the day after the Hamas massacres and before there was any fire to cease, because Israel had not yet attacked Gaza. The protests continued during the multiday pause in fighting that resulted in the release of one hundred hostages, and they will persist even if there is a longer cease-fire.

Nor have these protests called for the creation of a peaceful Palestinian state alongside Israel—a two-state solution. They demand one Palestinian state from the river to the sea, which means the end of Israel. The benevolent sounding call for a cease-fire serves to attract useful idiots to hold signs demanding the end of Israel "from the river to the sea."

This is not the first time in our history that young people have been led into bigotry by pied pipers of hate. In the 1930s, many young students at universities such as Harvard, Yale, Princeton, Oxford, and Cambridge were led by their elders to believe that Hitler and his Nazi Party were the only answer to Communism. On the other side, many students were seduced by their professors into believing that Stalin and Communism were the only answer to fascism. In the 1960s, many university students supported Castro and displayed pictures of his murderous accomplice Che Guevara on their dorm walls and t-shirts. Some supported Mao Zedong and even the genocidal Pol Pot. There is no limit to the naivete and willingness of some young zealots to embrace any cause that sounds exciting or bold, regardless of the harm it threatens.

Those who try to excuse, justify, or even explain the attractiveness of these unattractive causes to young people on the ground that "they are just kids," are ignoring the lessons of history. Many of these kids will

become our future leaders and will remain influenced by their exposure to these malevolent philosophies. Others will grow out of them and
regret their youthful indiscretions but will be hurt because of them in
their future careers, as former Communists were during McCarthyism.

There is no easy solution to the problem of young extremists who
refuse to listen to reason or learn from history. Each new generation of
zealots believes they have discovered "justice" and those who refuse to
go along are regressive.

Now, the spiritual heirs to these ill-informed past supporters of
hate are marching for Hamas which proudly claims responsibility for
massacring and kidnapping more than 1,500 Israelis. Some are even
saying they approve of Osama bin Laden—the terrorist behind the 9/11
murder of more than three thousand innocent civilians.

One disturbing similarity among these youthful cults of hatred
is that they all eventually blame "the Jews" for the evil they claim to
be combatting. As August Bebel once observed "antisemitism is the
socialism of fools." The description fits many of the current haters who
say they support "socialism" (though few are familiar with its mixed
history). They are indeed fools for following their evil pied pipers into
waters that drown principles, decency, and progress.

Stalin understood this phenomenon and exploited it by making
antis-Semitism a central part of his Bolshevik agenda because he
regarded most of his followers as easily manipulable fools.

Hitler, too, understood this, deliberately misnaming his fascist
followers as members of the "national socialist party." He, too, used
anti-Semitism to attract useful idiots among university students.

The leaders of the current protests understand, too, that there is
no overestimating the foolishness of many of today's lemming students
who will follow any radical opposition to establishment values. The
woke, progressive, intersectional, diversity, equity, and inclusion mindset is a path to disaster for our nation, and especially for Jews, Asians,
and white male heterosexuals who are excluded from their zero-sum
game. But it is the only game in town for many young students who
need to rebel against their parents, their heritage, and the values with
which they were brought up.

This is a generational battle, and we are losing it to the pied pipers of hate who are willing to exploit the ignorance and closed-mindedness that many current "educators" have inflicted on our children and grandchildren. Intergenerational battles are hard to win because our ideological adversaries, whose support for Hamas we may hate, are often people we personally love. That makes it even more important to engage thoughtfully and persistently. We cannot afford to give up on them and on our future.

CONCLUSION

What Can Be Done?

It's getting worse, not better, as the new McCarthyism becomes mainstream, especially among our young, educated future leaders. Appreciation for the values—indeed the necessity—of universal freedom of expression, due process, presumption of innocence, the right to counsel, the equal protection of the laws, the right to privacy, and other basic civil liberties is diminishing, especially among progressives and others on the left. Liberalism has become a condemnatory epithet for those who accept ignoble dangerous and often unconstitutional means to more quickly and efficiently achieve their "noble" goals, without the burdensome interference of process, procedure, and structural protections against authoritarianism, both malignant and benign.

Extremists, both right and left, have always rejected process. Republican zealots who opposed the impeachment of President Trump on the unconstitutional grounds of "abuse" and "obstructions" are now seeking the impeachment of President Biden on similarly unconstitutional grounds. They are emulating their Democrat opponents by weaponizing our criminal justice system against their political enemies, and by ignoring, or even rejecting, the procedural safeguards that are designed to protect all Americans. Now that rejection is moving to the center and threatening to become a majority, or at least a plurality, view. If this is permitted to continue unchallenged the new

McCarthyism will become the new Americanism—if not immediately, then certainly when the current generation of students and young professionals become our political, media, business, educational, religious, and "influencer" leaders.

Process and procedure, though they are the essence of liberty and the rule of law, have never garnered the same kind of popular support as concrete results. That is why, as a great civil libertarian once put it, "The struggle for liberty never stays won." But history shows that it can stay lost for a considerable period of time unless it is constantly maintained and renewed. It is being lost today, and unless we renew it with rigor, it threatens to destroy our precious liberties we have earned over the years.

The new woke McCarthyism has been embraced by many anti-Israel and anti-Jewish extremists in the wake of the Hamas barbarism of October 7 and the Israeli response to it. Instead of rational debate, we have seen violent efforts to harass speakers, suppress opposing views, and interfere with travel and other basic rights.

It is imperative, therefore, for all those who love liberty, whatever our views on other matters, to unite in opposing the new woke McCarthyism.